English Criticism in Japan

English Criticism in Japan

Essays by Younger Japanese Scholars
on English and American Literature

Compiled and Edited, with an Introduction,

by Earl Miner

UNIVERSITY OF TOKYO PRESS

© University of Tokyo Press, 1972

UTP 3098-87088-5149

Edited by Elizabeth W. Kodama,
designed by Takashi Suzuki,
composed in Bembo type,
and printed in Yokohama, Japan, by
General Printing Company.

Published by University of Tokyo Press

This book is available in the United States
through Princeton University Press.

For the other members
of the English Society of Japan

Contents

Preface

All teachers of English in Japan are acquainted with a monthly magazine bearing the title *Eigo Seinen*, with a somewhat freely rendered English co-title, *The Rising Generation*. This volume derives from that journal its principle of inclusion of the work of younger scholars. Perhaps it would be more accurate to say that the concept of a "Rising Generation" has operated as a convenience for exclusion. At the annual meeting of the English Society of Japan in Sapporo in 1961, I enjoyed the privilege of addressing the society, and in my lecture I devoted my remarks under the general heading of the future of English study in Japan to the thesis that it should be better known in the rest of the world where English literature is valued. The realization that I had raised some hopes and some expectations has made me feel ever since that an initial burden of responsibility lay on my thin shoulders. But how was such a responsibility to be discharged?

One of my first ideas was the compilation of a book of essays on English and American literature by Japanese. Another was the inclusion of essays by Japanese in compilations I might make on narrower subjects. Not long ago, the second possibility became a reality, and I included an essay on Donne by Toshihiko Kawasaki (who is, therefore, not represented in this volume) in a collection of essays on imagery in seventeenth-century English literature. But the larger effort still seemed required, and if it were not done by one who had made such a suggestion, and who owes so much to the Japanese and their literature, by whom, in all conscience, might it be done? But the task of selecting essays from numerous Japanese periodicals, many of them *Transactions* of this or that university, journals not to be found consistently in any American library, was not a beckoning prospect. Similarly how was I to choose between various famous professors, dead or alive, when standards of current interest and emphasis might direct me to someone quite junior whom most of the world did not know? Such problems seemed insoluble. Fortunately, a solution presented itself to me as I flew to Japan for a UNESCO conference on Japanese-Western cultural relations in September 1968. It came with the recollection of *The Rising Generation*.

By consulting with various professors, senior and junior, during my stay in Japan, I might (I thought) seek to compile a volume of essays on English and American literature, arranged in roughly chronological order by subject, by younger scholars in Japan. And what is meant by "younger"? My decision was to exclude anyone above forty at the time of the search and everyone who held a professorial chair. In practice this has turned out to mean mostly people in their mid or late thirties at the time of search, all of them what I have ventured to term adjutant professors. As the Introduction explains at somewhat greater length, the national universities are commonly organized, at least in a Faculty of Letters, into suites involving three ranks: *kyoju, jokyoju,* and *koshi.** Only the first, *kyoju,* translates into English or American usage easily as "professor." The last means something like (but is not the same as) "instructor" in American usage or "assistant lecturer" in the usage of most English universities. It is a post given to someone still working on his or her doctoral course and is given in the university where the "assistant" is working. It does not carry tenure or security of employment, and in that is almost unique in major Japanese appointments. The second term, *jokyoju,* illustrates how bothersome language and custom may become. Frequently translated, by analogy to American academic ranks, as assistant professor or associate professor, it differs from the former in carrying tenure and from the latter in being very much a junior post that does not entitle its holder to participation in the

---

* Throughout this book, diacritical marks have been eliminated, giving *kyoju* instead of *kyōju*, etc.

Committee of Professors, the crucial body that decides so much in Japanese universities. And in the national universities, as has been said, the post is commonly literally adjutant to the professorial chair. At all events, the distinction seemed to solve one aspect of my problem of inclusion and exclusion.

Consulting with friends and acquaintances in Japanese university circles, I soon discovered that, even with this definition of "younger," the problem would be an embarrassment of riches. I would need to exclude any essay I could find any formal pretext to exclude. Therefore, I decided that anyone who had taken a doctoral degree outside Japan should not be included. That covered such personal friends as Toshihiko Kawasaki of Nagoya University, whom I have already mentioned, Makoto Ueda of Toronto University, and Masao Miyoshi of the University of California, Berkeley, as well as some others. I further decreed that no one who had published in England or America an essay of some length would be included. This edict ruled out two other friends, Haruhide Mori of Kobe University, who had published on D. H. Lawrence in *ELH*, and Hiroshi Watanabe of Kyoto University, who had published on Henry James in *American Literature*. Both of these principles of exclusion follow naturally from the original goal of the project: to make English criticism by Japanese scholars better known in the rest of the world. Those who have studied or published in the West, I reasoned, have already gone a long way toward achieving this goal independently.

The truly essential matter of selection based on quality remained. It is no doubt true that quality is quality in literary studies throughout the world. But the nature of quality in Japanese criticism of English and American literature obviously presents some distinct elements. The purpose of the Introduction is to explain those features of the Japanese system of higher education that introduce considerations different from those known by most of the readers of this volume and to examine, at least in the closing pages of the Introduction, the distinctly Japanese elements in "English criticism in Japan." Such qualities, to be seen at their best, somewhat paradoxically required choosing essays that would also seem attractive by conventional English and American standards of judgment. In other words, what is distinctly Japanese would have to be found in essays meeting international criteria of excellence and therefore likely to appear, at least at first examination, very much like essays written by critics native to such places as England or the United States, Canada or Australia. Finally, selection was inevitably influenced by such factors as the length of essays and what I in my limited judgment thought most interesting to readers in England and the United States. One whose work lies to a considerable extent in seventeenth-century England is not the best judge of work in other centuries. But having bitten the bullet, I had to soldier on. I am pleased to say that I received nothing but cooperation from everybody approached. Authors whose essays I selected on the basis of their Japanese versions have translated them into English. All have borne with my editing, with my requests for citation (when the need arose) of other, more generally available editions, and with my recommendations for alteration, cutting, or expansion. It need hardly be said that the responsibility for the versions appearing here resides with me.

Some ten years ago, the harbinger of this volume was published by Frank L. Huntley, Professor of English at the University of Michigan: "Milton Studies in Japan" (*Comparative Literature*, 13 [1961]: 97–113). He has preceded me in studying seventeenth-century English literature, in teaching in Japan, and in writing on a subject like that in the Introduction that follows. He concluded his essay with these remarks: "We should encourage these Japanese scholars to write in an internationally accepted medium [English]; we should welcome them into the world's intellectual orbit. They need our criticism, and we their insight." These words seem axiomatic to one who has learned about Bacon from an edition of Donne annotated in Japanese, who has learned about Dryden from his Japanese students, who has learned about Yeats from a colleague in a Japanese university, and who has learned above all a good deal about art and life from Japan and its literature. The late Professor Motohiro Fukase of Kyoto University used to tell the story of his granddaughter's remark when he took her swimming at the beach. Seeing some Americans there, she exclaimed, "Grandpa, Americans have navels, too!" Along with such signs of our vital ties with our mothers, we share the common humanity of ties with literary culture. Such signs may be less visible, but there remains a sense in which literature in English is the *alma mater* of countless men and women throughout the world.

E. M.

Acknowledgments

A collection of this kind inevitably requires the assistance of many people. As much to assist my own memory as to express my gratitude in an intelligible way, I shall follow some of the steps by which this book became a reality. In Tokyo and Kyoto in September 1968, I had the opportunity to discuss with colleagues my plan to compile this book. Among my older friends, Professor Shiko Murakami at Osaka University along with Professor Yasuo Suga and Professor Yukio Oura at Kyoto University gave me valuable help. In addition, five of the contributors to this collection have advised me in numerous ways and assisted my communications with individual authors as well as the publisher. Among these five are three friends of some years standing. During my year in Japan as Fulbright Lecturer, I became acquainted with Haruhiko Fujii, who was in the doctoral course at Osaka University, and Tetsuo Kishi, who was in the master's course at Kyoto University. Yasunari Takahashi and I met in the North Library of the British Museum in 1962. I must also thank the other two, Shigeru Koike and Masayuki Sakamoto, and express my hope that the day of our meeting will not be too long deferred.

When the essays arrived, I assumed the role of editor as I have for other collections, suggesting changes and raising questions. During this time, two research assistants, Steven Sharp and Ruth Wolin, verified quotations, titles, and citations. So edited, the manuscript of each chapter was typed up by the UCLA Central Stenographic Bureau and a copy was then mailed to the author for change and approval. Since sizes of typing paper differ in Japan, England, and the United States, and since contributors were in all three countries, the usual reliable services of that bureau were more helpful than ever. Another friend and contributor to this volume, Minoru Fujita, a student of mine at Osaka University in 1960–61, happened to be at UCLA on a Fulbright grant when the book was being assembled. I am grateful to him for many kinds of help, including providing some information used in the Introduction. The five contributors mentioned in the previous paragraph also read the Introduction and made helpful corrections.

This book has been a matter of faith to me. I knew that it would be published because it deserved to be. But the chilling economic climate for university presses did not assist the chances of a collection of essays. I am grateful for the very helpful advice given me by Miriam Brokaw, associate director and editor at Princeton University Press and editor of one or two of my books. Having been born in Japan and having spent a year on a Fulbright grant at the University of Tokyo Press, Miss Brokaw was able to direct me to the publisher with good timing. At the University of Tokyo Press, its director, Shigeo Minowa, kindly gave the book his blessing, and thereafter the contributors and I benefited greatly from the careful editing of Elizabeth W. Kodama. I am most grateful to the press, and to the original Japanese publishers of the essays. Anyone with the unlikely combination of an ability to read Japanese and a bibliographical desire to compare the originals with the present versions would find that our constant effort has been to render everything as compactly and as clearly as possible.

The problems of having a book edited and typeset in Tokyo and checked and proofread in Los Angeles have required considerable good will and some assistance. I must thank Susan McCloskey, James Patch, and Saul Steier for help in reading proof, and Susan McCloskey for assistance with the Index.

I have reserved to the last my thanks to Robert H. Brower. Years ago, when we were collaborating on studies of Japanese court poetry, he instilled in my mind the belief that someone with mixed interests like my own should take the responsibility for making Japanese criticism of English and American literature known outside Japan.

This book was his idea, then, before it was my own, and I want to acknowledge my debt to him on this as well as so many matters over a period of twenty years. By working closely for fifteen months with a distinguished Japanese professor of Japanese literature, the team of Brower and Miner came to realize how much could be learned from Japanese literary students. It is with gratitude to many people, confidence in this book, and hopes for a widened perspective on English study that I direct attention to the new team of fifteen gifted younger scholars who have now come onto the field.

Notes on Contributors

SHINSUKE ANDO.* Adjutant Professor, Faculty of Letters, Keio University, Tokyo. B. A. (1955) and M. A. (1957) from Keio University; "recognized student" at Oxford University (1962–63) on a grant from the Keio University Fukuzawa Memorial Fund. Major interests: medieval and Renaissance English literature. In preparation: a study of medieval English drama; a translation of Nevill Coghill's *Geoffrey Chaucer*.

TSUGIO AOKI. Adjutant Professor of American Literature, Faculty of Letters, Kyoto University. B. A. (1955) from Shinshu University; M. A. (1959) from Kyoto University. Studied at Yale University (1955–56) on a Fulbright scholarship; visiting research scholar at New York University (1967–68) on a grant from the American Council of Learned Societies. Major interests: modern American literature, Henry James. Publications: largely studies of James, including a translation, with Yoshimi Kudo, of *The Ambassadors*; in progress are a translation of *The Wings of the Dove* and a study of James.

HIROICHIRO DOKE. Adjutant Professor, Kokugakuin University, Tokyo. B. A. (1955) and M. A. (1957) from the University of Tokyo. Research student at Corpus Christi College, Cambridge (1967–68). Major interests: seventeenth-century English literature and its relations with Christianity.

HARUHIKO FUJII. Adjutant Professor, Faculty of General Education, Osaka University. B. A. (1958) and M. A. (1960) from Osaka

* Given names precede surnames, as in usual Western practice. For an explanation of titles, see the Preface.

University. Studied at the University of California, Los Angeles (1964–65) on a Falk Foundation grant. Major interests: Renaissance English literature, Spenser to Milton, with publications chiefly on writers of that period.

MINORU FUJITA. Adjutant Professor, Faculty of General Education, Osaka University. B. A. (1956) and M. A. (1959) from Osaka University. Studied at the University of California, Los Angeles (1968–69) on a Fulbright grant and thereafter (1969) at the Bodleian Library, Oxford. Major interests: Shakespeare, Renaissance English literature, Western and Japanese drama. His publications are almost wholly on Shakespeare.

SOJI IWASAKI. Adjutant Professor, Faculty of General Education, Nagoya University. B. A. (1954) from Aichi University of Liberal Arts; Research Student, Churchill College, Cambridge University (1964–66); M. Litt. (1969), Cambridge University. Fellow, Folger Shakespeare Library, 1969. Major interests: Shakespeare and Renaissance English literature.

TETSUO KISHI. Adjutant Professor, Faculty of General Education, Kyoto University. B. A. (1958) and M. A. (1960) from Kyoto University. Graduate student, Columbia University (1960–61). Visiting Associate Professor of Japanese, Stanford University (1966–67). Major interests: English and American drama, with publications and theatrical productions in such fields, including translations of plays by Shakespeare, Shaw, O'Neill, and Pinter, and Jan Kott's *Shakespeare Our Contemporary*.

SHIGERU KOIKE. Adjutant Professor, Faculty of Humanities, Tokyo Metropolitan University. B. A. (1953) and M. A. (1955) from the University of Tokyo. Studied at Birkbeck College, London University, and the Victoria and Albert Museum (1963–64). Major interests: nineteenth-century English life and fiction. Publications include *The Fortunate Travellers* (1962), a study of the picaresque novel in English from Smollett to Dickens, and numerous other studies and translations.

HIDEKATSU NOJIMA. Adjutant Professor, Ochanomizu Women's University, Tokyo. B. A. (1953) from Tokyo University of Foreign Studies; M. A. (1955) from the University of Tokyo.

Studied at Columbia University (1964–65) as a Fulbright research scholar. Major interests: modern literature, Shakespeare, literary criticism. His books include: *Muse and Fate: A Study of Virginia Woolf* (1962); *Exiles at Work: Joyce, Eliot, and Lawrence* (1963); *Modern Literature: Fact or Fiction?* (1970); *Essays on Modern Japanese Literature: Don Quixotes in Return to Native Japan*; and three other titles in progress.

MASAYUKI SAKAMOTO. Adjutant Professor, Faculty of Letters and Education, Ochanomizu Women's University, Tokyo. B. A. (1953) from Okayama University; M. A. (1955) from the University of Tokyo. Major interest: American literature of the nineteenth and twentieth centuries. His books include *A Study of the American Renaissance* (1969); translations of Whitman's *Leaves of Grass*, Emerson's *Representative Men*, and novels and stories by Thomas Wolfe, Frank O'Connor, and Bernard Malamud.

TAKASHI SASAYAMA. Adjutant Professor, Faculty of Letters, Osaka City University. B. A., old style (1953), from Osaka University. Studied at Harvard University (1953–54) on a Fulbright grant. Major interests: classical and Renaissance English drama. He has translated and edited Middleton and Rowley's play *The Changeling* and is preparing a book on Jacobean drama. In 1971 he received the Prix Claudel for his translation of Henri Fluchère's *Shakespeare, dramaturge élisabéthain*.

YASUNARI TAKAHASHI. Adjutant Professor, Faculty of General Education, University of Tokyo. B. A. (1953) and M. A. (1955) from the University of Tokyo. Studied at Birkbeck College, London University, and the British Museum on a British Council grant (1962–63). Varied interests, as represented by a *Genealogy of Ecstasy* (1967), with essays on Donne, Marvell, Wordsworth, Coleridge, Arnold, Eliot, and Beckett; he is also the author of *Samuel Beckett* (1971) and is preparing a book on Lewis Carroll.

SHOICHI YAMADA. Adjutant Professor, Faculty of the Humanities, Tokyo Metropolitan University. B. A. (1953) and M. A. (1956) from the University of Tokyo. Major interests: modern English poetry and criticism; presently preparing a book on T. S. Eliot.

HISAAKI YAMANOUCHI. Lector in Japanese, Cambridge University. B. A. (1958) and M. A. (1960) from the University of Tokyo; M. A. (1964) from Columbia University. Studied at the University of Toronto (1963–64) and Cambridge University (1967–). Taught English at Tsuda College, Tokyo (1964–67). Major interest: romanticism in literature. Held a British Council grant (1967–68).

KIMIYOSHI YURA. Adjutant Professor, Faculty of General Education, University of Tokyo. B. A. in philosophy (1952) and B. A. in English (1954) from Gakushuin University, Tokyo; M. A. in English (1956) from Keio University. Major interests: English Romantic literature, critical theory, Japanese literature.

Introduction

T he essays that follow can best be examined without an officious guide. The history, and especially the recent history, of English literary studies in Japan may be considered another matter. In spite of the international character of Japanese scholarship and criticism of English and American literature, the essays collected here take root in an educational heritage markedly different from that familiar to the personal experience of any but a Japanese reader. No doubt many Western readers will think they find Japanese traits in these essays. But what seems more immediately remarkable to me is that an educational system with a history and practice so much its own should have become so international in so short a period of time.

Higher education and its problems are, however, not new to contemporary Japan. Some slender ties with the past may be briefly mentioned. In what is perhaps the greatest single work of Japanese literature, *The Tale of Genji* (ca. A.D. 910?), one finds an amusing episode involving an academic examination or ceremony conducted by some very pedantic doctors. And, in her *Pillow Book* (early eleventh century), Sei Shonagon, with characteristic wit, includes "Doctor of Literature" among "Words that Seem Commonplace but that Become Impressive when Written in Chinese Characters." We may hope that such pedants no longer exist in the world. But we owe references to them in classical Japanese literature to the fact that Japan had taken on a *pro forma* equivalent of the Chinese system of appointment to office by competitive examination after training in a "university" (*daigaku*). Whatever the strict letter of academic theory, and no matter how useful the education conducted may

have been, however, in Japan the Chinese system yielded to the
social realities of appointment by reason of family connection and
patronage. The professional character of modern Japanese universities in fact possesses only the slimmest of bonds with the "universities" of the Japanese court.

During the slow period of transition from a court society to a
nation ruled by a military aristocracy, the "university" of the court
increasingly lost what educational importance it possessed, and new
educational institutions emerged. Even during the heyday of the
court, Buddhist temples had naturally provided education, especially
of a religious kind, and as time passed they came to take on secular
educational functions as well by establishing temple schools. But the
Japanese genius for establishing social realities at variance with insti-
tutional forms also made it possible for numerous subjects—whether
the arts of poetry, medicine, or war—to be studied by what seem less
formal expedients. A given teacher of repute in his art would collect
students or disciples and establish a school of his own, a "school"
as much in the sense of poetic parties or lineage as of formal educational institutions. Such schools—which might be schools of actors
as often as schools of poets or priests—usually came to take on histories of their own. A teacher would take into his family by adoption
an unusually gifted student, and the recurrent Japanese capacity for
originality would enliven the recurrent Japanese capacity for following the leader. None of the attributes of Japanese education so far
alluded to has disappeared: titles, pedantry, originality, informal
institutions grown formal, schools of study emanating from a line
of important practitioners, and, above all, another characteristic, the
remarkable closeness of teacher and student, and of fellow students.

The imperial Meiji Restoration of 1868 marks the formal break,
however, with premodern educational forms. Prior to that event,
Japan was officially closed to outside contact, and only the Dutch
(and they limitedly, ignominiously) had contact with Japan. However limited such contact was, it became increasingly important, and
by the nineteenth century there was a group of "Scholars of Dutch,"
who were busy studying books brought by Dutch traders to Naga-
saki and were eager to obtain more. The thirst for knowledge of

Western arts and sciences was as much discouraged as welcomed by the government; but after Chinese, Dutch was then the second international language for Japanese in search of education. When Japan was opened by the efforts of Commodore Perry and of a strong movement inside the country, the Japanese government began to cast a wider net and to look about Europe and America so that it might choose selectively what a new age demanded.

The search led Japanese authorities to eclectic choices. It seemed to them that the Prussian constitution was most suitable to Japan, and the French legal system most pertinent. And in the early modern era, English literature, of a late Romantic variety or of a Victorian earnestness, seemed to answer the needs of an age not only in search of new ideals but also possessed of an extraordinary energy and a capacity for hard work. The English Romantic poets and the German idealist philosophers, who had in fact provided some philosophical bases for Romantic poetry, inspired the hearts, and perhaps sometimes clouded the minds, of young men and women far removed from the English Lake District and the *Seminars* of German universities. Along with such lofty ideals, practical interests required serving, and the books quickly translated into Japanese included numerous scientific or engineering studies, along with such exponents of the gospel of work as Samuel Smiles. The time would come when idealism and practical bustle would come into conflict in Japan, as they did in Victorian England, but in the last decade or so of the nineteenth century the formula seemed to work well in a nation just emerging from self-isolation.

Among other institutions that seemed to be required for a modern Japan was a system of universal education. The pattern that emerged would have seemed reasonably familiar to a French or German observer and would not have looked wholly foreign to English eyes. Its form, a basic three-tiered system, can easily be grasped, but in practice it found a distinctly Japanese expression. As the system evolved, at least in reference to English study, the three basic tiers were lower schools, middle schools, and higher schools. The lower schools were mandatory for all and soon provided Japan with the highest literacy rate in the world. The quality of Japanese newspapers and journals, as well as the avid reading habits of Japanese, testified to a revolution successful in realizing the educational aims of the government. Admission to the middle schools was based on competitive examinations at the end of lower school training, and similar examinations for entry into the higher schools screened boys yet more finely. Girls entered a separate stream after lower school, the girls' schools, again by examination. (Only recently has a woman, Chie Nakane, been appointed to a chair at the University of Tokyo, and her appointment caused enough stir to lead a major Japanese newspaper to characterize her as a "strong woman" in a series on "Personalities of the Seventies.") Finally, yet another competitive examination allowed boys to continue to universities.

Before considering the standard or elitist governmental higher education system itself, however, some complexities must be introduced. The government also sponsored some commercial or scientific institutions of higher learning, and alongside the governmental pattern there emerged private schools and universities, sometimes related to missionary activity, but more often—as with Keio University, Waseda University, and Kansai University—founded on secular lines. There even came into being some universities for women, experiments with coeducation, and schools for foreigners residing in Japan. Some of the private schools and colleges, as Americans would term them, were of a high standard. A Roman Catholic school like that of the Sacred Heart in Tokyo, missionary-supported universities like Rikkyo, Sophia, and Doshisha, and foreign schools like the Canadian Academy in Kobe all filled roles that were recognized by need and that often provided English instruction of high quality. Tsuda Women's College is one of a number of institutions that has long provided remarkable training in English for women. While touching on exceptions to the national system, some mention should also be made of the education of Japanese in England, Europe, and the United States. The Japanese genius for exception and for meeting needs in ways outside the general pattern of state formality certainly found recognition in the varied pattern of higher education.

That said, attention must be devoted to the egalitarian state system.

Of that it may be remarked that the spirit of the Chinese system of competitive examinations was at last realized after the Meiji Restoration of 1868. Influence from social powers and subtle determination of opportunity by accidents of economic class or place of origin certainly played their part in determining the success of an individual boy. But such factors probably counted for less than in any society contemporaneous with Meiji Japan. The examinations were open to all, and a bright boy usually found support from some quarter, perhaps a rich relative, an interested patron, or even a proud village or town. Education was given an exalted importance, and the examinations were scrupulously fair. As late as 1961, four sons of professors at Kyoto University took entrance examinations to the university, and all four failed on their first try. Whatever objections might be made to a system based on examination at set ages, the system aimed solely at selecting a meritocracy, long before the term emerged in England.

The process of selection severely limited the number of boys who went from one stage to the next. The educational pyramid, which was so broad for the lower schools, sharply narrowed in successive stages until it became an obelisk or needle at the top. Few students ever went as far as the eight governmental higher schools (the number of these schools grew subsequently with national need, however). And those schools therefore resembled not American high schools but English grammar and public schools or German *Gymnasia*. Two principal results followed from such restrictions, and these results have determined the spirit of Japanese education until the last few years. One result has been the development of a distinct hierarchy of status, prestige increasing almost geometrically as one goes up the educational ladder. Another has been the remarkable *esprit de corps* engendered in successively selected groups. No American could grasp without special experience the close ties between graduates of, say, a given higher school. Even today, older professors will think of their classmates in higher schools as a race apart. The bonds resemble, or perhaps exceed in strength, those of old Etonians and Harrovians, or those of students of the Ecole Normale Supérieure.

At the apex of the educational system and of the universities there stood, and still stands, its position modified but not challenged, the University of Tokyo. No educational system with which I am familiar has ever possessed so Dante-like a hierarchy leading to such a single peak. The young men who entered the University of Tokyo might well come selected in a complex process from all over Japan. But the young men who left the University of Tokyo were all but certain of capturing the important posts in the government and in other universities. Not Eton or Oxford, Harvard or Yale, could claim to exercise the preeminence of the University of Tokyo. To be a graduate of that university was tantamount to security of career, and as far as English study in the government system was concerned, the very point of the apex was a professorial chair at the University of Tokyo.

With the end of the Second World War and with the American, or allied, occupation of Japan, numerous changes were introduced, partly by force and partly through cooperation, in Japanese society. The change in the educational system was one of the most firmly resisted at the time. The change can be represented most simply in terms of the alteration in the pattern of schooling. Where formerly the pattern had been six years in the lower schools, four to five in the middle, three in the higher, and three at the university, the new pattern followed a common American model. The Japanese names might remain the same, but the new pattern is better designated by American terms: six years of elementary school, three years of junior high school, three of senior high school, and four of university. But the revision was far more fundamental in spirit. It was aimed, and it was seen to aim, at two central features of the prewar system: limiting control by the Ministry of Education (which had ordained, in effect, that all students in the lower grades were taught the same lessons by the same methods from the same books) by delegating responsibility to local school boards; and attacking the elitist meritocracy of prewar days. It was meant to be a revolution, and it did constitute a revolution in education. But, like all major changes, it had unforeseen results, including ultimately a greater continuity with the past than the Occupation revolutionaries had envisioned.

One result was the proliferation of institutions of higher learning.

The still current ancient Japanese term, *daigaku*, can mean either a college or a university in American usage, that is, either a four-year undergraduate institution or an institution with undergraduate and graduate faculties in the various professions, schools, and research centers that Americans designate a university. The proliferation meant that many teachers' colleges or academies became daigaku, and these as well as junior colleges have sprung up like unknown flowers in a fertile spring. Other new institutions sponsored by Buddhist groups, by the so-called new religions, by schools of flower arranging, and by other, less probable groups have become daigaku.

The result of such proliferation has been a major broadening of the base of higher education. But along with such changes, to which I shall return in treating other matters, there has been a reorganization of undergraduate and graduate education. A student "majoring in," or "reading," English language or literature and aiming at a teaching post will find the following stages in most of the government universities. (The excellent Tokyo University of Education and to a lesser extent the University of Tokyo provide some exceptions in organizational structure, and others are likely to follow suit. But most of the authors represented in this volume have gone through the system I shall describe.) After passing the fiercely competitive entrance examinations in March, they enter, in their first university term, a college of general education, where they study for two years. These colleges usually represent reconstitutions of the higher schools semi-related to various former imperial universities, or their equivalents, and in fact many of the professors in these colleges, especially during the early postwar transition period, have been former higher school teachers.

After two years of general education, students transfer to the faculty of letters, in which there is an English section or department. Such a section typically includes two sets, or suites, of faculty members, each including a professor, an adjutant professor, and an assistant. (It must be said again that "adjutant professor" is my own coinage: a *jokyoju* is very much junior to a professor, or *kyoju*, but possesses tenure and hopes of succeeding the professor.) In very many instances, the emphasis of such a dual system is like that of an

English university, one line involving English literature, the other English linguistic studies.

After graduation, the English student pursuing graduate work passes on to further study under the close supervision of the professors in the faculty of letters. On paper, he can expect to complete a master's course and win an M.A., and then the doctor's course and the Ph. D. But the new doctorate has proved hard to obtain. Before the war, a doctorate in literature was awarded rarely, and only after some major study had been published. Hence the problem: how could postwar neophytes win a degree of the same title, when many of their professors had not received it? At the time this volume was being compiled, none of its contributors had been awarded the doctorate, although many were nearly forty years of age. In some scientific fields students have won the new doctorate, but in English the rule has been that, the more prestigious the institution, the less willing it has been to award a doctorate in English. Compromise and transition have operated in the time-honored Japanese fashion. The last year in which the old-style doctorate could be earned was 1961. Since then, in the major government universities, various professors who received their education under the prewar system have received new-style doctorates. In the next few years we may expect that the postwar system will gradually become fully operative.

We now enter into matters yet more complex. I must enter a plea that my aim is descriptive rather than evaluative. Whatever the differences between Japanese practice and Western, it should be understood that Japanese ways involve as important a relation to society and traditions as do those of any other system, and that higher education in Japan is very much a lively thing. We may begin with what Japanese describe as something like the academic cartel, which comes down to the hegemony of the University of Tokyo, with Kyoto University running a somewhat distant second, and the rest following behind. Recent events have made major changes, but professors now teaching in Japanese universities are very much aware of these matters I treat as realities of their lives. Both in prewar days and at present, the University of Tokyo has occupied the central position described above. To consider the major chair at Kyoto University, the recently retired Professor Nakanishi was the second incumbent *not* to be a graduate of the University of Tokyo. His appointment, as a graduate of the second in the hierarchy, Kyoto University, was all but unprecedented, since most of the major professors at every national university are and have in the past been Tokyo graduates. (The major private universities have tended to appoint their own people.)

The preeminence of the University of Tokyo has been especially strong in the humanities. In the days after the Meiji Restoration of 1868, there were very few teaching posts, and the Tokyo graduates who won the coveted positions were selected by their professors with unsparing rigor of academic standards. Most graduates of the University of Tokyo hoped for a position at a higher school, and for English graduates from other universities, a post at a higher school was normally the summit of their ambitions. Such positions were, indeed, much coveted, and most graduates from other universities had to content themselves with far less. But all have recognized that the University of Tokyo set, and continues to set, standards of excellence for English study in Japan.

Even so briefly described, the hegemony of the University of Tokyo can easily be translated into the lordly position of Oxbridge or into the former dominance of the Ivy League in the United States. What is much more difficult to convey is the relationship between Japanese professors and their students.* Throughout Japanese society relationships once entered into have characteristically maintained at once an intimacy and an element of patronage unknown in English, "old" Commonwealth, and North American universities. The Japanese phrase for the relationship between a professor and his student, as also for numerous other social relations, is *giri to ninjo,* a phrase that pretty nearly defies translation. Giri derives from the mores of the warrior aristocracy and its Confucian ethic and means something like "obligation" or "indebtedness." It encompasses the ethical duties owed by a junior to his sponsor, whether the latter be a university professor, the head of a school of painting,

---

* I am describing here less the lives of contributors to this volume than a general pattern in Japanese society.

an officer in a corporation, or a leading politician. In theory, and to a very considerable extent in practice, such obligations on the part of the juniors are conceived of as lasting throughout their lives. The junior assists his senior in innumerable ways, sometimes helping to write books. The junior indeed gradually establishes his own school of juniors in a new generation, but his obligations to his senior continue.

The complementary concept of ninjo carries associations derived from the lives of commoners rather than from the aristocracy, and perhaps it may be rendered as "benevolence," insofar as any Western ethical concept resembles it. What the concept implies is the responsibility of the senior to his juniors. He owes them support, appointment to a post, and assistance when needed.

A professor who really takes his obligations to heart can work wonders for his students, getting them good posts, seeing that they are advantageously married, introducing them to profitable publishing ventures, solving numerous personal problems, and in short ensuring security, self-respect, and even a step to fame. Before World War II, Japanese professors were well paid (unfortunately, this is definitely not true today) and their power to do good for a bright lad of meager means was remarkable. Many of them have done so and have excited a passionate devotion in their juniors.

Such respect for one qualified by age, superiority, and professional status is not confined to Japan, nor are the relationships described. Everyone knows that the cabinets of the English government, Labour as well as Conservative, include a preponderance of graduates from Oxbridge and the major "public schools." If one does not know it, he soon discovers that in Canada and the United States university positions are best obtained by the working of networks of friends. What has been unique in Japan has been the thoroughgoing character of such relationships. Even today there is no public advertisement of posts available, as in England, Australia, and other countries; nor is there a system of application by candidates, as in Canada and the United States. The professor is expected to look after, and choose from among, his own. As social mores have been undergoing change, however, alternatives to the old system have gradually appeared, and the giri to ninjo system, though still strong, is perhaps on the wane.

Other unique features of higher education in Japan derive from the preeminence of Tokyo as the nation's capital, center of publishing, and first metropolis. Tokyo is not merely London, Paris, or Rome. Nor is it quite a London with an Oxford within its walls. It is something approaching the Rome of the empire with the Rome of the papacy, at least in the magnetism it holds for most Japanese. Such an attraction produces some interesting effects. Because many well-qualified postgraduates prefer to take a post in a lesser college or university, just to be in Tokyo, posts have come available in much better colleges or universities outside Tokyo for those who might otherwise have been denied them. Or again, the opportunities available to graduates and postgraduates of universities in Tokyo to enter profitable careers in such fields as journalism or broadcasting have meant that fewer have been available for desirable posts not in Tokyo. The result of such factors has been that universities outside Tokyo have taken on new independence and that a growing portion of important academic work, whether in teaching or research, is transacted outside Tokyo. As new centers form, local pride increases, a network of friends transcending university origin emerges, and a more various system of higher education begins to emerge.

As a discipline, English study in Japan presents some paradoxes. A Japanese university has a staff of men and women in English *much* larger than its staff in Japanese language and literature. This situation probably has no counterpart in any other country possessing so distinguished a native literary tradition and so advanced an economy. Perhaps the centrality of French in aristocratic circles of czarist Russia offers some comparison. But at the same time that English is the predominant second language, beyond comparison, in Japan, it has not been, since about 1910, the most popular area of foreign literature. French and Russian or Soviet literature have had far greater prestige, even though they have usually been read in translation. Similarly, American literature and history have not held major places in Japanese university curricula, in spite of the founding of colleges by American missionary efforts, the close if not always friendly relations between the two countries, and what is commonly referred to, seldom favorably, as the Americanizing of postwar Japan.

Some Japanese scholars before World War II took, as it were, a private interest in American literature, and in colleges and universities outside the government sector there were some who showed a teaching interest. But few books appeared before the war that treated American literature as something distinct from English, and in the national universities American studies were all but nonexistent. Japanese novelists showed more interest, and translators have not been idle. But only the now tragically cut Fulbright program effectively altered the role of American studies in Japanese universities and the role of American culture in Japanese intellectual life. Most Japanese professors of English can read French or German; the works they teach most often are English; and behind their soft Japanese intonation of English will often be heard American English, just as American spellings predominate in their writing.

Within such a slowly changing spectrum of English teaching in Japanese universities there have been certain other characteristics of some prominence. One legacy from the Meiji government has been an interest in translation. A foreign work is apt to appear in Japanese before it appears in any language other than its original, and major foreign classics often appear in numerous translations. As a distinguished and multilingual Czechoslovakian professor has aptly described it, to other countries their own literatures are historical, while English literature of all periods is contemporary. It exists in contemporary translations, and Shakespeare can be found in Japan, as in Germany and other countries, in varieties of Japanese from the near classical to the contemporary, reflecting changes in the language during the past century. A teacher of Shakespeare in Japan finds himself confronted with students who have read some of Shakespeare in Renaissance English and some in twentieth-century Japanese.

The emphasis of the Meiji government on translation as a practical necessity, as well as a means to national goals, has also affected methods of teaching English and other foreign languages. At the present time, linguistic study of English, whether theoretical or applied, goes on at a very advanced level indeed. Some students of literature in English complain that too many of their colleagues are turning to degrees in English linguistics as something easier than study of literature. That is as may be (one fancies that literature in English is capable of looking after itself, given a chance). But day in and day out in Japanese schools and universities, the teaching of English consists of exercises in translation. A harsh critic would say that a student who could learn English by such methods could learn anything. A somewhat less harsh critic would think of the Japanese insect whose weight as opposed to its wings and their gyrations theoretically prevents its flying, although fly it does. Certainly, English survives under hazard to the student—and to the professor, who runs (or perhaps walks) his students through translations when he would rather be teaching Milton or Melville.

The strong emphasis on translation or, more broadly speaking, on teaching English as a language as opposed to linguistics or literature becomes obvious when one looks at the numbers of faculty members occupied with teaching at different levels. In most of the government universities, four to six professors in the faculty of letters maintain the responsibility for teaching English literature, philology, and linguistics to upperclassmen and graduate students. The responsibility for teaching and conducting drill sessions for lowerclassmen in English as a language falls, on the other hand, on 38 dons at the University of Tokyo, 26 at Kyoto University, 22 at Tohoku University (in Sendai), and 17 at Osaka University. Because the training is the same for dons in each faculty—that is, either in literature or advanced linguistics—there is sometimes frustration, especially for literary scholars forced to teach language classes. Those in colleges of general education intermittently teach in faculties of letters or organize extracurricular groups performing plays, studying special literary topics, or editing literary magazines. In addition to such activities outside their usual teaching assignments, part-time teaching in other colleges or universities is necessary for a high proportion of professors. This pattern of moonlighting, especially among junior faculty members, is reinforced by the fact that salaries of professors have fallen far below their relative prewar levels. Thus, the professor tends to look outside his own university for part-time work both to alleviate his frustrations and to improve his finances.

The situation is far from ideal, as all educational situations are. But resident foreign instructors (the British Council has contributed effectively in this respect) and new methods of teaching with language laboratories have freshened the breeze for many a Japanese student. Colleges and universities with missionary affiliations have often brought English into the classroom with more life, because there have been more native speakers of English. For several decades such private institutions as Tsuda Women's College or Doshisha University have maintained splendid records for teaching English. More recently, the programs of Tokyo and Osaka Universities of Foreign Languages have proved effective. But it cannot be denied that a number of factors, with the teaching of English by translation among them, have led to English being conceived of as the linguistic arranged marriage, whereas the pleasures of the night seemed to be gained in French and Russian literature. A certain justice will be found in the fact that the Maison Franco-Japonaise occupies a stately building opposite a main gate of Kyoto University, whereas the attractive British Council is situated in a remoter nook, and the practical American Cultural Center will be found near the business district. Foreign countries appear to have found their own methods of translation.

To Lord Chesterfield's observation that nothing but a bishop benefits from translation we must add certain qualifications. The Japanese propensity for translation in the linguistic sense has given the nation the windows it has felt it needed upon an international scene. That many of the windows have been made of Japanese stained-glass is a reality that finds its counterparts everywhere. If we accept translation to mean something more like Chesterfield's wider sense, then we must consider two prime factors in English study in Japan: the "translation" into Japanese of foreign critical methods and the "translation" of individual Japanese to the United States and England. To look first at the former, the accidents of history have been such that the English literature in vogue in Japan has not always been that with the highest claim today. Post-Romantic and especially Victorian tastes held sway during the first decades of English literary

study in Japan. Wordsworth and Shelley were indisputably prominent, whereas Dryden and Pope, not to mention Donne and Herbert,
were formerly little read. Criticism of English literature tended toward the descriptive and the impressionistic. Since World War II,
major changes have transpired, especially under the impact of T. S.
Eliot. The postwar period has seen the rise of a criticism more
methodical, more analytical and psychological, but less popular than
before. Japanese poets might respond to the Imagists, to Yeats, or to
other writers, but Eliot's influence was strongest in the academies.
It is sometimes said that two lines of criticism exist in Japan, the
journalistic and the academic, although the line between a journalist
and an academic frequently puzzles me. But one must admit that
more Japanese professors earn money by journalism than do their
counterparts in the United States, or even in England. In Japan the
professor's views still matter very much.

Turning to the second factor in English study in Japan, the "translation" of Japanese abroad since World War II is the single most
significant fact, apart from the individual gifts of the authors, behind
this book and the present character of Japanese study of English and
American literature. Informal arrangements, Fulbright grants, and
British Council bursaries have radically if subtly affected Japanese
study of English and American literature. The opportunity to work
in well-stocked libraries, to handle, as it were, the Shakespeare first
folio, is an experience no student of English literature, Japanese or
otherwise, can escape unaltered. And the necessity of moving in a
world where only English is spoken does unalterable things to a
person whose conception of English was formed on translation,
narrowly defined, or on contact with missionaries, businessmen, and
resident Americans. To speak my own mind, whether in or out of
season, I shall say that the Japanese government, like its American
and English counterparts, has not spent enough money and has not
always spent it wisely, in sending Japanese professors abroad. The
Japanese Ministry of Education has had a curious institution of allow-
ing senior professors a round-the-world trip shortly before retirement. What this does for English study in Japan may be valuable as
a reward to devoted service, and no sane person could deny it. But

the same person could safely predict what it does to the digestion of a man in his sixties and how little it contributes directly to English study. These same funds might be used more profitably to send Japanese scholars to international conferences, or to sponsor such conferences in the fields of literature and linguistics in Japan. This pattern is well established in the scientific fields, and Japanese scientists have become familiar figures at professional gatherings, but at the Fifth Congress of the International Comparative Literature Society in Belgrade in 1967, only one Japanese professor appeared with travel paid by the Ministry of Education; and how many of us have ever attended an international literary conference in Japan? Of greatest value, however, would be sending younger Japanese scholars to places where they can work with English or American scholars, in major libraries, and in a university setting in which they are more than exotic flowers.

The governments of the United States and of England have sometimes understood these matters, but they have often moved with heavy foot and reluctant hand. They have not always understood what a Japanese *needs* abroad, and they have not often provided the funds to enable him to live above a subsistence level. Officials of the Ministry of Education or of British and American agencies can all too truthfully say that if they had the funds their work could be far more effective. And they have not always had the cooperation necessary from English and American universities, much less from their societies. The remarkable thing, after all, is probably that so much has been done, and that so many qualified younger Japanese have found their way into great university libraries and into the fast friendships that are essential to an international fraternity of scholars.

The contributors to this volume have worked entirely, or for the most part, under the postwar system of higher education in Japan. At the time of compilation, all but one or two had completed a doctoral course under the new program; yet none had been awarded a doctorate under the new system. All have considerable experience teaching and have published a number of articles or books. Most of them have visited the United States or England on Fulbright grants, on British Council grants, by private arrangements, or on teaching appointments (see the Notes on Contributors). It is obvious that some of the essays could not have been written without many hours spent in important research libraries in England or the United States, and the importance of residence abroad would certainly be stressed by all contributors. If this book should lead individuals or agencies in Japan, in England, in the United States, or in other English-speaking countries to increase funding for study abroad by Japanese scholars, the long-term benefits to English study in Japan, and elsewhere, would be incalculable.

One question that will arise in the minds of readers will be whether or not there is something distinctive about Japanese studies of English and American literature. The simplest answer is that there is no one school of English study in Japan. Or put another way, Japanese scholars are part of the international fraternity of students of literature in English, and they share methods of study with colleagues in, say, New York or London. All the same, differences exist. Japan has its own literary traditions extending over the centuries. The first major critical essay on Japanese literature, the preface to the first of the imperial anthologies, the *Kokinshu*, dates from ca. A.D. 905. If that date seems impressive, let it also be said that the standard edition of *The Great Compendium of Japanese Poetic Treatises* (*Nihon Kagaku Taikei*) consists of eleven unannotated volumes of critical works on Japanese poetry. Japanese professors of English literature are, after all, Japanese. They possess a perspective on literature, English included, that no other nation can lay claim to. And it is simply not true that, as some Western visitors have said, they are uninterested in their own literary heritage.

Without question, Japanese scholars or critics of English and American literature have a special vantage point. Their special view reflects in part their Japanese heritage and in part the special situation of Japan among the nations today. Certain less obvious differences, political ones for instance, distinguish their views. Unlike many of their colleagues in historical studies in Japan, few base their study on Marxist assumptions; but they are much more aware of Marxist thought than their English and American colleagues. Also, recent literature and criticism in French probably figure larger on their intellectual landscape than on that of the more intellectually self-sufficient, or self-satisfied, English dons in the United States and England.

There are certain more distinctly Japanese emphases. One of the most striking seems to me to reflect the accretive, sinuous character of Japanese literary forms. Many of the essays postulate an idea or set a question, proceed to develop its detailed associations, and then return to the topic in a different, more advanced guise. Association and iteration in a progressive flow: such a movement corresponds to our experience of much of the finest Japanese literature.

Two other emphases seem more consistent in these essays than they would be in a comparable collection originating elsewhere. One of these is a respect, or affection, for detail. The details matter not so much for their status as objective or statistical verities as for the almost sensuous texture of literature. In this respect, Japanese literary study seems almost to seek an answerable style, a critical or scholarly emphasis corresponding and responding to the rich detail of literary experience. No profound acquaintance with Japanese literature or esthetic preference is necessary for such a concern to be understandable. A second emphasis is concern with the human element. The pursuit engaged in by most of these essays is not after abstraction but after what proves telling about a character, about an author, or about men and women. To take two essays that spring at once to mind as illustrations of these emphases, Professor Fujita's examination of an abstract concept in Shakespeare's plays turns on the sensuous details that give such a concept human validity; and Professor Koike's study of Gissing rounds out the man's whole artistic and very human life. The subjects and methods employed by the authors vary enormously, but again and again the texture of detail and the definition of human experience prove to be the major emphases. With so much said, it need only be added that the rest must be left to the reader's discovery. And I confess to the confident expectation that he will first find himself immersed in essays interesting for what they tell of familiar authors and works, and that only thereafter will he reflect that the critic who has heightened his appreciation lives, not in England or the United States, in Canada or Australia, but in Japan.

English Criticism in Japan

Problems in Chaucer's
Description of Women

Shinsuke Ando

I t is widely recognized that the descriptions of women in medieval European literature were generally written according to patterns prescribed in the traditional rhetorical or poetic manuals. The same is evidently true of English poetry, and Chaucer's relationship to this tradition of European literature claims first attention in any investigation of the problems involved in his description of women.

Edmond Faral has presented what might be regarded as the established rules for the formal description of a person drawn inductively from various examples found in medieval authors.[1] He demonstrates the order of description the medieval poets generally followed, proceeding from the upper to the lower part of the human body, depicting the external appearance of a person from the head moving downward step by step toward the feet, on the basis of the order in which God or Nature (God's "vicaire") supposedly created the human being. Part of Maximianus's *Elegies* written in the sixth century is quoted by Faral as a very early illustration of this traditional pattern.

> Aurea caesaries demissaque lactea cervix
> Vultibus ingenuis visu sedere magis.
> Nigra supercilia, frons libera, lumina clara
> Urebant animum saepe notata meum.
> Flammea dilexi modicumque tumentia labra,
> Quae gustata mihi basia plena darent.[2]

---

[1] E. Faral, *Les arts poétiques du douzième et du treizième siècles* (Paris, 1924), pp. 79 ff.
[2] Ibid., p. 80; translated:

Together with the conventional order of description, it is important to note the qualities assigned to the woman in this passage: "the golden locks," "milky neck," "black eyebrows," "spacious forehead," "clear eyes," "lips . . . moderate[ly] swelling," and so forth. All these are distinctive characteristics which comprised the idealized form of the beautiful woman in European literature up to the end of the sixteenth century.[3] The portraits of women by such so-called rhetoricians as Matthieu de Vendôme and Geoffroi de Vinsauf[4] also conform to that ideal of feminine beauty demonstrated in Maximianus's *Elegies*, and a great many other examples of this kind can be found in vernacular literature of the Middle Ages. In Middle English romances and lyrics (secular lyrics in particular), we also find an extraordinary number of portraits of women endowed with those qualities that make up a stereotyped beautiful woman. Chaucer's women, as well as those in Gower's *Confessio Amantis*,[5] are depicted in very much the same way. Blanche (in *The Book of the Duchess*) and Criseyde and Emelye (in *The Knight's Tale*) also share the same idealized beauty. But then, even the Virgin Mary appears in the religious lyrics as a woman of the same type.[6] A consideration of this single subject, whether from a rhetorical or an esthetic point of view, would be sufficient to demonstrate the cultural unity of medieval Europe.

> Her golden locks and declining milky neck,
>   To simple-looking faces more befitting,
> Her black eyebrows, spacious forehead, clear eyes,
>   Burnt into my mind through frequent glances,
> Her flaming lips I loved with their moderate swelling,
>   Which, I wish, would bring me full sweet kisses.

[3] D. S. Brewer, "The Ideal of Feminine Beauty in Medieval Literature, Especially 'Harley Lyrics,' Chaucer and Some Elizabethans," *Modern Language Review*, 50 (1955): 257–69.

[4] Matthieu de Vendôme, "Ars Versificatoria," st. 1, lines 56, 57, in Faral, *Les arts poétiques*, pp. 129–30; Geoffroi de Vinsauf, "Poetria Nova," lines 554 ff., in ibid., pp. 214–15.

[5] See *The Complete Works of John Gower*, ed. G. C. Macaulay, 4 vols. (Oxford, 1901), 2: 188, lines 767 ff.

[6] See *The Harley Lyrics*, ed. G. L. Brook (Manchester, 1948), p. 16; hereafter cited as Harley Lyrics, with reference to poem and line.

The portrait of Blanche in *The Book of the Duchess* may be said to be the earliest example of a formal description of a woman in Chaucer. For, although a greater part of this portrait relies for its source on Machaut's *Jugement dou Roy de Behaingne*, it is not a translation, in the strict sense of the word, but a fairly free paraphrasing or adaptation, which clearly shows Chaucer's own technical expertise in formal description. But before we proceed to an analysis of this portrait, I think it would be relevant to examine some problems contained in the description of women in *The Romaunt of the Rose*, for this particular aspect of the *Romaunt* presents an appropriate point of departure from which to postulate a relationship between Chaucer and earlier or contemporary provincial English poetry, such as the Harley Lyrics and the tail-rhyme romances. I should like to quote Chaucer's description of Beaute side by side with the French text by Guillaume de Lorris.

Icele dame ot non Biautez,	This lady called was Beaute,
Ausi come une des cinc floiches.	As an arowe, of which I tolde.
En li ot mout de bones toiches:	Ful wel thewed was she holde,
El ne fu oscure ne brune,	Ne she was derk ne broun, but bright,
Ainz fu clere come la lune,	And clere as the mone lyght,
Envers cui les autres estoiles	Ageyn whom all the sterres semen
Resemblent petites chandoiles.	But smale candels, as we demen.
Tendre ot la char come rosee;	Hir flesh was tendre as dew of flour;
Simple fu come une esposee,	Hir chere was symple as byrde in bour;
E blanche come flor de lis.	As whyt as lylye or rose in rys,
Ele ot le vis cler e alis,	Hir face gentyl and tretys.
S'estoit graillete e aligniee.	Fetys she was, and smal to se;
Ne fu fardee ne guigniee,	No wyndred browis hadde she,
Car el n'avoit mie mestier	Ne popped hir, for it neded nought

De soi tifer ne afaitier.	To wyndre hir, or to peynte hir ought.
Les cheveus ot blondez e lons,	Hir tresses yelowe, and longe straughten,
Qui li batoient as talons.	Unto hir helys doun they raughten;
Nés ot bien fait e iauz e bouche. . . .	Hir nose, hir mouth, and eye, and cheke Wel wrought, and all the remenaunt eke. . . .
Briement el fu jonete a blonde,	For yong she was, and hewed bright,
Sade, plaisant, aperte e cointe,	Sore plesaunt, and fetys withall,
Grasse, graillete, gente e jointe.[7]	Gente, and in hir myddill small.[8]

Obviously Beaute is depicted as a beautiful woman in the traditional mold. She is "bright" and "clere," with golden hair, soft skin, a white complexion, well-proportioned features, and a slender waist. There are no essential differences between her and any of the beautiful women appearing in the *Roman*: it is clear that Guillaume portrayed various women according to the established ideal of feminine beauty. In corresponding with this idealized conception of beauty, Blanche (the Duchess), Criseyde, and Emelye can be seen to share much with the women depicted by Guillaume.

What should be underlined in this description of Beaute is the fact that Chaucer, while translating the French text, makes frequent use of the conventional diction which occurs over and over again in Middle English provincial poetry. The adjectives "bright," "gentyl," "gente," "tretys," and "fetys" in the above passage were, of course, conventional epithets for ideal feminine beauty in the romances and lyrics of the non-Chaucerian tradition.

Translating the *Roman* probably gave Chaucer an opportunity to acquire a practical technique for writing poetry. It might be

[7] Lines 992–1016, in *Le Roman de la Rose*, ed. Ernest Langlois, 5 vols. (Paris, 1914–24).

[8] Lines 1006–32; all quotations from Chaucer are taken from *The Works of Geoffrey Chaucer*, ed. F. N. Robinson, 2d ed. (London, 1957).

reasonable to argue that his own art of formal description of women was acquired much more through his actual experience translating or reading French poetry than from studying Geoffroi de Vinsauf's treatise on rhetoric. But was it only through French or Latin models that the young Chaucer established his art of poetry? It seems inconceivable that Chaucer's genius as a poet suddenly awakened only when he gained access to French poetry, without any previous knowledge of English literature. Rather, it seems more reasonable to imagine that Chaucer became acquainted for the first time with the art of formal description of women through popular English verse rather than through the works of Guillaume, Machaut, or Geoffroi. Chaucer the poet could not possibly have written a single line if he was a *tabula rasa*, in complete ignorance of the literary tradition in his mother tongue.

There are a number of significant indications of Chaucer's relationship with English provincial literature in his description of Beaute. "Byrde in bour" is a translation of "esposee." Although it was perhaps for the purpose of rhyming that Chaucer translated this French word, not into one word, "byrde," but into "byrde in bour," what is of special interest is the fact that he used a conventional phrase typical of Middle English romances and lyrics which might have been latent in his memory. As far as Chaucer's poems are concerned, this is the only instance of "byrde in bour," but this phrase appears so frequently as to be a cliché in many lyrics included in MS Harley 2253:

> Ichot a burde in a bour ase beryl so bryht . . .
> [Harley Lyrics, 3. 1]
> þat bird so breme in boure . . .
> [Harley Lyrics, 14. 17]

In both examples, this phrase is obviously employed alliteratively. "Bright in bour," another well-known alliterative phrase of the same kind, was used only once by Chaucer in the *Tale of Sir Thopas* (*The Canterbury Tales*, 7. 742).[9] This again is a conventional phrase constantly used in, for instance, *The Romance of Guy of Warwick* of the

---

[9] Reference is to fragment and line; hereafter cited as *CT*.

Auchinleck MS which Chaucer might very well have known.[10]
Sir Thopas is a superb parody of provincial literary conventions, and
Chaucer achieved a fine ironical effect by the deliberate display of
hackneyed words and phrases of this kind. These conventional
phrases, which Chaucer's *Sir Thopas* caricatures and parodies to make
a "rym dogerel," are used in a perfectly serious way in his early
writing. This will become clearer when we consider the portrait of
Alisoun in *The Miller's Tale* somewhat later.

"Rose on rys" was another of the conventional alliterative phrases
commonly used in Middle English romances and lyrics:

> Hire rode is ase rose þat red is on rys . . .
>
> > [Harley Lyrics, 3. 11]
>
> Lylie-whyt hue is,
> hire rode so rose on rys . . .
>
> > [Harley Lyrics, 5. 31–32]
>
> As rose on rys her rode was red . . .[11]

In the description of Beaute this phrase may be taken as Chaucer's
own insertion, since there is nothing that corresponds to it in
Guillaume's text. Apart from the poet's concern for rhyming, this
would appear to indicate that Chaucer was familiar with the conventional phrases used in depicting the ideal beautiful woman. The stock
of alliterative words and phrases of this kind that belonged to the
provincial literary tradition was therefore also available to the young
Chaucer when he began to write.

These two alliterative phrases, "byrde in bour" and "rose on rys,"
may reasonably be accepted as internal evidence of Chaucer's relation to Middle English provincial poetry. However, in Chaucer we
have only one instance of each of these phrases. Thus, it may be said

---

[10] See *The Romance of Guy of Warwick*, ed. J. Zupitza, Early English Text Society
(London, 1933), p. 380; and J. P. Oakden, *Alliterative Poetry in Middle English* (Manchester, 1935), p. 319. As regards the relationship between Chaucer and the Auchinleck MS, see L. H. Loomis, "Chaucer and the Auchinleck MS: 'Thopas' and 'Guy of
Warwick,' " in *Essays and Studies in Honor of Carleton Brown* (New York, 1940), pp.
111 ff.; also "Chaucer and the Breton Lays of the Auchinleck MS," *Studies in Philology*, 38 (1941): 14–33.
[11] *Sir Launfal*, ed. A. J. Bliss (London, 1960), line 937.

that the language of the *Romaunt* has a certain conservative and conventional nature, while the style gradually becomes more flexible and varied in Chaucer's later works. Perhaps it is unnecessary to deal in such detail with such other adjectives as "fetys" and "tretys," though they, too, clearly exhibit Chaucer's indebtedness to the Middle English literary convention. At any rate, the conservative nature of the phraseology of the *Romaunt* seems to prefigure Chaucer's later devaluation of the time-honored literary convention, such as in his excellent parody of it in *Sir Thopas*. This problem will be discussed subsequently in relation to the description of Alisoun in *The Miller's Tale*.

The portrait of Blanche in *The Book of the Duchess*, which, as already mentioned, depends for its source on Machaut, provides the most typical example in Chaucer of the formal description of an ideal lady. Compared with this, Criseyde is much less formally depicted (*Troilus and Criseyde*, 3. 1247–50; 5. 806–19). Chaucer describes the Duchess's hair, eyes, neck, shoulders, waist, arms, hands, nails, breasts, hips, and back; the description of her forehead, eyebrows, nose, mouth, teeth, chin, thighs, legs, feet, and flesh is omitted!

Chaucer's description presumably presents some points that show what the Duchess was actually like, but it cannot be said that Chaucer depicted her with a realist's eyes. Essentially, the beauty of the Duchess corresponds with the medieval ideal of feminine beauty. By thus idealizing the Duchess in the traditional manner, Chaucer expressed his wholehearted affection and sympathy for the deceased wife of his patron. The external attributes ascribed to the Duchess can be almost directly applied to Criseyde, as well as to Emelye. What is given to the Duchess, Criseyde, and Emelye, then, is no more than an idealized description based on the established type of the beautiful woman. Chaucer did not aim at the depiction of the individual characteristics of each woman: there is nothing here of the realism of the Prologue to *The Canterbury Tales*. It would be inappropriate, however, to assume that Chaucer relied slavishly on the conventional

devices of rhetoric. He never failed to seize the most effective opportunities for employing a traditional formula; thus the formal
description is so adapted as to comprise a moving eulogy for the
Duchess, and the stock formula is most ingeniously applied to
Criseyde when the emotion of love is wrought to the highest pitch.
What can be said with certainty is that Chaucer did not feel any
uneasiness with the rhetorical convention: his powerful use of it in
the most appropriate situations does not display the slightest touch of
mannerism. It is well recognized that Chaucer often commented
indirectly upon the rhetorical convention. His attitude toward
rhetoric, on the whole, seems quietly ironical. The words of the
Host in *The Clerk's Prologue* (*CT*, 4. 16 ff.), or those of the Franklin
in *The Franklin's Prologue* (*CT*, 5. 719 ff.) on the subject of rhetoric
have a certain flavor of irony. Moreover, the passage in *The Nun's
Priest's Tale* that begins with an invocation to Geoffroi de Vinsauf
(*CT*, 7. 3347 ff.) betrays an implicitly ironical attitude toward this
sovereign master of poetics. However, all the remarks on rhetoric
that occur in these passages should be viewed in the light of what we
know of Chaucer's temperament and his superb genius for caricatur-
ing himself: it would be unwise to take this ironical attitude toward
rhetoric as Chaucer's last word on the subject.[12]

As regards the description of the Duchess, the analogy with
Machaut's text has been discussed by various scholars, notably
W. Clemen,[13] G. L. Kittredge,[14] and B. S. Harrison.[15] Harrison per-
suasively argues against J. M. Manly's idea that Chaucer's portrait of
the Duchess is nothing more than a free paraphrasing of the description of a woman included in Geoffroi's *Poetria Nova*.[16] Harrison,
working from a comparative examination of the three texts by
Chaucer, Machaut, and Geoffroi, conclusively demonstrates that

[12] Cf. Dorothy Everett, "Some Reflections on Chaucer's 'Art Poetical,' " in *Essays
on Middle English Literature* (Oxford, 1955), pp. 172–74.
[13] *Chaucer's Early Poetry*, trans. C. A. M. Sym (London, 1963), pp. 54 ff.
[14] "Guillaume de Machaut and *The Book of the Duchesse*," *Publications of the Modern
Language Association*, 30 (1915): 1–24.
[15] "Medieval Rhetoric in *The Book of the Duchess*," *Publications of the Modern
Language Association*, 49 (1934): 428–42.
[16] J. M. Manly, "Chaucer and the Rhetoricians," *The Proceedings of the British
Academy*, 20 (1926): 95–113.

Chaucer is much nearer to Machaut than to Geoffroi. His article is a fairly early instance of the criticism of Manly's theory, and his conclusion seems definitely warranted.[17]

In a lecture delivered to the British Academy in 1926, Manly declared that much of Chaucer's technical art was learned from the poetical treatises, including Geoffroi's, rather than from French models. Ever since this historic lecture, what might be described as a "Manly Cult" has grown up in the study of Chaucer's art of poetry. But was Chaucer really under the direct influence of Geoffroi? Though it cannot be denied that Chaucer knew Geoffroi,[18] whether he had actually learned the *Poetria Nova* or not is a question that has not yet been answered satisfactorily. J. J. Murphy's recent article "A New Look at Chaucer and the Rhetoricians"[19] throws new light on this problem. He offers a penetrating criticism of the theory held by Manly and his followers, asserting that no irrefutable evidence can be found that Chaucer had read Geoffroi's manual. He further declares that the texture of Chaucer's style ought to be studied in connection with a wide range of sources.

Though not unduly emphasized in Murphy's article, this assertion opens up the possibility of investigating Chaucer's art of poetry in terms of the English tradition as well as the European tradition. As regards style and vocabulary, the description in *The Book of the Duchess* suggests a comparatively closer relationship between Chaucer and the French source than in the case of the *Romaunt*, although the latter is nearly a direct translation of the French poem. With so many provincial English elements, which seem to become less striking in *The Book of the Duchess*, the *Romaunt* frequently reminds the reader of the Harley Lyrics or tail-rhyme romances. The picture of Beaute is quite English in spirit and workmanship. A comparison of the description of Beaute with that of the Duchess would be enough to suggest the process of Chaucer's devaluation of the provincial stylistic convention. This convention, which Chaucer appears

[17] Cf. Robert O. Payne, *The Key of Remembrance* (New Haven and London, 1963), p. 128, n. 27.

[18] *The Nun's Priest's Tale, CT*, 7. 3347.

[19] *Review of English Studies*, n.s. 15 (1964): 1–20.

to have tried to divest himself of gradually, comes to life again in the *fabliaux* of *The Canterbury Tales* and in precisely this devalued format.

Chaucer's technique of formal description in *The Canterbury Tales* is best exemplified first of all in the portrait of the Prioress in the Prologue.

> Hir nose tretys, hir eyen greye as glas,
> Hir mouth ful smal, and therto softe and reed;
> But sikerly she hadde a fair forheed;
> It was almoost a spanne brood, I trowe;
> For, hardily, she was nat undergrowe.
>
> [*CT*, I. 152–56]

Much has been said of the delicate tone of irony in this portrait: Chaucer's subtle humor lies in the fact that the image of the Prioress is finely linked with that of a beautiful lady in the secular world. To the Prioress are attributed the very qualities that were ardently worshiped in the lyrics and romances of *fine amour*. The gray eyes, as well as the spacious forehead, were necessary characteristics demanded of the ideal feminine beauty.[20]

Chaucer's humor can be appreciated again in the portrait of the Miller's daughter, where the image of a lady overlays that of a wench.

> This wenche thikke and wel ygrowen was,
> With kamus nose, and eyen greye as glas,
> With buttokes brode, and brestes rounde and hye;
> But right fair was hire heer, I wol nat lye.
>
> [*CT*, I. 3973–76]

This is an excellent parody of the rhetorical convention: the juxta-

---

[20] D. S. Brewer, "The Ideal of Feminine Beauty," pp. 259–60. So far as I know, the only exception to the common description of the forehead is found in Hoccleve's *Praise of His Lady*: see *Secular Lyrics of the Fourteenth and Fifteenth Centuries*, ed. R. H. Robbins (Oxford, 1952), p. 223.

position of the "eyen greye as glas"[21] and the "kamus nose" (i.e.,
flat nose) creates an extravagantly farcical effect, suggesting an incongruous combination of a romance heroine and a quean. Chaucer's
irony lies in his attempt to describe the Miller's daughter within the
formal rhetorical structure primarily designed to depict an aristocratic lady. In this portrait, the idealization constantly seen in the
poetry in praise of courtly love has been entirely cast off. Another
comical effect of this kind produced by the incongruity between the
style and the subject can be found in the passage in *The Nun's
Priest's Tale* where the misfortune of a cock is lamented in high-
sounding terms that would be more appropriate to the death of a
king.[22] It is of special interest that Chaucer refers in this passage to
Geoffroi de Vinsauf, the great master of the art of poetry.

   This mock-heroic tone observable in the Reeve's and the Nun's
Priest's style seems to be much stronger in the description of Alisoun
in *The Miller's Tale*. Within the scope of the formal description of
women, it is in this portrait of a carpenter's wife that Chaucer's
comic spirit is most splendidly illustrated. Chaucer portrays her with
a realist's eyes. Whereas the Duchess, Criseyde, and Emelye are
depicted according to the conventional ideal of feminine beauty, to
Alisoun are attributed her own individual characteristics. Chaucer's
comic spirit may be said to have succeeded in creating a very realistic
picture of a woman by using the most formal devices of rhetorical
tradition. As J. L. Lowes pointed out, Alisoun is among the most
vivid of the *dramatis personae* created by Chaucer, along with
Nicholas, the shrewd student at Oxford, and Absolon, the lovable
but stupid parish cleric.[23] Chaucer depicts her as follows:

> Fair was this yonge wyf, and therwithal
> As any wezele hir body gent and smal.
> A ceynt she werede, barred al of silk,
> A barmclooth eek as whit as morne milk
> Upon hir lendes, ful of many a goore. . . .

[21] See the description of the Prioress in the previous quotation.
[22] *CT*, 7. 3347 ff.
[23] J. L. Lowes, *Geoffrey Chaucer* (Oxford, 1944), pp. 176–77.

And sikerly she hadde a likerous ye;
Ful smale ypulled were hire browes two,
And tho were bent and blake as any sloo.
She was ful moore blisful on to see
Than is the newe pere-jonette tree,
And softer than the wolle is of a wether. . . .

There nys no man so wys that koude thenche
So gay a popelote or swich a wenche.
Ful brighter was the shynyng of hir hewe
Than in the Tour the noble yforged newe.
But of hir song, it was as loude and yerne
As any swalwe sittynge on a berne.
Therto she koude skippe and make game,
As any kyde or calf folwynge his dame.
Hir mouth was sweete as bragot or the meeth,
Or hoord of apples leyd in hey or heeth.
Wynsynge she was, as is a joly colt,
Long as a mast, and upright as a bolt.
A brooch she baar upon hir lowe coler,
As brood as is the boos of a bokeler.
Hir shoes were laced on hir legges hye.
She was a prymerole, a piggesnye,
For any lord to leggen in his bedde,
Or yet for any good yeman to wedde.

[*CT*, I. 3233–70]

The Miller's Tale is in its entirety an ironical parody of the *fine amour* professed by the Knight in the preceding tale (*The Knight's Tale*), and the contrast between the narrators, the Miller and the Knight, brings out the very contrast between the two tales. Nicholas and Absolon can be taken as parodies of Palamon and Arcite, and Alisoun as a parody of Emelye. The comic tone in the description of Alisoun is of the same quality as that used for the Miller's daughter (*The Reeve's Tale*): Chaucer's humor lies in his ingenious twisting of the rhetorical convention, applying it to a carpenter's wife, as if she were an aristocratic lady. Her body is graceful and slender ("gent and smal"), and her "hewe" is "bright." Although she is thus provided with the typical nature of any heroine of romances, the elegance of her body is compared to that of a weasel, and her "hewe" to a new-minted "noble," a gold coin worth 6s. 8d. Her eyes are lecherous ("likerous"); few adjectives would be less proper than this for a noble heroine. Singing and dancing were the indispensable accomplishments demanded for an aristocratic lady, but Alisoun's voice is loud and eager ("loude and yerne") as a swallow's, and she skips about like a kid or calf. Still other instances of Chaucer's modification of conventional devices are easy to find. The courtly audience—well versed in the literary convention—must have burst out laughing when they listened to this exquisite parody by Chaucer. D. S. Brewer, in his excellent discussion of Alisoun's portrait, refers to the fact that "her very name is that of a lady of a famous song in the Harley Lyrics."[24] If Chaucer can be supposed to have known the lyric "Alysoun,"[25] this naming of a carpenter's wife after an aristocratic lady adds a further level of irony. There is no convincing external evidence to prove that Chaucer had read the Harley Lyrics, but E. T. Donaldson's essay "Idiom of Popular Poetry in *The Miller's Tale*"[26] is both suggestive and significant on this problem. Comparing *The Miller's Tale* and the Harley Lyrics, he has shown that there is much in common between the vocabulary of these two works. He observes that the peculiar nature of the vocabulary in *The Miller's Tale*, which differs from Chaucer's other poems, is a result of the poet's deliberate use of the conventional diction with a comic intent. Through what might be called a philological approach to this fabliau, Donaldson has offered an interpretation of Chaucer's dramatis personae as fascinating as the one by J. L. Lowes. His argument provides us with an appropriate point of return to the problem of the relationship between Chaucer and Middle English provincial poetry.

---

[24] Brewer, "The Ideal of Feminine Beauty," p. 267.
[25] Harley Lyrics, 4.
[26] Donaldson, "Idiom of Popular Poetry in *The Miller's Tale*," in *English Institute Essays* (New York, 1951), pp. 116 ff.

"Gent and smal" in the quotation from *The Miller's Tale* is an adjectival phrase commonly found in the Harley Lyrics;[27] and "gent," in particular, was a conventional epithet frequently used for women in romances and lyrics. We have, however, only two instances of Chaucer's use of this word for a person; namely, in the descriptions of Alisoun and Beaute. This adjective, used in all literal seriousness in the *Romaunt*, must have come to be merely an old-fashioned epithet to Chaucer's ear: it was only with a comic intent that he could revive this word in his fabliau.

Such a phrase as "whit as morne milk" can also be found in a song in the Harley Lyrics, though in a slightly different form.[28] Chaucer's ironic attitude toward this kind of hackneyed expression is best exhibited in his use of this phrase, commonly used to represent the whiteness of a woman's skin, to describe Alisoun's white apron. This noble phrase, with which a great many heroines of poetry had formerly been adorned, was completely devalued by Chaucer.

Donaldson has made a detailed analysis of the adjective "hende" (pleasant, courteous, gentle) to clarify the process of its devaluation in Chaucer's poems.[29] Here I should mention that "lemman" was another word which came to share this fate. The word "lemman" means "lover" or "sweetheart" and occurs over and over again in Middle English romances and lyrics. In religious lyrics of the thirteenth and fourteenth centuries the word is used very often even for Jesus Christ.[30] But in *The Manciple's Tale*, "lemman" is defined as a "knavish" word: "Hir lemman' Certes, this is a knavyssh speche!" (*CT*, 9. 206). It seems to be precisely in this sense that the word "lemman" is used in *The Canterbury Tales*: it is accepted in the devalued pejorative sense of "mistress" or "concubine":

Slepynge, his lemman kitte it with hir sheres;
Thurgh which treson loste he bothe his yen.
[*CT*, 3. 722–23]

[27] See Harley Lyrics, 23. 45.
[28] Harley Lyrics, 7. 77. Cf. The Prologue to *CT*, line 358: *The Romaunt*, line 1196.
[29] Donaldson, "Idiom of Popular Poetry," pp. 122 ff.
[30] See *English Lyrics of the Thirteenth Century*, ed. Carleton Brown (Oxford, 1932), nos. 34, 35, 36, 37, 63, 64, etc.; and *Religious Lyrics of the Fourteenth Century*, ed. Carleton Brown (Oxford, 1924), nos. 52, 78, etc.

Unto his lemman Dalida he tolde
That in his heeris al his strengthe lay,

[*CT*, 7. 2063–64]

In both cases the word identifies Samson's betraying "lemman,"
Delilah, and its pejorative sense as "knavyssh speche" is clear.

As regards Chaucer's own poems, it is only in *The Miller's Tale,
The Reeve's Tale*, and *Sir Thopas* that the word "lemman" is used in
the nonpejorative sense.[31] Whereas in *The Knight's Tale* the word
"lady" is chosen for a sweetheart, in *The Miller's Tale*, a kind of
parody of the former, "lemman" is constantly used. The difference
in the shade of meaning between "lemman" and "lady" should
demonstrate a striking contrast between a gay fabliau and a serious
romance in praise of courtly love. Chaucer's deliberate use of
"lemman" for a sweetheart in the fabliaux (the Miller's and the
Reeve's tales) clearly shows the poet's attention to the relevance of
style to subject matter. Moreover, it is easy to understand why the
word was also used in a nonpejorative sense in *Sir Thopas*, if we
remember that this was a parody of the conventional rhyming
romances.

What we should further note is that "lemman" is used four times
in the *Romaunt* (fragment A) in the nonpejorative sense.[32] Un-
doubtedly the word was no "knavyssh speche" to Chaucer's ear and
imagination when he was translating the *Roman* into English. It was
before the literary tradition in London English had been firmly
established that Chaucer attempted his translation of this great work
of French poetry. It may not be far from the truth to imagine that
what gave him a primary vehicle of expression in English was the
traditional diction which had already been long established in Middle
English provincial poetry. The instance of "lemman," together with
the other provincial elements we have considered, suggests the literary environment surrounding the young Chaucer. His changing attitude to this kind of literary convention needs to be examined
alongside his development as a master poet. Deliberately adopting

[31] *The Miller's Tale, CT*, I. 3278, 3280, 3700, 3705, 3719, 3726; *The Reeve's Tale,
CT*, I. 4240, 4247; *Sir Thopas, CT*, 7. 788.
[32] Lines 1209, 1272, 1290 (Fr. "amie"); line 1421 (Fr. "drue").

conventional diction, Chaucer finally attained a unique style of comedy.

Vocabulary is not the only problem that faces us. We should note also that Chaucer conveys the feel of alliterative verse in some of the lines in his description of Alisoun. The use of a succession of alliterative lines in this passage may also suggest Chaucer's subtle intention to present a carpenter's wife with a certain provincial aura about her.[33] Behind this comical portrait of Alisoun we should not fail to recognize Chaucer's implicit criticism of both the provincial literary convention and the literary taste of the Miller narrator. In *The Reeve's Tale* and *Sir Thopas* as well, we can recognize the same kind of critical spirit at work in Chaucer.

Various scholars—notably C. Schaar[34] and D. S. Brewer—have advanced fruitful suggestions about Chaucer's description of women. Pursuing this line of analysis, I have attempted to examine the relationship between Chaucer and Middle English provincial poetry. The technique of formal description, based essentially on rhetorical conventions, may well be assumed to have definite relevance to the establishment of Chaucer's "art poetical." Although the influence on Chaucer of French and Italian literature cannot be overemphasized, it is impossible to regard Chaucer's style as having been formed without relationship to the literary tradition in his mother tongue. Chaucer wrote in nothing but English; and his English heritage ought to be further investigated.[35] In view of the small amount of internal evidence, it may be too sweeping an assumption to relate Chaucer's art of poetry directly to English tradition, yet his description of women does seem to offer us valuable insights into this difficult but tempting subject.

[33] Regarding the problems of alliteration in Chaucer, see Dorothy Everett, "Chaucer's 'Good Ear,' " *Essays on Middle English Literature* (Oxford, 1955), pp. 139 ff.; F. Kuriyagawa, "Chaucer to Chihogen Bungaku" (2) [Chaucer and Middle English Regional Literature (2)], *Eigo Seinen* [The Rising Generation], 108, no. 4 (1962): 144 ff.

[34] *The Golden Mirror* (Lund, 1955).

[35] Recently one noteworthy tendency in the study of Chaucer has been to view him in the light of the English tradition. This attitude has been forcefully emphasized by D. S. Brewer in his essay "The Relationship of Chaucer to the English and European Traditions," in *Chaucer and Chaucerians*, ed. D. S. Brewer (London, 1966), pp. 1–38.

Time and Colin Clout, the Shepherd

Haruhiko Fujii

Time in Spenser's *Shepheardes Calender* has three aspects. There is, first, a cyclic stream of time rotating endlessly. Next, there are a few moments when time stops and the shepherds enjoy a fleeting but intense joy in living. Finally, Colin Clout has a personal consciousness of time as a never returning stream flowing toward a definite end: his death. The aim of the present essay is to examine the nature of these three aspects of time, especially the nature and function of Colin Clout's consciousness of time.[1]

The concept of time as a cycle is readily suggested by the plan of making a calendar of eclogues. This task completed, Spenser's envoy says:

> Loe I have made a Calender for euery yeare,
> That steele in strength, and time in durance shall outweare.[2]

It is a traditional conception, derived, as E. K. notes, from Horace and Ovid, to compare one's own work to steel or time. Ronsard also writes, "Plus dur que fer j'ay fini mon ouvrage."[3] Yet, while other

---

[1] In his valuable essay "The Implications of Form for *The Shepheardes Calender*," *Studies in the Renaissance*, 9 (1962): 309–21, S. K. Heninger, Jr., has anticipated my analysis of time as cycle and as forward stream, and he provides detailed information about likely sources for Spenser's temporal cyclicism. My aim lies not with the origins of Spenser's work but with the function of Colin Clout, its central figure, and with not two but three orders of time in which Spenser's shepherd finds himself involved.

[2] All quotations from *The Shepheardes Calender* are from *The Works of Edmund Spenser: A Variorum Edition*, vol. 7, *The Minor Poems, Part One*, ed. Charles Grosvenor Osgood and Henry Gibbons Lotspeich (Baltimore, 1943); hereafter cited as *Works*, vol. 7. In the text, references are to eclogues and lines in this volume.

[3] "Harder than steel I have finished up my work." Pierre de Ronsard, "A sa Muse," line 1, in *Poésies choisies*, ed. L. Becq de Fouquières (Paris, 1873), p. 163.

poets use these images to boast that their works are immortal because of their esthetic perfection, Spenser's lines have an additional meaning. He asserts that the essential value of his work consists in its enduring quality as an ideal calendar to be used perpetually by all shepherds. Once a perfect calendar is made, the time measured by this calendar seems to repeat the same course every year. In other words, the calendar forces time to flow in an enclosed, circular course of eternal return. The cyclical course of time set by the framework of the calendar finds corresponding patterns in the views of time held by some shepherds in what E. K. calls "moral" eclogues. In these eclogues, which show exemplary patterns for pastoral life, the good shepherds almost always interpret time as a wheel rotating everlastingly. In "Februarie," when Cvddie loudly complains about the bitterness of winter, Thenot instructs him:

> Must not the world wend in his commun course
> From good to badd, and from badde to worse,
> From worse vnto that is worst of all,
> And then returne to his former fall?
>
> [11–14]

These words reveal Thenot's belief in the medieval idea of the wheel of fortune. Indeed, he declares that he was never "to Fortune foeman" (21). While Thenot interprets the lifetime of an individual as a wheel, Piers, in "Maye," formulates a similar idea concerning the whole of human history when he predicts the return of the state of innocence.

> The time was once, and may againe retorne,
> (For ought may happen, that hath bene beforne)
> When shepeheards had none inheritaunce,
> Ne of land, nor fee in sufferaunce:
> But what might arise of the bare sheepe,
> (Were it more or lesse) which they did keepe.
>
> [103–08]

The interpretations of time by Thenot and by Piers share another common feature in that their perspective is from the lowest point in the cycle. Although both of them are firmly convinced of the return of happiness in the future, old Thenot is now afflicted by the cold weather and Piers lives in an age when the shepherds have reached the worst stage of their degeneration. In the "October" eclogue, Cvddie applies this interpretation to the history of poetry. In Virgil's times the poet was warmly patronized by Maecenas, but since then, Cvddie complains, there has been no hero worthy to be praised by poets, and poetry itself has been degenerating. In this lament, however, Cvddie never abandons the hope that there will be an age of great poetry sometime in the future.[4] Like Thenot and Piers, he views history as a cycle and his viewpoint is also from its lowest point.

The interpretation of time as a cycle provides Spenser with an effective means of introducing satiric elements into his pastoral. Traditionally the pastoral world is an ideal land detached from the evils of actual human society, but because of this very detachment shepherds can act as critics of social and religious evils. Drawing a contrast with the innocence of the simple world in which they live, they can point out the evils perpetrated by a sophisticated society. As the elements of social and religious criticism increase, however, the pastoral genre approaches satire proper and loses its identity. On the other hand, if the distance between the pastoral world and actual society is too great, the pastoral poem will be merely a pleasant daydream having no vital connection with reality. Spenser's use of cyclic time solves the problem: the alternate phases of misery and happiness make it possible for Spenser's shepherds to be properly satirical toward the evil around them without completely losing their vision of idyllic happiness.

There are a few shepherds in The Shepheardes Calender, however, who do enjoy moments of sheer happiness. To them the wheel of time seems to have stopped when they reach the top of the cycle. Willye and Thomalin, who talk about catching Cupid in "March," Hobbinoll, who recites Colin's colorful praise of the Queen in

[4] W. L. Renwick says about this poem: "In spite of the recurrence of the despondent mood, this is rather a declaration of faith in the poetic vocation, and of the ambitions of the New Poetry" (Works, 7: 374).

"Aprill," and Willye and Perigot, who are engaged in the heated singing match in "August"—these are the happy shepherds who can enjoy contentment. Willye's words urging Thomalin to tell the story show how impatiently they endeavor to forget the past and the future while plunging into the rapture of the present moment.

> Let be, as may be, that is past:
> That is to come, let be forecast.
> Now tell vs, what thou hast seene—
>
> ["March," 58–60]

In response to this demand, Thomalin tells what happened to him "vpon a holiday" (61). The singing match in "August" also begins with the lines:

> It fell vpon a holly eue,
> hey ho hollidaye.
>
> [53–54]

The happy idyllic world is the world of holiday. The term "recreative" by which E. K. classifies this group of eclogues is, therefore, most appropriate to denote this world. That holiday world of eternal youth which time seems to have no power to destroy is a characteristic aspect of pastoral. Marlowe's shepherd, dreaming of the world of eternal holiday, addresses his love, "Come live with me, and be my Love," though his plea is not granted by Ralegh's realistic nymph, who realizes that the dream is illusory and that "Time drives the Flockes from field to fold."[5] Milton's "Sunshine Holiday"[6] also shows continuity with Spenser in the image of pastoral holiday. The happy moments, however, are few in the world of *The Shepheardes Calender*. In "the mery moneth of May" ("Maye," 2) the ascetic Piers turns his back upon the merriment of youth. Even "August," which starts with a merry rollick, ends with the recitation of Colin's

---

[5] Christopher Marlowe, "The Passionate Shepheard to his Love," line 1, and Sir Walter Ralegh, "The Nimphs Reply to the Sheepheard," line 5, both in *English Pastoral Poetry: From the Beginnings to Marvell*, ed. Frank Kermode (London, 1952), pp. 146–48.

[6] John Milton, "L'Allegro," line 98, in *John Milton: Complete Poems and Major Prose*, ed. Merritt Y. Hughes (New York, 1957).

sad song. The keynote of this work is not delight but melancholy.
The main cause of the sorrowful tone is the depression of Colin
Clout, who appears in the four plaintive eclogues: "Januarye,"
"Iune," "Nouember," and "December." "Nouember" is a pastoral
elegy on Dido's death, but the other three poems are Colin's laments
over his unrequited love. Colin's laments, therefore, occupy the
three crucial places on the calendar, namely the beginning, the
middle, and the end. In some other eclogues as well, his fellow
shepherds recite his songs and regret that he has abandoned the poet's
mission because of his unfortunate experience. Thus Colin appears,
though intermittently, throughout the calendar. This central figure
of the calendar is a solitary poet standing apart from his fellow shepherds. In "Iune" Hobbinol addresses Colin:

> Lo *Collin*, here the place, whose pleasaunt syte
> From other shades hath weand my wandring mynde.
> Tell me, what wants me here, to worke delyte?
> The simple ayre, the gentle warbling wynde,
> So calme, so coole, as no where else I fynde:
> The grassye ground with daintye Daysies dight,
> The Bramble bush, where Byrds of euery kynde
> To the waters fall their tunes attemper right.
>
> [1–8]

This is one of the passages in *The Shepheardes Calender* where the
description approaches most closely the classical milieu of Virgil's
eclogues. Commentators have pointed out that shadow, cool wind,
bush, birds, and water are all conventional features of the classical
pastoral landscape.[7] But Colin, who cannot share this happy moment
with Hobbinol, replies:

> O happy *Hobbinoll*, I blesse thy state,
> That Paradise hast found, whych *Adam* lost.
>
> [9–10]

At this moment Hobbinol's happiness has the same quality as that of
those shepherds who enjoy the idyllic bliss of eternal youth, for

[7] See *Works*, 7: 310–11.

Hobbinol is in the garden where time does not exist. Actually Colin himself was once in such a blessed world. Hobbinol recalls that Colin composed words in praise of Eliza when "by a spring he laye, / And tuned it vnto the Waters fall" (" Aprill," 35–36). But now Colin is an unhappy wanderer pursued by angry gods. It is true that we find a similar situation in Virgil's first eclogue, where Tityrus, who has preserved his land, talks to his friend Meliboeus, who lost his. Yet while Meliboeus's loss of fields is an external misery, Colin's melancholy, caused by an inner affliction, is more subjective. His lament in the latter part of "August" also reveals his inner darkness. Here Colin chooses, as the fittest place to meditate on his misfortune, a deep forest where he can hear the night birds' ominous shrieks.

It is Colin's unrequited love for Rosalind that has driven him to this misery. Now he looks back upon his past and repeatedly compares his life to the changing of the four seasons. Although the comparison of life to the four seasons is conventional, Colin's keen sensitivity to the changes in the speed of time's flow during his life is remarkable. In "Januarye" he addresses the earth:

> Thou barrein ground, whome winters wrath hath wasted,
> Art made a myrrhour, to behold my plight:
> Whilome thy fresh spring flowrd, and after hasted
> Thy sommer prowde with Daffadillies dight.
> And now is come thy wynters stormy state,
> Thy mantle mard, wherein thou maskedst late.
>
> [19–24]

Spring and summer were happy but short, there was no autumn, and now Colin is in the midst of dreary winter. What does this change of seasons signify? Of course it could be an objective description of seasonal change in England. "As if nature were keeping balance," writes Ken'ichi Yoshida, "although England from spring to autumn is superbly lovely, England's winter is miserable and ugly. Moreover, in this country where winter comes in October, these two seasons are almost equal in length."[8] Yet even if the seemingly unendurable length of winter is an objective fact, whether

[8] Ken'ichi Yoshida, *Eikoku no Bungaku* [English Literature] (Tokyo, 1951), p. 15.

the memory of the past summer is near or far—like any consideration of time—is fundamentally a subjective question. The previous
summer could be recalled either as long past or very recent. The
word "late" describes not so much the objective speed of the
season's change as the speed of the flow of Colin's inner time. His
interior stream flows rapidly till it reaches winter:

> Such stormy stoures do breede my balefull smart,
> As if my yeare were wast, and woxen old.
> And yet alas, but now my spring begonne,
> And yet alas, yt is already donne.
>
> [27–30]

In "Iune" Colin's retrospection shows us another aspect of his
preoccupation with time: his sense of psychological freedom.

> And I, whylst youth, and course of carelesse yeeres
> Did let me walke withouten lincks of loue,
> In such delights did ioy amongst my peeres:
> But ryper age such pleasures doth reproue,
> My fancye eke from former follies moue
> To stayed steps: for time in passing weares
> (As garments doen, which wexen old aboue)
> And draweth newe delightes with hoary heares.
>
> [33–40]

The image of walking in these lines signifies the changes in Colin's
consciousness of inner freedom. And the core of his consciousness is
his awareness of time, for he recapitulates these changes in the
sentence "time in passing weares." Here "time" does not mean
objective time, since objective time which continues mechanically
forever cannot be worn out like clothes. C. H. Herford notes that
"the phrase is a blending of two ideas; 'time as it passes wears away
life,' and 'life, as time passes, *wears*' ('as garments doen')."[9] Time and
life, therefore, are inextricably entwined in Colin's consciousness.

Colin's fragmentary retrospections in "Januarye" and "Iune" are
completed in the longer retrospection in "December." Here again

---

[9] *Shepheards Calendar*, ed. C. H. Herford (London, 1895), p. 138.

Colin compares his life to the four seasons. First there was a spring when he could enjoy those carefree days which he erroneously supposed to be perpetual: "Tho deemed I, my spring would euer laste" (30). This thought contrasts with his recollection in "Januarye" that his spring had ended immediately. The two passages are different interpretations of the same experience resulting from a difference in point of view. When, as in "Januarye," he looks back on his spring, conscious of its having ended, it seems to have ended as soon as it began. But when, as in "December," Colin recalls what he actually felt in the midst of youth, he can remember that his spring then seemed as if it would continue forever. Colin's agony begins in the summer when he experiences love. Under its sway, he loses freedom. However violent his actions may be, he has lost the real freedom he had in the spring. The summer provides various kinds of knowledge, without affording a cure for his wounds. Time passes, bearing no fruit:

> Thus is my sommer worne away and wasted,
> Thus is my haruest hastened all to rathe.
>
> [97–98]

There is no harvest in Colin's autumn; and his life's winter is rapidly approaching:

> My spring is spent, my sommer burnt vp quite:
> My harueste hasts to stirre vp winter sterne.
>
> [128–29]

His situation in this poem is somewhat similar to that of Thenot in "Februarie." Thenot also looks back upon the past in the winter of his life. He, too, has had more sorrowful years than happy ones. There is, however, a marked difference between the recollections of the two shepherds. While Thenot calmly accepts his fate, believing in the return of happiness, Colin has no such happy expectation. What Colin feels is the stream of time gathering more and more speed as his life approaches the end. Near the end of "December" he says:

27

Winter is come, that blowes the bitter blaste,
And after Winter dreerie death does hast.

[143–44]

And again:

Winter is come, that blowes the baleful breath,
And after Winter commeth timely death.

[149–50]

In Colin's consciousness, life is a gradually accelerating stream of time flowing toward death. He seems to feel that, although the wheel of time seems to revolve perpetually for the other shepherds, his own life will be a line vanishing at the moment of his death. The best reaction he can muster to his fate is to call his end "timely."

The contrast between cyclic time and the stream of time culminating in the death of an individual is the nominal theme of "Nouember" as well. In this elegy, Colin laments Dido's death, asking why a dead person never returns to the world, although the wild flowers that wither in winter can revive in spring. This perennial human question is posed in "The Lament for Bion" by Moschus and has since formed a part of the convention of pastoral elegy. The Book of Job provides a biblical version of the same idea (14: 7–10). Here, as in many pastoral elegies, this question elicits the answer that, although Dido never returns to us, her soul has ascended to heaven to share the seat of the gods. For poets dealing with death, the ascension of the soul to the eternal world has often proved to be an effective way of resolving the contradiction between the continuity of cyclic time and the death of an individual. Half a century after Spenser, Milton made full use of this convention in *Lycidas* to reestablish his faith after the trial he underwent at the death of his friend. It is doubtful, however, whether the theme of "Nouember" is a serious meditation upon the real death of an individual. Death in this poem may rather be figurative, symbolizing some other crisis.[10]

[10] Paul E. McLane convincingly interprets Dido as Elizabeth I and the poem as "an elegy with ironic overtones which stated, in riddling fashion, the death of England and of Elizabeth, a death which seemed, in terms of the Alençon marriage, imminent in the last few months of 1579." See *Spenser's Shepheardes Calender: A Study in Elizabethan Allegory* (Notre Dame, Indiana, 1961), p. 60.

In any case, the poem proceeds so smoothly from sorrow to consolation that we find no mental struggle with the problem of death in this elegy. Colin's thoughts on death in "Nouember" are less dark than his melancholy in "December."

Colin's melancholy does not, however, drive him into helpless desperation. "December" ends with serene words of farewell:

> Adieu delightes, that lulled me asleepe,
> Adieu my deare, whose loue I bought so deare:
> Adieu my little Lambes and loued sheepe,
> Adieu ye Woodes that oft my witnesse were:
> Adieu good *Hobbinol*, that was so true,
> Tell *Rosalind*, her *Colin* bids her adieu.
>
> [151–56]

Moreover, the detailed accounts of his recollections in the earlier part of this poem, especially the memories of happy boyhood, show Colin's contented acceptance of each phase of his past life. Colin seems to be reconciled to time. Although his consciousness of time has been different from the other shepherds' cyclic concept of time, he is not disturbed by the thought that his life should disappear from that cycle. Indeed, ironically enough, Colin's calmness may be a result of his recognition that even though the time he lives may disappear from the cycle, the cycle itself will last forever.

Through his preoccupation with time, Colin Clout arouses the modern reader's interest in *The Shepheardes Calendar*. When these eclogues were written, Spenser's friends may have been more or less able to identify the shepherds with actual people, and this must have afforded his contemporaries a peculiar interest. Such identification is, however, extremely difficult for the modern reader.[11] We can be sure only that Colin Clout represents Spenser himself. Yet what is important about Colin's personality is, not the fact that he shares some experiences with the poet who created him, but the fact that Colin has a keen consciousness of his inner self, lacking in the other shepherds. Colin is the only shepherd in the *Calender* who speaks in

---

[11] McLane (see n. 10) attempts identification of the shepherds with contemporary characters.

the form of monologue. While the reader can only listen to other shepherds engaged in dialogue with each other, he can see directly into Colin's subjective world, which is colored by his melancholy view of time. It has been shown by several commentators that "December" imitates Clement Marot's *Eclogue au Roy*, in which another poet looks back upon his past in his life's winter; but while Marot's eclogue ends with the joyful recovery of hope, Colin calmly awaits his death.[12] The uniqueness of Colin's personality consists in his consciousness of time as a never returning flow.

Colin Clout lacks the dimensions of a tragic figure, however, as we can see by comparing his situation in "December" with that of Donne when he wrote:

> now mine end doth haste,
> I runne to death, and death meets me as fast,
> And all my pleasures are like yesterday.[13]

This comparison, however, is inappropriate, for death in "December" is not so much the death of a specific man as a figurative death signifying the end of a phase of life. The subject of this poem (as also to an important degree of Milton's *Lycidas*) is not the irrecoverable death of an individual but the end of youth, which also inevitably visits every person, yet without the annihilating threat of real death. In this sense, Spenser's prediction that these eclogues will be a universal calendar is justified. Colin Clout, the melancholic shepherd meditating on the past flux of his inner time, is a universal figure representing man at the end of his youth.

[12] *Works*, 7: 417–18.
[13] John Donne, "Holy Sonnets" (1635), no. 1, lines 2–4, in John Donne, *The Divine Poems*, ed. Helen Gardner (Oxford, 1959), p. 12.

The Concept of the
Royal in Shakespeare

Minoru Fujita

In his last tribute to Hamlet, Fortinbras says that he was likely "to have proved most royal." The ideals and values invested in the word *royal* make it a richly complex term, one no doubt owing something to politics and society in Shakespeare's day, but one more important to us for its symbolism and its representation on the Elizabethan stage. We may hypothesize that the idea had much to do with the civic tradition of pageantry and that Shakespeare shared with his audience theatrical as well as esthetic associations in their conceptions of "the royal." The evidence to support this can be discovered most readily in the history plays, through an examination of the connotations the word possessed. Other evidence and associations can be found in the tradition of pageantry. After exploring these "royal realms," we can seek to use the concept of "the royal" to help explain the nature of the tableau in the final scene of *Antony and Cleopatra*.

In his history plays Shakespeare sometimes employs the word *royal* in a manner apparently redundant and meaningless. It serves almost as an expletive, with little positive significance. For example, in the third part of *Henry VI*, we find the following:

> And now to London with triumphant march,
> There to be crowned England's royal king
> [2. 6. 87–88][1]

[1] All the citations from Shakespeare are to the New Shakespeare editions, numbers indicating act, scene, and line, respectively.

Or in the first part of the play, the adjective is attached to "queen":

> Therefore, my Lord Protector, give consent
> That Margaret may be England's royal queen.
>
> [5. 5. 23–24]

A king or queen, of course, belongs to a royal family and is royal by definition. Therefore the wording "royal king" or "royal queen" may seem tautological. In the above examples, however, the speakers are talking of the future enthronement of the persons concerned, and the epithet *royal* describes the speakers' own expectation or hope that those persons will prove to be truly equal to the office and dignity of majesty, or that, upon their accession to the throne, they may be richly invested with the bliss and glory befitting a king or a queen. The apparent redundancy of this epithet is by no means meaningless.[2]

When, therefore, Shakespeare says "royal king" we may understand that the words connote the idealization of a king and are not necessarily meant to give a real description of him. In *Richard II* we find England idealized by Gaunt, and the word *royal* harmonizes well with his praise:

> This royal throne of kings, this sceptered isle,
> This earth of majesty, this seat of Mars, . . .
> This blessed plot, this earth, this realm, this England,
> This nurse, this teeming womb of royal kings, . . .
>
> [2. 1. 40–41, 50–51]

Royal is a word that can heighten a happy and congratulatory feeling; there is felicitation involved in the pomp and majesty of royalty, and other such words, like *kingly* and *regal*, cannot vie with *royal* in its rich connotations and its joyful, auspicious mood. In a tragedy, the effect of this adjective may enhance the tragic feeling. As we have seen, young Hamlet's death is felt the more painful and pathetic, "For he was likely, had he been put on, / To have proved most royal."[3]

---

[2] See also *Richard III*, 3. 7. 20–22. The *OED* says of the word *royal*: "In a number of Shakespearean passages . . . the adj. has a purely contextual meaning, the precise force of which is not always clear" ("Royal," A. adj.).

[3] *Hamlet*, 5. 2. 396–97.

The sense of rejoicing conveyed by the word *royal* has to do with a public, ceremonial world transcending ordinary experience. It conveys feelings aroused by royalty on public view. Although it represents something above the workaday lives of the time, it retains its universal, irresistible appeal. On Shakespeare's stage we often find that the auspicious joy suggested by the adjective *royal* takes a concrete, visible form and appeals directly to the senses of the spectators. In *Henry VIII*, act 4, scene 1, we see a stage version of Queen Anne's coronation procession *"pass over the stage in order and state."* The nature of the visual appeal obtained from this spectacle can well be understood from its detailed stage direction.[4] Attention to appropriate detail is evident. Costly items such as *"sceptre of gold," "robe of estate," "coronal of gold,"* and so on, embellish the parade in this scene, and under the canopy borne by four of the Cinqueports goes *"the Queen in her robe, in her hair, richly adorned with pearl, crowned."* Seeing the sumptuous sight, one of the stage spectators speaks admiringly: "A royal train, believe me" (4. 1. 37). "Royal" here is meant to describe the impression of the spectacular beauty which the costumes, properties, and procession as a whole present to the audience. The *OED* cites this line as the basis for the definition "finely arrayed; resplendent; grand or imposing."[5] What is interesting here is that, although the beauty portrayed in the stage procession is directly borrowed from the world of royalty, the word *royal* does more to qualify the nature of the beauty itself than to suggest the initial relationship of that beauty to kingship. In other words, the kind of beauty termed "royal" is, despite its origin in kingship, now felt to form an independent esthetic category which is complete in itself and distinguished for its gorgeous, stately splendor.

Another interesting example of the use of the adjective *royal* is found in *Henry VIII*. In act 1, scene 1, Norfolk reports upon "the earthly glory" displayed by the British and French kings meeting in the Field of the Cloth of Gold:

> . . . men might say,
> Till this time pomp was single, but now married

[4] *Henry VIII*, 4. 1. 36 s.d.
[5] *OED*, "Royal," adj. II. 8. b.

To one above itself. Each following day
Became the next day's master, till the last
Made former wonders its. To-day the French,
All clinquant, all in gold, like heathen gods,
Shone down the English; and to-morrow they
Made Britain India: every man that stood
Showed like a mine. Their dwarfish pages were
As cherubins, all gilt; the madams too,
Not used to toil, did almost sweat to bear
The pride upon them, that their very labour
Was to them as a painting. Now this masque
Was cried incomparable; and th' ensuing night
Made it a fool and beggar. The two kings,
Equal in lustre, were now best, now worst,
As presence did present them: him in eye
Still him in praise; and being present both,
'Twas said they saw but one, and no discerner
Durst wag his tongue in censure.

$$[\text{I. I. } 14\text{--}33]$$

This may well sound like an extravagance, and Buckingham quite naturally responds by saying, "O, you go far." But in Norfolk's opinion even this is not likely to have given satisfactory expression to what he has witnessed in the spectacular encounter of the two kings, and, full of admiration, he says, "All was royal."

Norfolk's story is remarkable for its references to gold and for its intimations of the contemporary fashion of pageantry. The first matter bears very much upon the second. The magnificent appearance of the two kings and their parties is likened to the visual effect of gold. In order to make his audience experience the utmost splendor of the kingly meeting, Shakespeare felt no hesitation in appealing outright to that sense of beauty and visual imagination which had been universally cultivated among people through their years of contact with pageantry. And doubtless the brilliance of gold was a source of pleasure to people's sense of sight. In a pageant it always took the lead in affording the feeling of luxury and splendor to the spectacle. Chroniclers tried to strengthen the impression of magnificence by giving all the sumptuous details of a spectacle. In his chronicles, Hall records the Christmas kept by the king in 1512:

> . . . within the Castle wer six Ladies clothed in russet satin laide all over with leves of golde, and every owde knit with laces of blewe silk and golde: on their heddes, coyfes and cappes all of gold. After this Castle had been carried about the hal, and the Quene had behelde it, in came the Kyng, with five other appareled in coates, the one halfe of russet satyne, spangled with spangels of fine gold, the other halfe rich clothe of gold; on ther heddes cappes of russet satin embroudered with works of fine gold bullion.⁶

Neither historians nor theatre audiences were bored by the artless repetition of "gold." And it is interesting to note that, in British pageantry and historical writing at this time, the idea of conspicuous costliness, sheer sumptuousness, was an important index of the concept of the beautiful. Apart from political or sociological implications, then, the adjective *royal* implied the costly beauty that had traditionally been associated with kingship. People were conscious of royalty as the office, dignity, and power of a prince, and at the same time they felt it was a basis of their cult of beauty.

In the descriptions of public pageants, the word *royal* was often used to deepen the sense of luxury and magnificence. On his return from Agincourt in 1415, Henry V was welcomed by a pageant show. According to a contemporary account, the king was "riolly receyvet with procession and song," and when he entered London

> the stretes were riolly hanget with rich clothes, & in Corn-hylle was made a riol toure full of patriarches syngyng. . . . And the cros in the Chepe was riolly arrayet like a castell with toures pight full of baners.⁷

---

⁶ John Nichols, *The Progresses, Public Processions, &c., of Queen Elizabeth*, 3 vols. (London, 1823), 1: 70.
⁷ Cited from Robert Withington, *English Pageantry*, 2 vols. (Cambridge, Mass., 1918–20), 1: 132–34.

When Queen Elizabeth was crowned at Westminster on January 15, 1559, Westminster-hall where she dined "was richlie hoong, and everie thing ordered in such roiall maner as to such a regall and most solemne feast apperteined," and this feast was "celebrated with all Roial Ceremonies and high solemnities."[8]

In the same vein, James I, Queen Anne, and Prince Frederick were received with several pageants when, in March 1604, they visited the City of London. The entertainment was designed by Thomas Dekker. According to his own explanation, a "Device" was "made up, as the first service to a more Royall and serious ensuing Entertainment," and in the structure of the Italians' pageant "King Henry the Seventh was royally seated in his imperiall robes; to whome King James . . . approches, and receyves a scepter." There followed the pageant of the Dutchmen; and "it was a Royall and magnificent labour."[9] In 1610, on the day when King James' son was created Prince of Wales and granted other titles, "after a most Royall and sumptuous tilting, the water-fight was worthilie perfourmed."[10] Later, in 1679, there was a Lord Mayor's Show, of which the third pageant showed "A delicate stately rich Royal Chariot." The adjective *royal* does not mean "belonging to a king" here, since, pointing to the chariot, the presenter of the show says, "*This Rich and Royal Piece of Art you see/Is call'd* The Chariot of Loyalty."[11] Such a usage conclusively proves that the word *royal* may be used to describe a thing of beauty not specifically connected with kingship.

The visual, esthetic concept of kingship is carefully elaborated in Shakespeare's history plays. In the first part of *Henry IV*, the King discusses the importance of the visual effect that a royal figure should produce on public eyes.

Thus did I keep my person fresh and new,

[8] Nichols, *Progresses of Queen Elizabeth*, 1: 60–61.
[9] John Nichols, *The Progresses, &c., of King James the First*, 4 vols. (London, 1828), 1: 338, 346, 349.
[10] Ibid., 2: 322.
[11] Thomas Jordan, *London in Luster* (London, 1679), pp. 13, 16.

My presence like a robe pontifical,
Ne'er seen but wond'red at, and so my state,
Seldom but sumptuous, showed like a feast,
And won by rareness such solemnity. . . .

[3. 2. 55-59]

And he goes on to talk about people's "extraordinary gaze, / Such as is bent on sun-like majesty, / When it shines seldom in admiring eyes." From this we may glean some important information about the popular, visual conception of royalty. In the people's mind a king was the essence of sumptuousness, the likes of which they seldom had the opportunity to see with their own eyes; when they were fortunate enough to see it on such an occasion as a Royal Entry, it was a rare visual feast, a solemn, majestic show which people "wond'red at" with "extraordinary gaze." The popular, conventional view of kingship developed, not from abstract speculation about it, but from real experience of the people when they had the rare opportunity to witness the pageantry of royalty.[12]

A king's presence in a royal procession remained a source of sumptuous, spectacular beauty comparable only to the fully arrayed magnificence of the pope in his ceremonial dress. People attached both spiritual and esthetic values to royalty, just as to papacy or episcopacy, and the two kinds of values were so closely amalgamated that it was difficult to appreciate one separately from the other. When people admired the costly beauty embodied in kingship, it necessarily meant also appreciation of the divine quality of an annointed king. The idea of such beauty was not discrete; it was discussed without much discrimination between the moral or spiritual value of the thing and the beauty it incorporated.[13] Popular experience of royalty involved, therefore, the perception of the visible, esthetic qualities of the essentially transcendental idea of kingship. This paralleled a

---

[12] Dekker reports that the "presence" of James I in an entertainment "did most graciouslie feede the eyes of beholders." See Nichols, *Progresses of King James*, 1: 358.
[13] Johan Huizinga, in this connection, says, "The very notion of artistic beauty is still wanting. The aesthetic sensation caused by the contemplation of art is lost always and at once either in pious emotion or a vague sense of well-being" (*The Waning of the Middle Ages* [London, 1924], p. 245).

religious experience expressed in terms of the esthetically organized outward symbolic forms of rituals.

"Admired" or "wondered at" is the description of the way people generally responded to the "sun-like majesty" portrayed in a public ceremony of royalty or on an occasion of civic pageantry. In an earlier scene in the first part of *Henry IV*, we again find the pattern of popular response to visualized royalty. After Falstaff and his crew have made their exit toward the end of act 1, scene 2, the Prince, remaining on stage, reveals his secret intention of pretending to be a prodigal in order later to show his own royal quality the more effectively.

> I know you all, and will awhile uphold
> The unyoked humour of your idleness,
> Yet herein will I imitate the sun,
> Who doth permit the base contagious clouds
> To smother up his beauty from the world,
> That when he please again to be himself,
> Being wanted he may be more wond'red at,
> By breaking through the foul and ugly mists
> Of vapours that did seem to strangle him.
>
> [1. 2. 187–95]

The pattern is repeated with slight variation later.

> By being seldom seen, I could not stir
> But like a comet I was wond'red at.
>
> [3. 2. 46–47]

"Wonder at," it should be noted, describes, not the individual's incipient surprise at the solemn, sumptuous sight of royalty, but rather the common mold of action in which popular emotion was excited by spectacle. The generalization, however, proves that there was a long course of time in the history of man's experience when access to a royal show invariably meant awe and admiration at the sight of "sun-like majesty." As a dramatist, Shakespeare was well aware of this reaction to such spectacles. He also knew that he could best treat royalty in his plays by dealing with it in the visual, esthetic terms understood by his audience.

One of the remarkable aspects of the staging of Shakespearean history plays is that the *idea* of kingship is discussed along with presentation of its concrete, visual correspondents. In the second part of *Henry IV*, a crown is found placed at the king's bedside, and the Prince, seeing the crown, deplores the heavy cares a king must endure.

> O polished perturbation! golden care!
> That keep'st the ports of slumber open wide
> To many a watchful night! . . .
>   O majesty!
> When thou dost pinch thy bearer, thou dost sit
> Like a rich armour worn in heat of day,
> That scald'st with safety.
>
> [4. 5. 23–25, 28–31]

The crown lying on the king's pillow in this scene may have been merely an ordinary stage property, but to the spectators' imaginative eyes it must have seemed to glow with an inexpressible radiance when the Prince addressed it, when, somewhat like the presenter of a dumb show, he explicated the bitter hardships its glitter symbolized. In the first part of *Henry IV*, the Prince predicts that his future reformation will absorb people's admiring eyes, and when he does reform himself in the final act of the second part, the audience again has a visual correlate of royalty. The Prince appears in a royal robe, saying to the Lord Chief Justice,

> This new and gorgeous garment, majesty,
> Sits not so easy on me as you think.
>
> [5. 2. 44–45]

Here, too, as with the crown in act 4 of the play, the "gorgeous garment" is explicitly equated with "majesty." Royalty thus visually translated does not subject itself to logical analysis; it is something esthetic to be wondered at, to be experienced. The idea of royalty formed by popular esthetic sensations, an idea seemingly primitive and unintellectual, had acquired a strong currency in Shakespeare's theater. In other words, the knowledge of royalty derived from its sumptuous show transformed itself into an integral part of the dramatic experience of Shakespeare's plays. Prince Hal's reformation is fully portrayed in the final scene of the second part of *Henry IV*, and the dramatist provides the scene with the coronation procession of the new king, in order to augment the auspicious, spectacular beauty in the drama's finale, where the rejection of Falstaff takes place. The rejection of the "foul" figure[14] is, in my view, subordinate to the triumphant display of the rich, joyful spectacle of royalty, which, as the main issue of the play, has been predicted in the first part of the play to take place in the way the sun suddenly breaks "through the foul and ugly mists." Shakespeare's audience would have been justly expected to "wonder at" the Prince's reformation portrayed in such a stage spectacle.

The total dramatic effect of the closing scene of the *Henry IV* plays is less one of realism than one of pageantry, and this is due largely to the rich esthetic cult of kingship in the pageants. The visual impression of "a sun breaking through the clouds after a thunderstorm" was a subject favored in painting in the fifteenth century, and painters were "occupied with the problem of fixing the light-effect of a moment."[15] In pageantry, too, this theme seems to have been used repeatedly. Upon the battlements at Fenchurch in London was set a miniature City of London when King James was received on his way to his coronation in 1604. The whole frame of the city "was couered with a curtaine of silke, painted like a thicke cloud, and at the approach of the K[ing] was instantly to be drawne." The allegory of this device is that "at the rising of the Sunne," which means the king, "all mists were dispersed and fled," and people in London enjoy the idea of the sun breaking through the clouds.[16] In the Lord Mayor's Show of 1613, Middleton produced the idea of a "Mount Triumphant." The beauty and glory of the Mount is "*over-spredde*

---

[14] The foulness in Falstaff's costume is referred to in places preceding the rejection scene. See *2 Henry IV*, 5. 5. 11–14, 24–27.

[15] Huizinga, *Waning of the Middle Ages*, p. 266.

[16] Herford and Simpson, eds., *Ben Jonson*, 11 vols. (Oxford, 1941), 7: 90.

with a thicke sulphurous darkenesse," which is *"a fog or mist raisde from* Error, *enviously to blemish"* the Mount, or London. Truth's chariot then approaches, and she says, "with this fanne of starres I'll chace away" "that foule cloude to darken this bright day." The mists vanish, the cloud suddenly rises, and it *"changes into a bright spredding canopy, stucke thicke with starres and beames of gold, shooting forth round about it, the mount appearing then most rich in beauty and glory."*[17] Or, in 1675, the Lord Mayor's Show had, in its first pageant, an allegorical figure of Triumph, who hailed the Lord Mayor and, addressing him, said:

> *You are the Sun beams that break through the Cloud,*
> *The Sun in* Aries, *who are this year*
> *Brightly to shine in* LONDON's *Hemisphere.*[18]

The popular idea of royalty, not legally or philosophically authorized, was developed, then, through people's immediate visual contact with kingship as often as through their reading of historians' descriptions of kings. Shakespeare's study of man in his history plays was conducted upon the basis of this popular, intuitive knowledge of kingship. This is well illustrated in the lines referring to "ceremony" in *Henry V.* A king is gorgeously adorned with "ceremony," and that is what distinguishes him from a common man. But to him nothing is more real than the fact that "his ceremonies laid by, in his nakedness he appears but a man." The King apostrophizes the "ceremony" that causes him to suffer "more / Of mortal griefs than do thy worshippers":

> I am a king that find thee: and I know,
> 'Tis not the balm, the sceptre, and the ball,
> The sword, the mace, the crown imperial,
> The intertissued robe of gold and pearl,
> The farced title running 'fore the king,
> The throne he sits on: nor the tide of pomp
> That beats upon the high shore of this world:

---

[17] Nichols, *Progresses of King James*, 2: 690–91.
[18] Thomas Jordan, *The Triumphs of London* (London, 1675), p. 11.

No, not all these, thrice-gorgeous ceremony,
Not all these, laid in bed majestical,
Can sleep so soundly as the wretched slave.

[4. 1. 255–64]

We may understand from this remark that "ceremony" here implies what the royal costume, throne, and regalia stand for: the emblematic, gorgeous attributes of kingship.

The recurrent Shakespearean theme of a king's dual nature is discussed in this monologue, and we see, unmistakably, a fatal, irredeemable split in his dual nature. He strongly feels that he is no more than a mortal man, but at the same time he cannot but realize that he is "twin-born with greatness." The outward form of "ceremony" is a sign pointing to the "greatness" or the body divine which lies within him, often divorced from his natural body. A king is, therefore, a difficult, essentially impossible, combination of the two conflicting natures, godhood and manhood. The "gorgeous" "ceremony" that a king has to wear is the external manifestation of the "indelible character of the king's body-politic, god-like and angel-like."[19] The esthetic response of the audience to the sumptuous, pageantlike stage image of royalty was induced more fundamentally by the nature of a ceremony that stood for the immortal divinity of kingship. The sight of royalty was, accordingly, more than a matter of visual enjoyment; it created "adoration," "awe and fear" among its "worshippers."[20]

Turning now to *Antony and Cleopatra*, we can understand the significance of the crowning and robing of Cleopatra as she is about to commit suicide. That the dying heroine should wear a crown and be attired in a royal robe is a matter already decided in Plutarch's *Lives* and is by no means due to Shakespeare's theatrical genius. But the dramatist without doubt knew both the spectacular virtues of the regalia and his audience's capacity to respond esthetically to the

[19] Ernst H. Kantorowicz, *The King's Two Bodies* (Princeton, 1957), p. 27.
[20] *Henry V*, 4. 1. 238 ff.

pageant arrangement of the final scene. Cleopatra wants to have herself attired like a queen:

> Now, Charmian!
> Show me, my women, like a queen: go fetch
> My best attires. I am again for Cydnus,
> To meet Mark Antony. Sirrah Iras, go.
>
> [5. 2. 225–28]

And when Iras returns to Cleopatra with her crown and robe, she says:

> Give me my robe, put on my crown, I have
> Immortal longings in me. Now no more
> The juice of Egypt's grape shall moist this lip.
> Yare, yare, good Iras; quick. Methinks I hear
> Antony call; I see him rouse himself
> To praise my noble act; I hear him mock
> The luck of Caesar, which the gods give men
> To excuse their after wrath. Husband, I come:
> Now to that name my courage prove my title!
> I am fire and air; my other elements
> I give to baser life . . .
>
> [5. 2. 279–89]

What the Shakespearean audience saw here disclosed was a vision of life transcending all baser elements of earthiness; it was a vision of transformation from the natural and material to the beautiful and eternal. People had been educated in the appreciation of "royal" splendor, and they were able to apprehend abstract ideas of royalty in regal emblems. Shakespeare could justly expect his audience to experience an enhanced poetic vision from this pageantlike scene and for that purpose he did not hesitate to bring the elements of "ceremony" into the scene.

Cleopatra wishes to wear her crown and robe, and her reason for this is unequivocally stated: "I am again for Cydnus, / To meet Mark Antony." An idea parallel to this is heard when she says, "Give me my robe, put on my crown, I have / Immortal longings in me."

Logically there seems to be no necessary relation between her wearing a crown and a robe and her feeling "immortal longings." Her
longings may be explained as her desire to meet Antony in the
eternal world, which she terms "Cydnus." To Shakespeare's mind,
however, the relation between the two things was real enough,
since the "ceremony," considered in the light of pageantry, was
easily interpreted by his audience as a visual, esthetic correlative of
the divine, transcendental nature of royalty. Cleopatra's putting on
her crown and robe made itself felt in Shakespeare's theater as the
visible counterpart of her longings for immortality, a desire for her
new sublimated being, her new royalty. As a royalist and as a playwright, Shakespeare knew of the close link between the sumptuous
portrayal of royalty on the stage, to which his audience responded
by "wondering" at it, and the idealized vision people generally had
of the divine and eternal associated with the crown. Contemporary
audiences of the play no doubt felt a subtle but unmistakable correspondence between the sight of the queen's pompous attire and her
remark "I am fire and air; my other elements / I give to baser life."
   In her imaginative vision, Cleopatra's death involves going again
to "Cydnus, / To meet Mark Antony." The "Cydnus" here referred
to is, of course, understood as alluding to Enobarbus's description
in act 2, scene 2, of the occasion when "she first met Mark Antony
. . . upon the river of Cydnus." "Cydnus" is a metaphor that indicates
what lies beyond the limits of the earthly world, and at "Cydnus"
she is able to achieve self-realization, her immortal royalty. Enobarbus's description of the queen in a barge on the Cydnus is based on
Sir Thomas North's rendering of Plutarch's *Lives.* How closely
Shakespeare followed North's version is easily seen when we compare his passage with that in Plutarch:

> . . . the poope whereof [i.e., of the queen's barge] was of
> gold, the sailes of purple, and the owers of silver. . . . And
> now for the person of her selfe, she was layed under a pavil-
> lion of cloth of gold of tissue, apparelled and attired like the
> goddesse Venus, commonly drawne in picture.[21]

[21] *Plutarch's Lives . . . Englished by Sir Thomas North,* vols. 7–12 in *The Tudor
Translations,* ed. W. E. Henley (London, 1896), 12: 25.

It may not be wide of the mark to suppose that Shakespeare's contemporaries imagined something resembling their own water pageants in the way this fabulous scene was rendered by both Shakespeare and North. In the Lord Mayor's Show, water processions were common enough, and for that purpose companies hired barges. "From the middle of the fifteenth century, there seems to have been an increase in the splendor of the water-progresses."[22] As early as 1478, on the occasion of the coronation of Elizabeth, Henry VII's queen, her royal entry was accompanied by the pomp of a water pageant.

> And at ther commyng fourth from Grenewiche by water, ther was attendyng uppon her ther, the Maire, Shirffs, and Aldremen of the Citie . . . in barges fresshely furnysshed with baners and stremers of silk richely besene . . . and in especiall a barge called the Bachelers Barge, garnysshed and apparellede, passing al other, wherein was ordeynede a great red dragon spowting flamys of fyer into temmys. And many other gentilmanly paiants wele And curiously devysed to do her highnesse sport and pleasure with. . . .[23]

Even in this early account of a pageant we can locate the general pattern of spectacular description that would, when visualized in the popular mind, afford esthetic pleasure. Shakespeare apparently noted in North's translation a passage that was fairly well in tune with the general esthetic pattern of pageant description and elaborated it into "Cydnus," which is a key metaphor of the play. In order to increase the impression of pageantlike splendor, Shakespeare introduced the image of "throne" into his own version:

> The barge she sat in, like a burnisht throne
> Burned on the water: the poop was beaten gold;
> Purple the sails, and so perfumed that
> The winds were love-sick with them: the oars
> were silver . . .
>
> [2. 2. 191–94]

[22] Withington, *English Pageantry*, 2: 10.
[23] Ibid., 1: 161.

"Cydnus" is instinct with the joyful, pleasurable sensation characteristic of the sumptuous pageantlike beauty best connoted by "royal." This "Cydnus" is the place, no longer geographical but placeless and idealized, where Cleopatra is going to "meet Mark Antony." The poetic vision Shakespeare called up in the final scene of *Antony and Cleopatra* is the acme of the traditional idea of beauty cultivated in the history of royal pageantry.

After Cleopatra has died invested with royal costume and regalia, the other characters repeatedly refer to the heroine as "royal." Charmian says when she sees the queen dead,

> . . . golden Phoebus never be beheld
> Of eyes again so royal!
>
> [5. 2. 316–17]

She further remarks on Cleopatra's noble suicide:

> It is well done, and fitting for a princess
> Descended of so many royal kings.
>
> [5. 2. 325–26]

Caesar follows suit, admiring her final act:

> Bravest at the last,
> She levelld at our purposes, and being royal
> Took her own way.
>
> [5. 2. 333–35]

Even before the queen's robing and crowning, we hear Iras address her as "Royal queen," and Shakespeare gives such variations as "Most noble Empress" and "Most sovereign creature." During the time Cleopatra is alluded to in this way, the Shakespearean audience contemplates the idealized figure embellished with her crown and robe. What is displayed on the stage is no longer an active drama but a static, iconographic presentation of an idea. The dead queen remains in the audience's sight, silent and still, gorgeously arrayed, placed, probably, at the center of the stage, while Caesar enters and the action continues around her. This is, in a way, a variation of the Elizabethan dumb show, and Charmian and Caesar are none other than the presenters of the show. As often as the presenters speak of Cleopatra as being "royal," they help to make explicit the emblematic significance implied in the appearance of the queen in full dress. By "royal" the audience must have understood that unexcelled superiority of queenly beauty now immortalized in her. The presenters' comments on Cleopatra's "royal" nature, revealed outwardly in her "eyes," and also in her genealogy and her noble act of suicide, serve for the audience's ultimate apprehension of the essentially nondiscursive idea of "the royal" now rendered visible in the dumb show.

Before Shakespeare used a variation of the dumb show in the final scene of *Antony and Cleopatra*, these shows on the Elizabethan stage had developed under the influence of the rich spectacles of pageantry. It is interesting to note that the English classical dramas, which were purely rhetorical and declamatory in origin, had to include dumb shows when they were produced in England.[24] With all its allegorical implications, the dumb show preceding the first act of *Jocasta* has much in common in its spectacular quality with the last scene of *Antony and Cleopatra*.

> . . . there came in vppon the Stage a king with an Imperial crown vppon his head, very richely apparelled: a Scepter in his righte hande, a Mounde with a Crosse in his lefte hande, sitting in a Chariote very richely furnished. . . .[25]

Again, in the dumb show before the second act of *Gorboduc*, we see "a King accompanied with a nombre of his nobilitie and gentlemen" enter the stage and place "him self in a chaire of estate." From the earliest period of Elizabethan drama, the pageantlike effect of royal splendor was one of the main features of the dumb show. In Shakespeare's *Richard II*, act 3, scene 3, the King and his attendants enter the upper stage, which theatrically represents Flint Castle, and these characters place themselves side by side in a symmetrical manner

---

[24] The dramatists, according to Dieter Mehl's valuable study, had the "desire to make abstract spiritual experiences and conflicts visible as concrete scenes and to impress a moral idea on the spectators by appealing directly to the senses" (*The Elizabethan Dumb Show* [London, 1965], p. 17).

[25] John W. Cunliffe ed., *Early English Classical Tragedies* (Oxford, 1912), p. 69.

with the King in the center. Then Bolingbroke, as a presenter, describes the impression of the King in this stage tableau: "King Richard doth himself appear, / As doth the blushing discontented sun / From out the fiery portal of the east." The medieval king on the upper stage is, of course, dressed in apparel of state and luxury, and the other characters flanking him are similarly attired. The princely splendor of this dumb show is commented on by another presenter, York:

> Yet looks he like a king! behold his eye,
> As bright as is the eagle's, lightens forth
> Controlling majesty; alack, alack, for woe,
> That any harm should stain so fair a show!
>
> [3. 3. 68–71]

It should be observed that Shakespeare used the word "show" to indicate what is presented by the visual scheme of the dumb show.

What Shakespeare did in the final scene of *Antony and Cleopatra* was to create a new kind of poetic effect, making advantageous use of the rich popular sensibility to the esthetic concept of "the royal." And the effect is considerably enhanced by the emblematic tableau of royalty arranged in the manner of a pageant dumb show. Needless to say, the polyphonic effect of imagery and music in Shakespeare's language is more strongly responsible for making the whole world of the play glorious and magnificent. My purpose in this essay is fulfilled if it is understood that, with all Shakespeare's incandescent exhibition of verbal skill in the play, there is a moment when he reverts to the primitive, stylized method of a dumb show.[26] The atavism of having recourse to the traditional ability of people to read an abstracted moral from an emblematic picture on the pageant stage was a kind of necessity for Shakespeare when he tried to render

---

[26] M. C. Bradbrook outlined a lecture in these words: "Taking a conventionally historic view, I shall try to recover traces of the archaic spectacular tradition from which Shakespeare first started and to which, in the richly transmuted form of his final plays, he returned" (*Shakespeare's Primitive Art* [London, 1965], p. 215). As to the dumb show, Mehl's idea is as follows: "The dumb show was a convenient means . . . of conveying to the audience something which the authors were apparently unable or unwilling to express through the medium of speech" (see p. 33).

perceptible the visionary idea, a new "Cydnus," that Cleopatra finally attained through her death. The word *royal* used by both Charmian and Caesar is the index to the ethereal quality of the idealized "Cydnus." It is this word that can evoke the rich and varied connotations of sumptuous beauty, blessed happiness, and ethereal divinity in the mind of the audience.

Shakespeare crowned and robed Cleopatra in order to reveal a truth. In *King Lear*, the "nature" of humanity is discovered by taking off all the outward kingly garments, or "ceremony." Seeing Edgar's "uncovered body," Lear says, "Is man no more than this? . . . thou art the thing itself. Unaccommodated man is no more but such a poor, bare, forked animal as thou art." Then the king *"strives to tear off his clothes,"*[27] crying, "Off, off, you lendings! Come, unbutton here!" What Lear does here is to see the true state of human existence beneath "what thou gorgeous wear'st."

> Take physic, pomp;
> Expose thyself to feel what wretches feel,
> That thou mayst shake the superflux to them
> And show the heavens more just.
> [3. 4. 33–36]

Antony and Cleopatra does not deny the truth that we find in *King Lear*. There are two types of truth; one is to be apprehended from the outward show of a thing and the other to be sought in the inward reality. The former asks us to be idealistic and visionary; the latter asks us to face realities. Both kinds of truth are given their due in Shakespeare's plays. The idea of "the royal" in *Antony and Cleopatra* was created by Shakespeare only in the wake of the long tradition of popular interest in the spectacle of royalty in English pageantry. The dumb show in the concluding scene of the play was the sure and decisive mode of feasting the audience's eyes with the dramatist's final, quintessential poetic vision of "the royal."

---

[27] Dover Wilson's stage direction in his edition of *King Lear*, 3. 4. 109.

Time and Truth in *King Lear*

Soji Iwasaki

1

The problems of *King Lear* center on the father-daughter relationship between Lear and Cordelia. The other characters are more or less subsidiary, supplying the main themes with antitheses, analogies, variations, intensifications, and ironies. And the issues concerning Cordelia are much less complicated and more appropriate as a starting point than those of Lear, for the heroine as a role and as a character is "drastically simplified and, as we may say, dehumanized,"[1] her life as wife and queen being rather strangely shut out of the play. Lear as a role and a character alters in stages. The obvious changes in the early stage of the dramatic action are from king to beggarman, from a wrathful old man to an innocent and powerless victim of evil, and from a man who sins to a man who is sinned against. But Cordelia remains the same from the moment of her first appearance till her reappearance in act 4, scene 4, after a long absence. And this undeniable fact of her long absence is the first point I would like to note about Cordelia. The second point is this: if Cordelia is unchanged throughout the play, what does she represent? Or, what is her significance to Lear, to the world of the play, and to us? Some may say she represents filial love, others nature, but what the opening scene insistently emphasizes is her truth.

The first scene, set in the court of King Lear, is predominantly ritualistic in tone.[2] The situation and the speeches are public, deliber-

---

[1] D. G. James, *The Dream of Learning* (Oxford, 1951), p. 101.
[2] Cf. William Frost, "Shakespeare's Rituals and the Opening Scene of *King Lear*," *The Hudson Review*, 10 (1957–58): 577–85 (reprinted in an abridged form in *Shakespeare's Tragedies*, ed. L. Lerner [Harmondsworth, Mddx., 1963], pp. 161–68).

ate, and formal. The speeches are more or less predictable, because the participants in such a ritual usually know what they are expected to say and how, and they play the parts assigned to them rather than express what they really feel. In his "darker purpose" of testing his daughters' love and dividing the kingdom to give each her share according to the love she bears for her father, Lear expects nothing but words of love simply conforming to his planned course of events. Goneril and Regan know their father's mind and how to please him for their own advantage. The theme of flattering speech versus silent truth is ironically introduced by Goneril:

> Sir, I love you more than word can wield the matter;
> Dearer than eye-sight, space and liberty;
> Beyond what can be valued rich or rare;
> No less than life, with grace, health, beauty, honour;
> As much as child e'er lov'd, or father found;
> A love that makes breath poor and speech unable;
> Beyond all manner of so much I love you.
>
> [I. I. 55–61]

Regan also follows the expected line of the ritual, introducing the theme of "true heart" and "deed of love" in contrast with what one "profess[es]" (I. I. 69–76). Everything goes on in a highly ritualistic tone till we come to Cordelia's answer to her father:

> LEAR: . . . Now, our joy,
>   Although our last, and least; to whose young love
>   The vines of France and milk of Burgundy
>   Strive to be interess'd; what can you say to draw
>   A third more opulent than your sisters? Speak.
> CORDELIA: Nothing, my lord.
> LEAR: Nothing?
> CORDELIA: Nothing.
>
> [I. I. 82–89]

This sudden "Nothing" of Cordelia's is indeed "a violent momentary break in the [ritualistic] proceedings,"[3] contrasting strikingly with

---

[3] Frost, "Shakespeare's Rituals," p. 581.

the "blank verse of a Byzantine stateliness"[4] in which the scene has been conducted throughout.

By her way of speaking, or rather by her reticence, Cordelia is thrown into relief against her sisters' fair speeches and mouth-honors. It is ironic enough that she stands for the "true heart" and the "love that makes breath poor and speech unable" which her sisters profess as theirs. The fact is that Cordelia's line of conduct is "Love, and be silent," and she seems well nigh obstinate in being true to her motto. She never professes her love but only her truth.

> LEAR: So young, and so untender?
> CORDELIA: So young, my Lord, and true.
> LEAR: Let it be so; thy truth then be thy dower.
>
> [I. I. 106–08]

Cordelia, whose only "dower" is now her truth, is not unlike the traditional Patient Grisel, who, after suffering trials given by her husband, leaves his house with nothing other than her plain clothes. The truth of Cordelia thus leaves Lear's court, and the plainness of Kent is also banished.

The two points I mentioned at the beginning now come into focus. Cordelia represents—and, in a symbolic sense, is—truth, and she is driven away from the world by untruthful speeches mistakenly approved by childish innocence, even ignorance, till at last time brings her back to the world, now as the confirmed truth. Does this not conform with the traditional idea of *Veritas filia temporis*? Shakespeare, as I have tried to show in another discussion, surely had this idea in mind when writing *Lear*, and it may not be too much to say that his intention in writing this play was to dramatize this particular emblem.[5] Cordelia's last words before she departs for France in the

---

[4] Ibid.

[5] In my Cambridge B. Litt. thesis, "The Sword and the Word," that discussion precedes this on *King Lear*. For present purposes I shall reproduce Geffrey Whitney's emblem (Plate I) and quote its application:

Veritas filia temporis
Three furies fell, which turne the worlde to ruthe,
Both Enuie, Strife, and Slaunder, heare appeare,
In dungeon darke they longe inclosed truthe,
But Time at lengthe, did loose his daughter deare,

opening scene bear great significance in this context. According to the Quarto, whose reading of the particular lines I would like to restore, the words go:

> Time shall unfold what pleated cunning hides,
> Who covers faults, at last shame them derides.
>
> [I. I. 280–81][6]

This is indeed the prophecy of the rest of the action of the play and almost a summary of it, and because of the significance of these lines my preference for the Quarto reading must be explained.

The lines are read differently by recent authorities. G. I. Duthie,[7] Peter Alexander,[8] and C. J. Sisson[9] follow the Folio:

> Time shall unfold what plighted cunning hides,
> Who covers faults, at last with shame derides.

Kenneth Muir in his New Arden edition gives the same reading except that the changes the comma at the end of the first line into a semicolon.[10] And he, following Duthie,[11] notes that "who" refers to "Time." But the fact is that it is very difficult, when we have examined the tradition of the idea of *Veritas filia temporis*, to assume Time as that which "covers" faults, for Time's proper office is to *unfold* them. Slander, Envy, and Strife usually cover faults, but Time

---

> And setts alofte, that sacred ladie brighte,
> Whoe things longe hidd, reueales, and bringes to lighte.
> Thoughe strife make fier, thoughe Enuie eate hir harte,
> The innocent though Slaunder rente, and spoile:
> Yet Time will comme, and take this ladies parte,
> And breake her bandes, and bring her foes to foile.
> Dispaire not then, thoughe truthe be hidden ofte,
> Bycause at lengthe, shee shall bee sett alofte.
>
> [G. Whitney, *A Choice of Emblems* (Leyden, 1586), p. 4]

[6] *King Lear, 1608 (Pied Bull Quarto)*, Shakespeare Quarto Facsimiles, no. 1 (London, 1939). As to the line numbering, I follow Kenneth Muir's edition of *King Lear*, The Arden Shakespeare (London, 1952); reference is to act, scene, and line.

[7] G. I. Duthie, *Shakespeare's King Lear: A Critical Edition* (Oxford, 1949).

[8] *William Shakespeare: The Complete Works*, ed. Peter Alexander (London, 1951).

[9] *William Shakespeare: The Complete Works*, ed. C. J. Sisson (London, 1953).

[10] *King Lear*, ed. Muir.

[11] Duthie himself says he follows Schmidt (Duthie, *Shakespeare's King Lear*, p. 129).

does not. Besides, Time is not usually derisive, while Shame is. The editors of the New Cambridge Shakespeare, Duthie and J. Dover Wilson, read,

> Time shall unfold what plighted cunning hides,
> Who covert faults at last with shame derides.

And in their note they rightly comment, "It is 'plighted cunning' not Time that covers faults"; but they again say, "Time is the antecedent of 'who.' "[12] If "who" refers to "Time," the second line sounds rather redundant and flat compared with the lively Quarto reading. Apart from this, the point is still valid that Time is not derisive, though Shame is. Although the word is abused by Goneril in her mistreatment of her father (1. 4. 254), Shame is actually to visit Lear before his reunion with Cordelia. Kent says of Lear:

> A sovereign shame so elbows him: his own unkindness,
> That stripp'd her from his benediction, turn'd her
> To foreign casualties, gave her dear rights
> To his dog-hearted daughters, these things sting
> His mind so venomously that burning shame
> Detains him from Cordelia.
>
> [4. 3. 43–48]

After all Alexander Dyce was right in saying, "I adhere to the Qq, because I feel convinced that 'Who' refers to people in general," though he failed to recognize the iconographical overtones which could have justified his reading of the lines.[13] The only critic, so far as I know, who is aware of this implication is R. A. Fraser in his *Shakespeare's Poetics*. He reads,

> Time shall unfold what plaited cunning hides.
> Who cover faults, at last shame them derides.[14]

This is virtually the right reading of the lines, though it seems un-

[12] *King Lear*, ed. J. Dover Wilson and G. I. Duthie, The New Cambridge Shakespeare (Cambridge, 1960), p. 154.
[13] Quoted in *King Lear*, ed. H. H. Furness, New Variorum Edition (New York, 1963), p. 39.
[14] R. A. Fraser, *Shakespeare's Poetics: In Relation to King Lear* (London, 1962), p. 41.

necessary to read "cover" for the Quarto's "covers"; "plaited" or "pleated" hardly matters.

Several other minor points concerning Time and Truth in *King Lear* are pointed out by Fraser:

> Truth, manifest in Goneril's letter to Edmund, will be re-
> vealed to Albany "in the mature time." (4. 6. 277–9) Edgar,
> the instrument of the revelation, will appear to confirm it,
> "When time shall serve." (5. 1. 48f.) Even Edmund bears
> witness to the empery of Time. For the evil he has done, he is
> sure that "the time will bring it out." (5. 3. 162f.) His assur-
> ance is verified. "He that covereth his sins, shall not prosper,"
> but not because Polonius might have said so. Edmund's lines,
> and Cordelia's, and the Biblical Proverb (xxviii. 13) on which
> her couplet depends are sustained by the action of the play.[15]

The critic is right, but the problem has hardly been thoroughly explored. At least we have already found that Cordelia is, or is play-ing, Truth in this play. And if she is playing Truth, and if the idea of *Veritas filia temporis* is working as a formative principle in the play, then, first, who is playing Time, and second, what is happening in the interval between the rejection of Truth and her recovery?

My answer to the first of these questions is Lear. In act 5, scene 3, when he enters with Cordelia dead in his arms, the scene is, I think, precisely the embodiment of *Veritas filia temporis*: Time has at last brought Truth to light. This is the most symbolic and most telling moment in the whole action of the play. But if so, why is Cordelia dead? This problem, however, had best be deferred. For the moment I will turn to the second question: what is happening in the middle part of the play? And by trying to answer this, we shall come to identify the changing role and character of Lear, until we reach an apprehension of the emblematic significance of the last scene, which will hopefully confirm my proposed answer to the first question.

---

[15] Ibid., p. 44.

2

As truth is significantly hidden, and envy and slander reign in sonnet 70,[16] so when Cordelia has been driven away, and Edgar, her counterpart in the subplot, has disguised himself as Poor Tom, the world of Lear's England is ridden with envy, slander, and strife. These evils working against truth in the world of *Lear* are represented by Goneril and Regan in the main plot, and by Edmund in the subplot, though the names of Cornwall and Oswald might be added to complete the list. Of this evil party, Edmund is the most openly professed and active member, and in our discussion of evil in *Lear* he is the right person to begin with.

Like other Shakespearean bastards, Edmund takes his position as an outsider, hating the insiders. He is first of all envious and contentious as regards his brother Edgar, legitimate son of Gloucester, and by slander and fraud he tries to drive him out. By promoting falsehoods, he creates hostility between Gloucester and Edgar, and, when he has succeeded in getting rid of Edgar, he approaches Goneril and Regan and swears his love to both, planning to make use of them for his swelling ambition for the throne. "I am rough and lecherous" (1. 2. 137–38) he says, but he is actually much more than that. He is disobedient to his father, envious, contentious, and slanderous vis-à-vis his brother, always ambitious for a higher state, Machiavellian in his pursuit of his will. By being "pleated cunning" itself, he hides the truth of Edgar, as the sisters do that of Cordelia in the main plot.

Edmund is a Machiavel and his policy consists chiefly in slander and creating false "opinion."[17]

> Some blood drawn on me would beget *opinion*
> Of my more fierce endeavour.
>
> [2. 1. 34–35; italics added]

He is unmistakably disobedient, envious, and contentious. We can

---

[16] My earlier discussion of the sonnet must also be dispensed with in this essay.
[17] Cf. *Lucrece*, line 937.

Plate 1. *Veritas temporis filia.* Woodcut in Hadrianus Junius, *Emblemata*, Antwerp, 1565; and also
in Geffrey Whitney, *A Choice of
Emblems*, Leyden, 1586.

safely argue that he is in fact playing Slander, Envy, and Strife, those
persecutors of Truth in Whitney's emblem of *Veritas filia temporis*
(see Plate 1). He is a hypocrite who cunningly disguises himself under
a mask of truth. His seeming truth, with which credulous Gloucester
is easily deceived and made to believe in his love and Edgar's murder
plot, is in marked contrast to Edgar's real truth, which is ironically
disguised and hidden in Poor Tom, in the peasant, and in the gentleman, until he reveals himself again. And this contrast of an apparent
falsehood and the covered truth in Edmund and Edgar is designed to
reflect and enhance the contrast between the other sisters and Cordelia in the main plot. The presentation of Cordelia as Truth is, as
we have already seen, no less clear and unmistakable than that of
Edmund as Slander, Envy, and Strife. In the opening scene, we
remember, Shakespeare is using, as it were, a fairy-tale method[18] in
establishing this clear-cut contrast between the truth of Cordelia and
the falseness of the sisters, between their false speeches and Cordelia's
"Nothing."

   Now, the antithesis between false speeches and plain truth is no
less than the basic design of those iconographical tableaux of *Veritas
filia temporis* in which the evil speaker is represented as Calumny[19]

---

[18] Cf. James, *Dream of Learning*, p. 101.
[19] See the woodcut from Adriaen Willaert, *Cinque Messe* (Venice, 1536), reproduced in Fritz Saxl, "Veritas Filia Temporis," *Philosophy and History: Essays Presented
to Ernst Cassirer*, ed. R. Klibansky and H. J. Paton (Oxford, 1936), fig. 2.

or Hypocrisy.[20] In Hadrianus[21] and in Geffrey Whitney, Slander is allied with Envy and Strife, but the antithesis of plain truth and false speeches is still clear.

Other vices conceived as enemies of truth in various versions of the "Veritas" emblem—for example, fury, greed, and perfidy in Bronzino,[22] avarice, insolence, oppression, and adulation in *Respublica*,[23] disobedience in *Temporis Filia Veritas*,[24] and malice, pride, and debate in *Horestes*[25]—may properly be considered the attributes of evil in *King Lear*. And also those symbolic animals like Bronzino's dog, lion, wolf, and serpent, and William Marshall's bat, dragon, and snake[26] may be compared with *Lear*'s abundant animal images, especially those related to Goneril and Regan.[27]

Goneril and Regan are, first of all, flatterers, who speak fair words in answer to *Lear*'s test of love, but their hidden envy and hypocrisy are also revealed to us in their private conversation just after the banishment of Cordelia. They seem to have been envious of their younger sister, whom their father loved most. Because they are selfish and avaricious like Edmund, they find an enemy in everyone who is not useful to their own interests. And now that Cordelia is gone and they have established themselves as duchesses, their next interest is in gaining as much as possible from their father, or spending as little as possible on him, who now holds one hundred knights

[20] See the woodcut from William Marshall's *Goodly Prymer in Englyshe*, 1535, reproduced in Saxl, "Veritas Filia Temporis," fig. 4.

[21] *Hadriani Iunii Medici Emblemata, ad Arnoldum Cobelium. Eiusdem Aenigmatum Libellus, ad D. Arnoldum Rosenbergum* (Antwerp, 1565). See Donald Gordon, " 'Veritas Filia Temporis': Hadrianus Junius and Geoffrey [sic] Whitney," *Journal of the Warburg and Courtauld Institutes*, 3 (1939–40): 237.

[22] Erwin Panofsky, *Studies in Iconology* (New York, 1962), p. 84; see also Panofsky's fig. 61.

[23] *Respublica: A Play on the Social Condition of England at the Accession of Queen Mary*, ed. Leonard A. Magnus (Early English Text Society, 1905). Magnus suggests that Nicholas Udall (1505–56) is the author (p. 12).

[24] *Temporis Filia Veritas: A mery devise called The Troublsome travell of Tyme, and the daungerous delivery of her Daughter Trueth*, 1589. There is a modern reprint: *Temporis Filia Veritas*, ed. F. P. Wilson, Luttrell Society Reprint, no. 16 (Oxford, 1957).

[25] John Pickering, *The Interlude of Vice: Horestes* (1567), ed. Daniel Seltzer, Malone Society Reprint (1962), lines 1380–81.

[26] See n. 20 above.

[27] I shall return to the problem of the animal imagery from a different point of view.

apart from "the name and all th' addition to a king." The sisters are selfish, but so far as they share an interest in depriving their father, they remain friends and conspirators. Their private conversation at the end of the first scene is conducted in a common, homely prose which is clearly contrasted with their high sentences in blank verse spoken in the earlier ritualistic passage.

The sisters' selfishness is soon brought into the open. Goneril outspokenly slanders Lear:

> I do beseech you
> To understand my purposes aright:
> As you are old and reverend, should be wise.
> Here do you keep a hundred knights and squires;
> Men so disorder'd, so debosh'd, and bold,
> That this our court, infected with their manners,
> Shows like a riotous inn: epicurism and lust
> Makes it more like a tavern or a brothel
> Than a grac'd palace. The shame itself doth speak
> For instant remedy . . .
>
> [1. 4. 246–55]

Plate 2. *Justice, Truth, and Reason persecuted by Fraud.* Woodcut by Albrecht Dürer, based on the Tapestry of Michelfeld, wrought in the early fifteenth century and discovered in 1524. (From *The Complete Woodcuts of Albrecht Dürer,* by Albrecht Dürer, Dover Publications, Inc., New York, 1963. Reprinted through permission of the publisher.)

Regan also calls Lear's attending knights "riotous" and slanders innocent Edgar as "ill affected" and as having planned Gloucester's death (2. 1. 94–99). Regan and Cornwall put Kent in the stocks, when he is sent as Lear's messenger to Regan at Gloucester's house, calling the old man of plain truth a "stubborn ancient knave, [and] reverend braggart" (2. 2. 127). The stage tableau in the scenes at Gloucester's castle, act 2, scenes 2 and 4, is strikingly emblematic, resembling "Justice in the Stocks," where, in Dürer's version, Justice, together with Truth and Reason, is put in the stocks by tyrannous Fraud (Plate 2).[28] In the latter of these scenes, the angered Lear answers Regan's recommendation that he return to Goneril:

> LEAR: [Rising]   Never, Regan.
> She hath abated me of half my train;
> Look'd black upon me; struck me with her tongue,
> Most serpent-like, upon the very heart.
> All the stor'd vengeances of Heaven fall
> On her ingrateful top!
>
> [2. 4. 159–64]

Plate 3. *Invidiae descriptio.*
Woodcut in Whitney,
Choice of Emblems.

[28] See also Peter Flettner's woodcut, reproduced in T. W. Craik, *The Tudor Interlude* (London, 1958), pl. 5 and its description, p. xi; also cf. pp. 93–95.

What Lear sees in Goneril—black eyes, a serpent-like tongue and a "wolvish visage"[29] on whose youthful brow he invokes "wrinkles"[30] —corresponds in more than one respect to Whitney's emblem "Invidiae descriptio" (Plate 3), and here we understand that Envy and Slander are an inseparable pair.

What hideous hagge with visage sterne appeares?
Whose feeble limmes, can scarce the bodie staie:
This, Enuie is: leane, pale, and full of yeares,
Who with the blisse of other pines awaie.
    And what declares, her eating vipers broode?
    That poysoned thoughtes, bee euermore her foode.

What meanes her eies? so bleared, sore, and redd:
Her mourninge still, to see an others gaine.
And what is mente by snakes vpon her head?
The fruite that springes, of such a venomed braine.
    But whie, her harte shee rentes within her brest?
    It shewes her selfe, doth worke her owne vnrest.

Whie lookes shee wronge? bicause shee woulde not see,
An happie wight, which is to her a hell:
What other partes within this furie bee?
Her harte, with gall: her tongue, with stinges doth
    swell.
    And laste of all, her staffe with prickes aboundes:
    Which showes her wordes, wherewith the good
    shee woundes.[31]

Indeed Lear himself is no less abusive than the sisters, calling one of them kite, serpent, wolf, vulture, dog, and so on, and he even curses all humanity. All this does no harm to anybody, because his anger is

[29] I. 4. 317.
[30] I. 4. 293.
[31] Whitney, *Choice of Emblems*, p. 94. In relation to this emblem of Whitney's, Henry Green cites *Merchant of Venice*, 4. I. 125–26; *Richard II*, I. 3. 129–32; *2 Henry VI*, 3. 2. 310–15; *Cymbeline*, 2. 5. 33–35; *Henry VIII*, 5. 3. 43–45; *Pericles*. 4 intro., 12; *Troilus and Cressida*, 2. 3. 18. See Green, *Shakespeare and the Emblem Writers* (London, 1870), pp. 432–33.

utterly impotent and ineffectual now that he is no longer a king or a father.

The sisters' envy and slander are accompanied by strife. Bitter dissension in the main plot is first brewed between ungrateful Goneril and offended Lear. It is reported to Regan as their "differences" (2. 1. 123). Then it is followed by another quarrel between Lear and Regan (2. 4). As early as act 2, scene 1, the rumor is current of an impending war between Cornwall and Albany (2. 1. 11–12). In act 3, scene 1, Kent knows of it, the "snuffs and packings of the Dukes," though "the face of it is cover'd with mutual cunning." And the French power is reported to have secretly landed in the kingdom. The same news is told by Gloucester to Edmund (3. 3), and the dissembler informs Cornwall of it just after (3. 5). The actual violence occurs between Cornwall and Gloucester, who is sided with by an honest servant of Cornwall, Gloucester losing both his eyes, the servant and Cornwall their lives (3. 7).

Then the disparity between Goneril and Albany is revealed. He fears her disposition and her sister's, and calls them "Tigers, not daughters." To him Goneril is a "devil" and "fiend" in a woman's shape (4. 2). Now Regan is a widow, and she knows that Goneril does not love her husband. She enviously suspects the love between her sister and Edmund (4. 5). The sisters, who were envious of their father's love of Cordelia, now envy each other Edmund's love (5. 1); and at last it happens that Goneril poisons Regan and kills herself (5. 3). Thus Strife is closely linked with Envy, which, as we have seen, is leagued with Slander. Where Truth is absent, Envy, Slander, and Strife reign. Here there is no harmonious relation of man to man, no love but love of self.

In this particular emblematic context in which the sisters and Edmund stand for the evil forces of Slander, Envy, Strife, and "pleated cunning," Lear stands for Innocence. Before he suffers Goneril's slander and leaves her house, he is utterly ignorant of the nature of each of his daughters, of what it means to divide a kingdom and give it away. He cannot see the truth of Kent, who has served him all his life, and banishes this loyal servant. Lear, who has been a king and has been obeyed by everybody, childishly believes in the authority of his own will. Though his love may be great indeed, he, as Goneril and Regan say, has "poor judgment" and "hath ever but slenderly known himself" (I. I. 291–94). Like his love, his wrath is great, but it is again a blind outburst of his misguided passion, under no control of self-knowledge and reason. He is, as Wilson Knight says, "mentally a child; in passion a titan."[32] He is innocent and ignorant, a fool who gives all and takes nothing, nothing but misery and suffering. As Gloucester, another fool, credulous and deceived by false opinion, is a victim of Edmund, Lear is a victim of his evil daughters. He is a child persecuted by Slander, Strife, and Envy. He is what Whitney calls "the innocent" whom "Slaunder rente, and spoile."

> Thoughe strife make fier, thoughe Enuie eate hir harte,
> The innocent though Slaunder rente, and spoile:
> Yet Time will comme, and take this ladies
> [i.e., Truth's] parte,
> And breake her bandes, and bring her foes to foile.[33]

The fire which Strife makes in Whitney's emblem and Envy's heart, which she herself bites, seems to have contributed much to the vision of Shakespeare's *Lear*. In the play the words "fire" and "heart" frequently occur,[34] and the two images do much to convey Lear's passion, his tempestuous suffering, his uncontrollable anger, and his mental agony rendered into physical torture. And these two notes, ringing throughout the play, reach their highest points in the "two very remarkable images of Lear's sufferings: vulture at the heart and the wheel of fire."[35]

LEAR: . . . O Regan! she hath tied

---

[32] G. Wilson Knight, *The Wheel of Fire* (London, 1949), p. 164. L. C. Knights says, "Lear, at the opening of the play, is the embodiment of perverse self-will" (*Some Shakespearean Themes* [London, 1959], p. 93).
[33] Whitney, *Choice of Emblems,* p. 4.
[34] The only other Shakespearean play in which the word "fire" occurs as often is *Caesar,* and "heart" appears with comparable frequency only in *Antony* and *Richard II.*
[35] W. M. T. Nowottny, "Some Aspects of the Style of *King Lear*," *Shakespeare Survey,* 13 (1960): 50.

Sharp-tooth'd unkindness, like a vulture, here.
                    [*Points to his heart.*]
                                        [2. 4. 135–36]
CORDELIA: How does my royal Lord? How fares
    your Majesty?
LEAR: You do me wrong to take me out o' th' grave;
    Thou art a soul in bliss; but I am bound
    Upon a wheel of fire, that mine own tears
    Do scald like molten lead.
CORDELIA: Sir, do you know me?
                                        [4. 7. 44–48]

The power of these images to convey the agony of the hero comes, not only from the images themselves and their aptness for the tenor, but also from their larger dramatic context. The vulture biting Prometheus's heart is in itself a powerful image. But when this greedy bird is associated with the "pelican daughters" (3. 4. 75) who suck their parent's blood, fusing a pagan image of heroic suffering with a twisted Christian image of inverted charity, and also when Prometheus's heroism is linked with Lear's titanic passion and his endless suffering, to which he is inescapably bound, then the picture proves the more telling. And such a fusion as this must have been an easily acceptable invention, judging from the popularity of the stories alluded to and their emblems (Plates 4 and 5).

Plate 4. *O vita, misero longa.* Woodcut in
    Whitney, *Choice of Emblems.*

Plate 5. *Quod in te est, prome*. Woodcut
in Whitney, *Choice of Emblems*.

The wheel of fire is that to which Ixion was bound for his impious
presumption,[36] and the story was one of the popular subjects of the
emblematists (Plate 6). The wheel torment is found in one of Dürer's
woodcuts, which represents a quarrel at the gaming table punished
by death on the wheel,[37] and also in the story of Saint Catharine and

Plate 6. *Ixion bound to the wheel.*
Rollenhagio, *Nucleus Emblem-
atum Selectissimorum*, Cologne,
1611. (Reprinted, with permission, from R. A. Fraser,
*Shakespeare's Poetics in Relation
to King Lear,* London: Rout-
ledge and Kegan Paul, 1962.)

[36] Pindar, *Pythia*, 2. 21; Ovid, *Metamorphoses*, 2. 461; Virgil, *Aeneid*, 2. 601;
Boethius, *Consolation*, 3. *metrum* 12, 34.
[37] *The Complete Woodcuts of Albrecht Dürer*, by Albrecht Dürer (New York, 1963),
pl. 19.

the Emperor Maxentius, whose representations are found again in Dürer[38] and in a stained glass window in West Wickham Church, Kent, reproduced in William Hone's *The Every-Day Book*.[39] Fire, which sometimes accompanies the wheel, is traditionally a characteristic feature of Hell and Purgatory, as we see in various pictures of these dark places.[40] Thus the "wheel of fire," another fusion of two popular images of torment, conveys the unbearable, endless quality of Lear's suffering, and the contrast of "a soul in bliss" and "a wheel of fire" in our play seems to embrace a cosmic range from Heaven to Hell.[41]

Plate 7. *Souls burn in hellmouth and are in bliss in heaven.* Engraving by Theodore Galle in Jan David, *Occasio Arrepta,Neglecta,*Antwerp, 1605.

[38] Ibid., p. 102.

[39] William Hone, *The Every-Day Book* (London, 1827), vol. 1, cols. 1505–06. Also the Prado Museum has Yanez's "Saint Catharine" (ca. 1520).

[40] E. g., Theodore Galle's engraving, "Souls burn in hellmouth and are in bliss in heaven" (Plate 7 in the present volume), reproduced in Samuel C. Chew, *The Pilgrimage of Life* (New Haven, 1962), fig. 49; "Hell-castle as represented in the Doom," formerly in fresco on the church arch in the Chapel of the Holy Cross, Stratford-on-Avon, reproduced in *Shakespeare Survey*, 19 (Cambridge, 1966): 2. Cf. *Macbeth*, 2. 3. 21: "th' everlasting bonfire"; and *Hamlet*, 1. 5. 11–13: ". . . confined to fast in fires, / Till the foul crimes . . . Are burnt and purged away."

[41] Cf. Galle's engraving mentioned above, n. 40.

Each of these images of a wheel of fire and of a vulture biting man's heart has independently a great symbolic power against its general traditional background, and at the same time each is closely related to the speaker's character and the dramatic situation. What I would like to emphasize is that these images form part of the pattern of the *Veritas filia temporis* theme working as a formative principle in the play. Of course what Shakespeare is creating is a dramatic vision of *Veritas filia temporis*, which is essentially far from Whitney's didactic statement in its rather spatial presentation of the idea. In Shakespeare's pattern Lear is Innocence, but he is more than that. He is also, as I have already proposed, Time himself. How can Innocence and Time be represented in one single person? This is our next problem. And the answer will be that it is only possible in time that Lear can grow out of Innocence into Time. But quite naturally it takes a long while for Innocence to change into Time, for it is, as it were, a lifelong journey from the child to the old man. The play tells us, rather, that Innocence must first come down to nothing before it is reborn as Time. To trace Lear's downward journey will be the concern of the next few pages.

3

While Truth is absent, or covered by cunning, and while Envy, Slander, and Strife are prosperous, what is Lear doing? Is he doing nothing? Yes and no. He is suffering the tempest, he is awakening out of his old folly into a dawn of truth; but at the same time he is playing a fool, a beggar, a nothing; he *is* nothing.

But is not truth, according to Cordelia's manner of speaking, also nothing? In answer to Lear's request for her expression of love, Cordelia says, "Nothing, my lord." And,

> LEAR: Nothing?
> CORDELIA: Nothing.
> LEAR: Nothing will come of nothing: speak again.
> [I. I. 88–90]

What Cordelia means in this particular context is that she can *say* nothing "to draw / A third more opulent than [her] sisters." But in the larger context of the whole play, this "Nothing" is the beginning of all the tragedy, and as the action goes on everything seems to come to nothing, and come out of nothing. In this sense Lear is completely mistaken when he says, "Nothing will come of nothing." For the play is, as we shall see, a tragic "Much Ado about Nothing."

In the dungeon of Pomfret Castle, Richard II recalls his dethronement by Bolingbroke and meditates on what are called the king's two bodies—the body natural and the body politic.[42]

> Sometimes am I king;
> Then treasons make me wish myself a beggar,
> And so I am. Then crushing penury
> Persuades me I was better when a king;
> Then am I king'd again, and by and by
> Think that I am unking'd by Bolingbroke,
> And straight am nothing.[43]

King Lear gives his kingdom away and dethrones himself, and like Richard he straightway becomes nothing. But being innocent and simple enough to believe the two elder daughters' professed love, he expects to enjoy a king's name and privileges, free from the cares and burdens that a king should duly undertake. To have the nominal authority of a king and a hundred knights for hunting and banqueting, however, is in fact to be a holiday king, or a Lord of Misrule. But the festive holiday must always turn out to be an illusion, an appearance, a matter of nothing, when the time comes, and the participants in the festivity must come to realize the hard reality of the everyday world. This is what Lear does not understand, and thus he has committed his first folly.

The second folly of Lear is that he has, as it were, unfathered himself. By giving authority to his elder daughters, and thus making his daughters his mothers (1. 4. 179–80), and by renouncing his youngest daughter, who will not throw away her proper role as

[42] Ernst H. Kantorowicz, *The King's Two Bodies: A Study in Mediaeval Political Theology* (Princeton, 1957), pp. 7–41.
[43] *Richard II*, 5. 5. 32–38.

child and subject and turn the natural order upside down, he has completely unfathered himself. By giving up his role as king and father, Lear is now doubly nothing, nothing to his subjects and nothing to his family. This is what the Fool means when he says to Lear, "now thou art an O without a figure. I am better than thou art now; I am a Fool, thou art nothing" (1. 4. 200–02). By rejecting the truth of Cordelia and the plainness of Kent, which might have checked his follies, the king and father becomes a fool, beggar, and child. Thus the moral significance of the first part of the play is: Innocence and Wrath, unchecked by Plain Truth and Patience, go their way to nothing. The irony is that Lear is right *and* wrong when he says, "Nothing will come of nothing": he is wrong in that the whole tragedy comes out of Cordelia's "Nothing"; he is right in that his fall to nothing will come out of Cordelia's "Nothing."

Lear's fall from king to fool is dramatically represented by his being accompanied by the Fool. Because a fool is a Lord of Misrule, a comic element quite naturally enters with him into the world of *Lear*.[44] In comical songs and witty sarcasms the Fool can speak the serious truth, for a fool has the license to speak freely, unlike Cordelia, who was allowed to speak only in accordance with the heartless conventions of Lear's court. And thus, ironically, the Fool plays the role of Wit and with his rodlike tongue—an ironic reversal of Slander's "most serpentlike" tongue which beats Lear's heart—the Fool whips Lear, who is now a fool in the court of Misrule.

> FOOL: Truth's a dog must to kennel; he must be
> whipp'd out when the Lady Brach may stand
> by th' fire and stink.
> LEAR: A pestilent gall to me!
>
> [1. 4. 117–20]
> FOOL: . . . thou hadst little wit in thy bald crown
> when thou gav'st thy golden one away. If I
> speak like myself in this, let him be whipp'd that
> first finds it so.
> *Fools had ne'er less grace in a year;*

---

[44] Cf. Knight, *Wheel of Fire*, pp. 160–76.

For wise men are grown foppish,
And know not how their wits to wear,
Their manners are so apish.

LEAR: When were you wont to be so full of songs,
sirrah?

FOOL: I have used it, Nuncle, e'er since thou mad'st
thy daughters thy mothers; for when thou gav'st
them the rod and putt'st down thine own breeches,

Then they for sudden joy did weep,
And I for sorrow sung,
That such a king should play bo-peep,
And go the fools among.

Prithee, Nuncle, keep a schoolmaster that can
teach thy Fool to lie: I would fain learn to lie.

LEAR: And you lie, sirrah, we'll have you whipp'd.

FOOL: I marvel what kin thou and thy daughters are:
they'll have me whipp'd for speaking true, thou'lt
have me whipp'd for lying; and sometimes I am
whipp'd for holding my peace.

[I. 4. 169–92]

In these passages the images of a fool, his breeches pulled down, of
whip and rod, of schoolmaster and wit, remind us of the emblem of
the "Whipping of Folly." In the picture on the title page of *The
Scourge of Folly* (ca. 1610) and of *A Scourge for Paper-Persecutors* (1725),
both by John Davies of Hereford, Folly with a fool's cap and with his
breeches pulled down is mounted on the whipping post of Time, an
old man with a scythe and a glass put aside, and Wit is beating
Folly's buttocks with a whip (Plate 8).[45]

When Lear has dethroned himself into Folly, he is, as it were,
whipped by the Fool, who is now a wit as a result of Lear's reversal
of order. Whipping, however, must go on for a long time, because
Folly cannot be cured so easily. The words printed with the John
Davies picture go:

O could'st Thou whip these Bedlams till they bleed
Thou whipp'st in vaine: wee'le whip anon indeed.

Plate 8. *Time as the whipping post for Folly.*
Title page in John Davies of Hereford, *A*
Scourge for Paper-Persecutors, London, 1625.

So Lear, even when he has found Goneril ungrateful and unnatural,
and strikes his head saying, "O Lear, Lear, Lear! / Beat at this gate,
that let thy folly in, / And thy dear judgment out!" (1. 4. 279–81),
still foolishly believes in Regan, who he is sure "is kind and comfortable" (1. 4. 315). Lear must be "whipped" again.

Lear's meeting with Regan at Gloucester's house affords him a
second chance to be whipped. He finds his messenger, the disguised
Kent, in the stocks, and Regan, who has left her house so that she
may more definitely refuse to accept her father, is found far from
kind and comfortable. Lear sees her take Goneril's hand when the
latter hurriedly comes. Regan, no less unkind and ruthless than is
Goneril, tells Lear to curtail the number of his followers and go back
to Goneril's. Lear's heart almost bursts: "O sides! you are too tough;
/ Will you yet hold?" (2. 4. 199–200). He feels his madness gathering,
yet he tries to learn patience, saying, "I can be patient; I can stay
with Regan" (2. 4. 232). But again he and his hundred knights are
rejected by Regan, who now insists on reducing the number of his
followers to twenty-five. Lear chooses Goneril, who seems to consent to maintaining twice the number of men. He is still so foolish as

[45] Cf. Chew, *Pilgrimage*, p. 18.

to believe that love can be measured by numbers, and he still clings to the foolish idea that man is not a beast because of some superfluous thing he possesses:

> our basest beggars
> Are in the poorest thing superfluous:
> Allow not nature more than nature needs,
> Man's life is cheap as beast's.
>
> [2. 4. 266–69]

As long as he holds to this view of man and expects something that is not essential to man, Lear is bound to find nothing, for "non-being always appears within the limits of a human expectation."[46] To realize what man really is, Lear must still be whipped. He is afraid he is going to be mad, and he asks Heaven for patience: "You Heavens, give me that patience, patience I need!" (2. 4. 273). His heart is breaking, his mind is collapsing, and the coming madness threatens him. A storm is heard in the distance.

In the storm scene, Lear's mental agony is rendered into a palpable physical torture. His unguarded body is actually whipped by the storm with thunder and lightning. Time, who tests both good and evil,[47] is giving him a severe trial. In the woodcut on the title page in Giovanni Andreo Gilio's *Topica Poetica*,[48] Time, the winged old man with an hourglass on his head, carrying a whip instead of his usual scythe, is running across the country[49] with the sun and the moon above him (Plate 9). The meaning of the picture is probably that Time watches and punishes Folly day and night, wherever Folly goes.[50] The same thing is happening in the storm scene of *Lear*. Time is no longer the whipping post for Folly but the whipper himself, and therefore here Storm and Time can be identified as the Whipper. Lear is one of those "wilful men" to whom "The injuries that they

---

[46] Jean-Paul Sartre, *Being and Nothingness*, trans. H. E. Barnes (London, 1957), p. 7.

[47] Cf. *The Winter's Tale*, 4. 1. 1–2; *The Mirror for Magistrates*, 24. 308.

[48] Giovanni Andreo Gilio, *Topica Poetica* (Venice, 1580). See Chew, *Pilgrimage*, p. 18, and his *The Virtues Reconciled* (Toronto, 1947), p. 91.

[49] In Stephen Batman's emblem of "The trauailed Pilgrime" the open space or "the fielde" is called "Time." See Craik, *Tudor Interlude*, pl. 9.

[50] Cf. *Hamlet*, 3. 1. 70: "For who could bear the whips and scorns of time . . . ?" and *Macbeth*, 1. 3. 148: "Time and the hour runs through the roughest day."

Plate 9. *Time with a whip*. Woodcut on title page in Giovanni Andrea Gillio, *Topica Poetica*, Venice, 1580.

themselves procure / Must be their schoolmasters" (2. 4. 304–06), in a more tragic sense than cruel Regan means by these words.

In the storm, Lear himself is suffering another storm; his whole mind and body are shaken by an unbearable, maddening passion. As outward Nature is in chaos and destructive confusion, so is Lear's inner nature.

> And thou, all-shaking thunder,
> Strike flat the thick rotundity o' th' world!
> Crack Nature's moulds, all germens spill at once
> That makes ingrateful man!
>
> [3. 2. 6–9]

The Fool keeps a fool's sanity and speaks the childish truth: "here's a night pities neither wise men nor Fools" (3. 2. 12–13). Lear desperately tries to learn patience: "No, I will be the pattern of all patience; / I will say nothing" (3. 2. 37–38). And it is significantly ironic that, as Gloucester more or less by accident begins to see the truth after he has lost his eyes, Lear, by his own metamorphosis, begins to learn something of man's essential nature when he is losing his wits.

My wits begin to turn.
Come on, my boy. How dost, my boy? Art cold?
I am cold myself. Where is this straw, my fellow?
The art of our necessities is strange,
And can make vile things precious. Come, your hovel.
Poor Fool and knave, I have one part in my heart
That's sorry yet for thee.

[3. 2. 67–73]

But it is only "one part" of him that begins to see things in the right way. He has still some distance to go.

Lear encounters Edgar disguised as a madman. Edgar is now Poor Tom in "the basest and most poorest shape / That [ever] penury, in contempt of man, / Brought near to beast" (2. 3. 7–9), and his words, "Edgar I nothing am" (2. 3. 21), imply that he is nothing in the same sense that Cordelia, as the buried Truth, is nothing. Yet an important difference between Edgar and Cordelia is that Cordelia is plain and simple truth, while Edgar is truth in the disguise of a beggar. He is nothing not only in that he is Truth but in that he is a beggar, a madman, even a bare, filthy animal. He is the "image of utter destitution,"[51] the image of nothing. Lear meets Poor Tom and, crazed now, he sees the beggar as the very essence of man: "the thing itself; unaccommodated man . . . a poor, bare, forked animal" (3. 4. 109–10). And this is exactly what the mad Lear himself is; or rather it is not Poor Tom but Lear who is "the thing itself . . . a poor, bare, forked animal," for Poor Tom is only a role that Edgar is playing, while Lear is not playing, but is, a mad beggar and bare, forked animal, a nothing.

Thus the animal imagery, whose "references are scattered broadcast through the whole play,"[52] is given new significance. In this particular context it does not simply represent man's vices—wolfish avarice, tigerish cruelty, and so on—as in the medieval system of animal symbolism, nor does it symbolize the lower level of human

[51] John F. Danby, *Shakespeare's Doctrine of Nature: A Study of King Lear* (London, 1949), p. 29.
[52] A. C. Bradley, *Shakespearean Tragedy* (London, 1904), p. 266.

nature in general, with its contrasting level in that higher human nature with whose grace Miranda and Marina are intrinsically chaste.[53] Nor is it applied to character description,[54] nor does it form part of the image cluster of the theme of *Veritas filia temporis*. Poor Tom is less than a fool; he is an animal. And this animality is precisely the outward manifestation of man's essential nothingness. Lear, who has been a fool followed by the reflective image of the Fool, is now accompanied by Poor Tom, the reflection of Lear's own essential state, a mad animal, a nothing, to which blind Gloucester is a witness: "O ruin'd piece of Nature! This great world / Shall so wear out to naught" (4. 6. 136–37). This is perhaps the end of Lear's downward journey, the utter nothingness.

What Lear has learned through such suffering is the nothingness of human nature and its acceptance, and perhaps patience. The king who was Innocence and Folly, beaten by Time's whip, has now in his madness learned to be nothing. The flatterers' speech haunts him still, but he now knows that

> they are not men o' their words: they told
> me I was every thing; 'tis a lie, I am not
> ague-proof.
>
> [4. 6. 106–08]

Now we see that the two parallel changes of Lear from king to beggar and from father to child have in fact been accompanied by a third change, a change from everything to nothing. It is only by becoming *nothing* that Lear has come to understand Cordelia's Nothing.

Lear has now realized his error and repents. Therefore "a sovereign shame . . . elbows him" (4. 3. 43 *s.d.*) when Cordelia comes to rescue him. Shame, as William Perkins expounds, is a sign of the working conscience and has regenerative force.[55] The "burning

---

[53] Cf. Northrop Frye, "Nature and Nothing," in *Essays on Shakespeare*, ed. G. W. Chapman (Princeton, 1965), p. 38.

[54] Cf. Bradley, "As we read, the souls of all the beasts in turn seem to us to have entered the bodies of these mortals; horrible in their venom, savagery, lust, deceitfulness, sloth, cruelty, filthiness" (*Shakespearean Tragedy*, p. 267).

[55] William Perkins, *The Workes of That Famovs and Worthy Minister of Christ in the Vniuersitie of Cambridge, Mr. William Perkins*, 3 vols. (London, 1616), 1: 536.

shame" (4. 3. 47) affords a kind of purgation to Lear before he is brought to Cordelia.[56] Lear's passion is burning for the last time, and reason in self-knowledge is now found working in him. Since Lear has been reduced to nothing, his redemption must be out of nothing; or rather it must be a re-creation out of nothing, not a return to the old Innocence or Wrath.

4

In the scene preceding the reunion scene, Lear is "fantastically dressed with wild flowers" (5. 6. 81) and looks almost like a part of wild nature. And at the moment of his reunion with Cordelia, he first regards himself as a soul tormented in the purgatorial fire. But, as he gradually awakes, his wakening seems almost a rebirth, a Persephonite return to the world from the underworld where he has been confined. When he fully wakes, enlightened out of his former folly, he kneels down before Cordelia.

> CORDELIA: No, Sir, you must not kneel.
> LEAR: Pray, do not mock me:
> I am a very foolish fond old man,
> Fourscore and upward, not an hour more or less;
> And, to deal plainly,
> I fear I am not in my perfect mind.
> Methinks I should know you and know this man;
> Yet I am doubtful: for I am mainly ignorant
> What place this is, and all the skill I have
> Remembers not these garments; nor I know not
> Where I did lodge last night. Do not laugh at me;
> For, as I am a man, I think this lady
> To be my child Cordelia.
> CORDELIA: And so I am, I am.
>   [4. 7. 59–70]

---

[56] Cf. L. C. Knights, "*King Lear* and the Great Tragedies," in *The Age of Shakespeare*, Pelican Guide to English Literature, no. 2 (Harmondsworth, Mddx., 1963), p. 238.

This simple repetition of the plain "I am" marks the moment of resumption of the bond of father and daughter. They reacknowledge each other as parent and child, and when Lear recovers his role as father he significantly feels himself not a beast but a man, however foolish, fond, and old.[57] And Cordelia's "holy water from her heavenly eyes" (4. 3. 31) again drops "As pearls from diamonds" (4. 3. 23). And so forgiveness is most readily given to Lear.

After Goneril and Regan die unnatural deaths and Edmund repents, Cordelia is hanged, quite unnecessarily: "Our great thing forgot." Absurdity. Lear enters with dead Cordelia in his arms. Upon this moving scene, W. M. T. Nowottny comments:

> ... visual language reaches sublimity here, putting all the play has said into one visible word and bringing the whole plot to its point. Along the receding planes keyed into this tableau we see in an instant of time Lear's sin and its retribution, the wider evil that has struck both, the full fatherhood of Lear bearing his child in his arms whilst at the same time the natural course of life is seen reversed (Lear senile, so lately cared for by Cordelia), the world's destruction of the love and forgiveness that had transcended it—for the reverberation of the reunion is still strong and the language of that scene has opened the way to those suggestions of a saviour's death which now make it inescapable that Cordelia dead in her father's arms and displayed by him to the world, should strike deeply into responses that lie midway between religion and art. "Howl, howl, howl": there is to be no language for meanings such as these.[58]

The full weight of Lear's suffering is driven home. In a sense, the whole action of the tragedy has prepared for this one moment. Lear's journey has been a long one, and Edgar's words at the very end of

---

[57] The garment image here is strikingly effective in expressing humanity regained out of utter destitution.

[58] Nowottny, "Some Aspects of the Style of *King Lear*," p. 56.

the play, "The oldest hath borne most: we that are young / Shall never see so much, nor live so long," ring true. With all his suffering, Lear surely has lived longest. Edwin Muir aptly says, "Lear is very old, almost Saturnian in his legendary age; the kingdom in him exists as a memory and no longer as a fact."[59] Lear is now almost a spiritual being, far from Folly, Wrath, or Bestiality. He has completed his own education, "till Time presents him with a Crown,"[60] a crown, of course, not of gold, but of wild flowers, of truth sprung out of soil. Now he is a man, a new man, a father, and a Saturn who has lived to be of legendary age and has found truth. Lear the character has almost disappeared, and Lear the symbol emerges. Lear is Father Time, Father of Truth, and also Ripeness and Patience itself—Patience in the sense of "the power to suffer with calmness and composure and . . . forbearance with the faults of others"[61]—which he has been trying so hard to learn.

Lear, who was once Innocence, has now grown into Time, and his image as he appears with Cordelia in his arms is exactly Shakespeare's version of the emblem *Veritas filia temporis*. We can put beside Shakespeare's stage tableau of dead Cordelia in Lear's arms Rubens's paintings of the "Triumph of Truth" (Plate 10) and "Triumph of the Eucharist,"[62] or Poussin's "Ceiling Decoration for Richelieu" (Plate 11), in each of which Truth, a naked woman, is either lifted by Father Time with both arms, or embraced by him.

But one point of supreme importance precludes an explanation of *King Lear* in conventional emblematic terms. This point is Cordelia's death. This is one of the two vital points in which Shakespeare the emblematist differs from Whitney and other iconologists. And because of this, the message conveyed by Shakespeare's *Veritas filia temporis* cannot be summarized in Whitney's or Hadrianus's applica-

---

[59] Edwin Muir, *The Politics of King Lear* (Glasgow, 1947), p. 23.
[60] Henry Godyere, *The Mirrovr of Maiestie: Or The Badges of Honovr conceitedly emblazoned* (1618), Emblem 28: "Indvstriam Tempvs Coronat"; facsimile reprint, ed. Henry Green and James Croston (London, 1870), p. 55.
[61] James, *Dream of Learning,* p. 95.
[62] Saxl, "Veritas Filia Temporis," fig. 6.

Plate 10 (left). *Triumph of Truth.* Painting on the Medici-Cycle by Pierre-Paul Rubens, 1621–25, Paris, Musée du Louvre.

Plate 11 (right). *Triumph of Truth.* Ceiling decoration for Richelieu by Nicolas Poussin, ca. 1641, Paris, Musée du Louvre.

tion of the emblem, or in any usual praise of the triumph of Truth. The fact is that the *Veritas* tableau of Shakespeare's tragedy tells us something more essential and immediate about human nature than is expressed by the emblem books. What Lear has reached at this particular moment of revelation is not simply the triumph of Truth, nor its defeat. It is both crowning triumph and utter defeat at the same time. By this supreme irony Shakespeare reveals a truth beyond our verbal expression.

Lear, like Shakespeare, does not imagine that this message can be conveyed by words, especially after the flatterers and slanderers have defiled words. In this play the most moving lines are simple repetitions of very plain words, like "Howl, howl, howl," "No cause, no cause," "I am, I am," "Then, kill, kill, kill, kill, kill, kill," and "Never, never, never, never, never!" These are more gestures than

words. At these moments "words . . . get out of mere verbal meaning [and] they become gesture."[63]

This idea of the ineffectuality of words before an intense actual
experience is the second vital point at which Shakespeare has parted
with Whitney and all other emblematists. Shakespeare knew that the
truth of *Veritas filia temporis* stated in an emblem is unsatisfactory,
because the truth this emblem is trying to express is essentially concerned with the temporal level of human existence and requires
affirmation in man's experience in time. Drama, Shakespeare's
medium of exploration and expression of human truth, was far
better than the emblematists' medium for the purpose of treating
this kind of temporal truth.

5

I must now return to those larger issues I have left half discussed
or kept more or less in abeyance: (1) Lear's last journey out of nothing, and (2) the message conveyed by the stage-tableau of *Veritas
filia temporis*. And I think these issues, together with that Nothing
which Lear hears on Cordelia's lips at the moment of his death, will
come into a single focus.

I have already said that if Lear is to be redeemed he will be redeemed out of the nothing to which he was reduced. His redemption
cannot but be creation out of nothing. Theologically, however,
creation *ex nihilo* is possible only for God, for any agency less than
God can make but nothing out of nothing. In other words, "to
bring finite (which hath no proportion with infinite) out of infinite
is . . . in GODS power,"[64] though "It is true, if the word (*nothing*)
bee taken in the affirmatiue; and the *making*, imposed vpon Naturall
Agents and finite power; That out of nothing, nothing is made."[65]
The point is that the world was not created *ex materia praeexistente*

---

[63] R. P. Blackmur, *Language as Gesture* (New York, 1952), p. 13.
[64] Walter Ralegh, *The History of the World* (London, 1614), sig. D4ʳ.
[65] Ibid., sig. D4.

nor was this matter the cause of itself, but God created us and the world *ex nihilo*.

> It is a power from without us, which hath brought us out of Notbeeing into beeing. . . . For otherwise, from out of that nothing which wee were (If I may so terme it,) we should never have come too be any thing at all. Now betweene nothing and something, (how little so ever that something can bee) there is an infinite space. Needes therefore must it be that the cause thereof was infinite (at leastwise if it may bee called a cause,) and that is the very same which we call God.[66]

The problem of creation *ex nihilo* is sometimes related, as Paul A. Jorgensen points out, to the *Contemptus Mundi* theology which affirms "the original nothingness surrounding creation and the essential nothingness of all temporal things," and also with "part of the literary tradition that produced mock encomia like Erasmus's *Praise of Folly*,"[67] which, I think, is echoed in the Fool scenes of *Lear*. Lear's recognition of nothingness began first of all with the discovery of the nothingness of the flattering speeches of envious men, but it has grown deeper and deeper and reached the nothingness of his own self and of all humanity. In the end of his journey is his beginning. The way down is the way up, toward another existence, another creation *ex nihilo*.

The new life brought to Lear by his stormy experience of nothing is, in a sense, analogous to the refreshed senses strangely effected by another kind of nothing, i.e., a "pleasant slumber" in William Lisle's verse:

> Excess of studie in a traunce denies
> My ravisht soule her Angel-winged flight:
> Strugling with *Nothing* thus my bodie lies
> Panting for breath, depriv'd of sences might.

---

[66] Philip Sidney, "A Woorke Concerning the Trewnesse of Christian Religion" (1587), in *The Prose Works of Sir Philip Sidney*, ed. Albert Feuillerat, 4 vols. (Cambridge, 1912), 3: 206–07. Paul A. Jorgensen cites part of the passage in *Redeeming Shakespeare's Words* (Berkeley and Los Angeles, 1962), p. 25.

[67] Jorgensen, p. 24.

At length recovered by this pleasant slumber,
The strange effects from Nothing, thus I wonder.[68]

Shakespeare himself is thinking in *Timon*, in a more serious tone than
Lisle, of another kind of sleep, another kind of nothing, which will
bring all things to Timon:

> My long sickness
> Of health and living now begins to mend,
> And nothing brings me all things.[69]

This "nothing" is what Richard II means by his last "nothing,"
which is different from that other "nothing" which he becomes
when dethroned by Bolingbroke.

> what'er I be,
> Nor I, nor any man that but man is,
> With nothing shall be pleas'd, till he be eas'd
> With being nothing.[70]

Shakespeare in *King Lear* was probably aware of the Christian
doctrine of being and nothingness discussed in theological treatises
of his day, but he definitely shut any direct Christian association out
of the play. Though he knew the old play *King Leir*, in which
the Biblical and Christian ethos is clearly observed, he brought the
Lear story back to its original pagan setting where the gods are Apol-
lo and Jupiter. It even seems as if "Shakespeare set himself to divest
his play of any framework of Christian belief and deliberately denied
himself any occasion for its expression."[71] The fact is that in the
pagan setting of *King Lear* Shakespeare is searching and examining
the basic truth of man—universal man, and not a Christian, much
less a Roman Catholic or a Protestant, man. It is for this purpose of
searching and presenting universal truth that Shakespeare did not

[68] William Lisle, "Nothing for a New-Yeares gift" (1603), second stanza, reprinted
in *Fugitive Tracts, Second Series* (London, 1875), no pagination. Cited in Jorgensen,
p. 28.
[69] *Timon*, 5. 1. 185–87. Cf. Jorgensen, pp. 36–37.
[70] *Richard II*, 5. 5. 38–41.
[71] James, *Dream of Learning*, pp. 120–21.

bring the idea of the Christian God—or even of Christian Justice or Mercy—into the world of the play. Lear, whose last wish is simply to have Cordelia alive, says, "if it be so, / It is a chance which does redeem all sorrows / That ever I have felt" (5. 3. 265–67), and yet he is deprived even of this small redemption. Cordelia is dead, although Lear brings her truth out to the world. And Lear also dies. Everything now seems dead, Truth and all.

All seems to have come to nothing, everything for which Gloucester, Edgar, and Kent, as well as Lear himself, have paid so much. So it seems. But this is not really the case. Shakespeare definitely created something out of nothing: love. This has been the destination of Lear's last journey, a journey from his nothing to Cordelia's Nothing.

Shakespeare's formula of creation *ex nihilo* is a paradox. It is somewhat like John Donne's formula of love in his *Songs and Sonnets*. In love, Donne says, one and one make one, not two. Shakespeare's arithmetic, or rather magic, of love is this: in love nothing and nothing make everything. A man is nothing, but two people, if they share the natural bond of love, can create something, even everything. Lear's former arithmetic of love in terms of the number of his followers has proved utterly wrong.

When Lear found this magic and miracle of love, he was *really* redeemed. For this discovery of love is a rebirth, a new creation. It is not only Lear's new creation but also, I think, all humanity's. The answer to our last question has now been given. The truth the dead Cordelia represents in Lear's arms, and what the whole tableau tells us, is the same truth that Lear at his moment of death heard on her lips: "Nothing." After all, Cordelia's Nothing has turned out to be the Truth, the Word beyond words.[72] This is what Shakespeare is saying in *King Lear*. This is the ultimate affirmation of human value that he has found in the nothingness of man. Only love can create

---

[72] The word "nothing" implies a theological idea which Dame Helen Gardner points out in Donne's "Negative Love," i.e. "the doctrine that God, the absolute perfection, cannot be known and can only be described negatively, since to attempt to define him by attributes is to limit his perfection." Gardner, *The Business of Criticism* (London, 1959), pp. 63–64.

ex nihilo. Love is the Creator. And Love is the Word. Here is the basic idea of the Christian God: God is Love. In this sense, *King Lear* is definitely a Christian play. It reveals the Word to us.

Exit the Fool

Hidekatsu Nojima

S o Lear cries out just before his death. And then, embracing the
body of Cordelia, he dies of frantic joy, believing her lips to move.
The words have an unquestionable dramatic actuality on the stage.
In the context of this scene, "my poor fool" must refer to Cordelia.
This is today the interpretation supported by most critics. There is,
however, another theory, that this phrase should be literally applied
to the Fool, who vanished from the stage with the enigmatic words,
"And I'll go to bed at noon," long ago, in act 3, scene 6. It is no
wonder indeed that an affectionate remembrance of the Fool's
destiny might come up in the mad brain of the dying Lear, because
the Fool is Lear's favorite, the one who stayed with him through the
storm on the heath. Also, for the sake of the audience, which loves
the Fool, it seems both a duty and a courtesy for the author to tell
something of this character's end. And although the expression
"poor fool" is surely a term of endearment, as many critics insist, the
phrase is usually applied to an inferior person (i.e., the Fool). William
Empson, although he supports the theory that the phrase refers to
Cordelia, frankly admits the impossibility of catching this use of
"fool" in his delicate net of sense equations. He remarks, following
A. C. Bradley, that Lear's "mind has wandered so far that he no
longer distinguishes the two . . . he must be utterly crazy to call one
by the name of the other."[1] Is this comment not a finely distorted
tour de force?

How is our Fool, after all? Is he dead, or still alive somewhere?
Although the question is still open, I think that Lear's "poor fool"

And my poor fool is hang'd! No, no, no, life!

---

[1] William Empson, *The Structure of Complex Words* (London, 1952), p. 152.

means Cordelia: that is to say, I think that the Fool's destiny is undecided.

It is very common in Elizabethan drama for characters suddenly to leave the stage and be heard of no more, so Shakespeare is not extraordinary in this point, particularly since, as Bradley proves, *King Lear* is a play full of dramatic inconsistencies. Bradley seems to ascribe the Fool's suspended destiny to the playwright's carelessness, to a failure to follow through to the last.[2] The role the Fool plays in this drama, however, seems too important to be ascribed only to the author's carelessness and haste. Shakespeare himself must have loved the Fool. There is no fool in the *Chronicle History of King Leir*, which Shakespeare directly drew upon as his source. Nor is there a fool in Holinshed's *Chronicle*. Because the Fool is Shakespeare's original character, he, the poet, is responsible for everything about the Fool. Can it be that the author would forget the very person whom he has created with great effort and love? On the contrary, I believe that Shakespeare *consciously* left the Fool's end ambiguous, and that this is related to the essential dramatic function of the Fool.

"And I'll go to bed at noon" (3. 6. 83).[3] These are the last words the Fool speaks. They provide a witty rejoinder to Lear's saying "We'll go to supper i'th morning," when he has become quite exhausted and is about to go to bed. The Fool's words may represent nothing but his usual jesting with words, it being his profession to turn everything upside down. But the last speech, no matter whose it may be, is of great concern. Curious and fussy Shakespearean scholars, naturally, never leave it alone. Edward Capell, for example, remarks that "this facetious speech of the Fool is meant as a preparation for losing him; for 'tis towards 'noon' with the play (that is, towards the middle of it) when he takes his leave of us in that speech."[4] Cowden Clarke, to cite another example, remarks in tears that the dramatist "seems by this last speech to let us know that the gentle-hearted fellow who 'much pined away' at Cordelia's going into France, and

---

[2] A. C. Bradley, *Shakespearean Tragedy* (London, 1952), p. 258.
[3] All quotations from *King Lear* are from the New Variorum Edition, ed. H. H. Furness (New York, 1963), with reference to act, scene, and line; hereafter cited as Furness, New Variorum.
[4] Quoted by Furness, New Variorum, p. 214.

who has since been subjected to still severer fret at his dear master's miseries, has sunk beneath the accumulated burden, and has gone to his eternal rest even in the very 'noon' of his existence."[5]

These are very interesting opinions, but they do not seem to supply a decisive clue to the enigma of the Fool's destiny. What can safely be said is only that it is the last speech of the Fool. Where does he go after that speech? Why has the author banished, halfway through the play, this nonpareil character of his own creation? We are back to the original question again.

Clarke raises the interesting question of the Fool's age, suggesting that this character is "a petted lad," fragile, weak in frame, suscepti-ble in temperament, on account of either his "pining away" on Cordelia's departure from England or his "sensitiveness to churlish weather and sharp night air."[6] Is this a valid inference? When the Fool first enters at act 1, scene 4, Lear speaks to him: "how now, my pretty knave!" The term "pretty knave" is the phrase on which Clarke bases his view that the Fool is "a boy." But do these words necessarily imply "a boy"? Bradley seems to think so: "[The Fool] is frequently addressed as 'boy.' This is not decisive; but Lear's first words to him . . . are difficult to reconcile with the idea of his being a man, and the use of this phrase on his first entrance may show Shakespeare's desire to prevent any mistake on the point." He con-cedes that this interpretation is not necessarily valid but goes on nonetheless to argue for the "boyishness" of the Fool, insisting that he "must be imagined as a timid, delicate, and frail being, who on that account and from the expression of his face has a boyish look."[7] Clarke's and Bradley's image of the Fool as "a boy" is doubtless derived from W. C. Macready in the early nineteenth century.

We must pay tribute to Macready, who revived the original Shakespeare in preference to Nahum Tate's version of King Lear, after a century and a half of neglect. Tate's Lear is a bad play, not only because of its notorious happy ending, but also because of the omis-sion of the Fool. On this account, it totally loses the multifarious

---

[5] Ibid., p. 214.
[6] Ibid., p. 68.
[7] Bradley, Shakespearean Tragedy, p. 313.

meanings of the dramatic world Shakespeare's play dynamically inhabits. What is the storm scene, for example, without the Fool? It is reduced to a stale pastoral scene in the vein of tragi-comedy. Macready revived the Fool with some apprehension, for he could not be assured of the success of the Fool on the stage. But he wrote in his *Diary* on January 5, 1838: "Speaking to Willmott and Bartley about the part of the Fool in *Lear*, and mentioning my apprehensions that . . . we should be obliged to omit the part, I described the sort of fragile, hectic, beautiful faced boy that he should be, and stated my belief that it never could be acted. Bartley observed that a woman should play it. I caught at the idea, and instantly exclaimed, 'Miss P. Horton is the very person.' I was delighted at the thought."[8] Now, a woman has come to play the part of the Fool! This is, I think it is evident from the quotation, because in Macready's mind there existed the image of the Fool as a delicate and beautiful boy. In the same year, C. A. Brown drew a portrait of the Fool as follows: "He appears to me of a light delicate frame, every feature expressive of sensibility even to pain, with eyes lustrously intelligent, a mouth blandly beautiful, and withal a hectic flush upon his cheek."[9] This is almost the same portrait as Macready's. Edmund Blunden's image of the Fool as an "inspired child," sensitive like "a scarlet pimpernel," follows, of course, from this portrait.[10]

These too romantic figures of the Fool seem to me irrelevant. The romantic taste for the fragile and rosy lad, in accordance with the decline of Romanticism, would bring up that *pierrot* under the moon. The pretty boy with a "hectic" face would change himself into the self-conscious pale-faced fool coated in pathos. This metamorphosis surely has nothing to do with the Shakespearean idea of the Fool.

Lear's Fool cannot be a pretty boy with a hectic flush on the cheek. Though "my pretty knave" is indeed a term of endearment, it is not necessary for it to be applied directly to "a pretty boy" or "a boy." Whether the Fool is a small, ugly man or an old man is no

---

[8] Furness, New Variorum, p. 67.
[9] Ibid.
[10] Edmund Blunden, "Shakespeare's Significances," in *Shakespeare Criticism 1919–1935* (Oxford, 1951), p. 336.

matter. If he is old and ugly, the expression of endearment "my pretty knave" may have a deeper meaning. If an endearment usually directed toward a pretty boy is used for the Fool because he is not such a boy, Lear's intimate and tender jesting with him becomes the more lively and merry. It is the Fool's profession to poke fun at persons around him, but it must be remembered that his essential form of existence is to be made a standing jest, a laughing scapegoat. Mocking and mocked, the intimate relationship between master and fool matures through this reciprocity.

The fool has been an ugly, grotesque, and uncanny being since ancient times. Without his sinister shape, he could not have performed his function satisfactorily. There was, of course, an ancient belief that misshapen, ugly, abnormal people were immune from the Evil Eye,[11] as the fashionable dwarf-fools of Rome illustrated well. The fool was, in a word, equivalent to a mascot, or talisman. Where people chose such human agencies to safeguard themselves and their families against misfortune, "domestic fools" must have come into being. For it is not convincing to contend that fools were freely allowed to attend on kings, lords, and superior bishops with licensed raillery, merely to supply laughter. Their licensed raillery itself is a form of magic protection against the Evil Eye. The point I wish to make here is that if Lear's Fool were merely "a pretty boy" he would be efficient enough to attract the Evil Eye and to lure the Devil, but he could never be a safeguard against them. In Shakespeare's mind, too, when he created the Fool, there must have lived the traditional belief in such magical powers of fools; or at least whether he believed this or not, he must have drawn on this tradition when he created his Fool. Touchstone and Feste, for that matter, must be mascots and counterparts in this sense for the romantic epithalamia of their plays.

If the Fool is not a boy, however, he is not necessarily an old man either. H. H. Furness, in particular, analyzes the Fool's age. "His [the Fool's] wisdom is too deep for any boy, and could be found only in a man, removed by no more than a score of years from the king's own age; he had been Lear's companion from the days of Lear's

---

[11] Enid Welsford, *The Fool* (New York, 1961), p. 73.

early manhood."[12] If Lear is eighty years old, in Furness's reckoning, the Fool is more than sixty.

There is no use making the Fool an old man of sixty. In my opinion, if only it is agreed that he is not "a boy," it is a matter of no significance if his age remains ambiguous and indefinite. The essential quality of the Fool lies in such ambiguity. As a matter of fact, the Fool himself says: "This prophecy Merlin shall make; for I live before his time" (3. 3. 95).

Shakespeare's source, Holinshed's story of Leir, sets Leir's reign in pre-Arthurian times: "Leir the sonne of Baldud was admitted ruler ouer the Britaines, in the yeare of the world 3105, at what time Joas reigned in Juda."[13] The Fool, that is, lived historically before the Arthurian Merlin. He is not wrong in saying that. Shakespeare seems to be stressing to his audience something of the nature of his source and suggesting the pre-Christian background of the play. But it is the Fool himself who tells us of these matters. What should be borne in mind here is that the Fool's remark frees him from the restraint of time. His time *prevents* (in the archaic sense) Merlin's time. The past ("I live *before* his time") also contains the future ("This prophecy Merlin *shall* make"). Moreover, the Fool, who has once jumped out of the *Leir* story, now steps out of the dramatic time of *King Lear* itself and also stands in the Elizabethan present. For he is now speaking directly to the audience in front of him, and his prophecy, given immediately before these remarks, is nothing but a satire of the contemporary world in an inverse light such as that used in More's *Utopia*. Thus, all times coil up within the Fool: "The wheel comes full circle" (5. 3. 175).

"The wheel" is, for that matter, one of the dominant images in *King Lear*. King and Fool, Fool and Knave, Wisdom and Folly, Reason and Madness, Eyes and Blindness, Good and Evil, Man and Beast—these antitheses are recognized as constituting the great themes of *King Lear*. And yet, at the same time, these antitheses slide into each other and take the place of each other. This is what Lear

---

[12] Furness, New Variorum, p. 69.
[13] *Holinshed's Chronicle*, ed. Allardyce and Josephine Nicoll (London and New York, 1927), p. 225.

calls "handy-dandy" (4. 6. 151), an ambiguity within which the complicated and serious meanings of this drama are focused. "The wheel" provides the very image of circling that "handy-dandy" demands. And "handy-dandy" is, as John Danby says, the Fool's form of existence.[14] It is no exaggeration to say that the Fool's ambiguity is related to the ambiguity of the whole play. If there is a still point in this tempestuous and furious tragedy, it is no doubt that of the Fool rendering himself in the image of "the wheel" or laughing agilely while standing on the shaft, that is, on the *punctum indifferens* or point of rest.

I have been following a tracery of issues. How relevant is the question of the Fool's age, for example? Surely it is the uncertainty that matters. If he were told that he is "a boy," he would immediately answer, "I am very old." If he were told that he is very old, he would rejoin that he is "a boy." He must be so ambiguous in point of age that such "handy-dandy" can be admitted. The player of the Fool must be dressed and must act to that effect. To say he is eternally old and eternally young is to say we see in him the central figure of the world in Erasmus's *Praise of Folly*.

Thus, he is a protean character. But where has he gone? To know where he has gone, as I said before, is vital to understanding his nature and dramatic function. Perhaps behind Lear's Fool lives the long tradition of fools since the Middle Ages. Let us quit considering licensed fools in kings' courts, or the Vatican and the domestic fools in the houses of lords and bishops. Let us pass over fools active in *The Feast of Fools, les Sociétés Joyeuses*, and morris dances, leaving them to such erudite scholars as E. K. Chambers and E. Welsford. Let us take up, instead, fools in dramatic tragedy.

Olive Busby writes, "Usually the clown disappears, jesting still, before the fifth act. His duty is to serve as relief to the minor tragedies which lead up to the final disaster."[15] Unfortunately, we find astonishingly few instances of fools in Elizabethan tragedies. The fools in Marlowe's *Faustus*, Strumbo in the anonymous *Locrine*, and

---

[14] John F. Danby, *Shakespeare's Doctrine of Nature* (London, 1961), p. 102 ff.
[15] Olive Busby, *Studies in the Development of the Fool in the Elizabethan Drama* (Oxford, 1923), p. 36.

Lollio in *The Changeling* are among the few that come readily to mind. How many of us could name another half dozen outside Shakespeare's plays? Such as there are play that role of comic relief and buffoonery described by Busby. They cannot be dealt with on a level with Lear's Fool, who takes part, not in "minor tragedies," but in the mainstream of the tragedy. Certainly, Shakespeare is outstanding in his use of the fool as a central dramatic element. But, after *King Lear*, even Shakespeare did not represent on the stage a character apt enough to be called a fool. The clown in *Antony and Cleopatra* who presents the asp to Cleopatra cannot be called a true Shakespearean fool. He may as well be described as a mere "rustic" in the *dramatis personae*, not as "clown." In the tragi-comedies of Shakespeare's last phase, no fool appears. The late romances of Shakespeare seem almost a *tour de force* in turning tragedy into comedy without the help of a Touchstone or a Feste.

Again, I must go back to our Fool. He completely fills a role as provider of comic relief, but if this is his sole purpose, he ought to stay longer, for Lear's madness and misery really begin at the Fool's exit. He could still bring relief. For example, when Lear, now completely driven into madness, enters "fantastically dressed with wild flowers" on the stage where blind Gloucester and Edgar have lately been (4. 6), the Fool might have been with Lear. This would have made possible then a very interesting and significant combination of Lear, Gloucester, Edgar, and the Fool, different from both the previous Lear-Kent-Fool combination (3. 2) and the Lear-Kent-Edgar-Fool combination (3. 6). The stage which this combination makes up would have been another, more meaningful arena for the Fool's activity. The scene, above all, is quite a paradoxical one, where the heroes of both the main plot and the subplot, each through madness and blindness, face reality—"the thing itself"—for the first time and so realize at last that the world is the "great stage of fools." It would have been a very fitting place for the Fool to wield his wits.

Is the dramatic function of Lear's Fool, however, really comic relief? I would contend rather that the Fool's function is equivalent to the function of the Vice in Morality plays. The Vice tempts the hero into evil; the Fool certainly draws Lear into madness. Though they differ in the meanings they bear, the dramatic functions they carry out are very similar.

Bradley argues in effect that it is Edgar, "the last man who would willingly have injured Lear," who drives him into madness. When he is at last persuaded to enter the hovel in the tempest scene, act 3, scene 4, Lear says, "I'll pray and I'll sleep." "If he could go in," remarks Bradley, "and sleep after his prayer, as he intends, his mind, one feels, might be saved: so far there has been only the menace of madness. But from within the hovel Edgar—the last man who would willingly have injured Lear—cries, 'Fathom and half, fathom and half! Poor Tom!' . . . at sight of Edgar, in a moment something gives way in Lear's brain, and he exclaims: 'Hast thou given all / To thy two daughters? And art thou come to this?' Henceforth he is mad."[16] Believing that the immediate cause of Lear's madness is the man the most faithful to him, Bradley reads the irony of "the relentless fate" that urges Lear on. This interpretation is worthy of serious consideration.

But is it not rather the Fool who is the messenger of Lear's "relentless fate"? From the first entrance "he uses his folly like a stalking-horse, and under the presentation of that he shoots his wit" (*As You Like It*, 5. 5. 102–03) at Lear's folly. Lear is struck without fail. "A pestilent gall to me!" (1. 4. 109), "bitter Fool!" (1. 1. 131)— Lear's bitter cries attest to the Fool's aim. At last Lear, who has been deeply wounded by the Fool's sharp knife of words, cries:

> Oh, let me not be mad, not mad, sweet heaven!
> Keep me in temper; I would not be mad!
>
> [1. 5. 43–44]

However, the Fool never softens in his baiting of Lear, and sometimes he seems without sympathy for his master. He may be called cold and relentless. Presently he comes to sing the ribald song beginning with the stanza "The cod-piece that will house / Before the head has any, / The head and he shall louse." This song drives the last blow home to the heart of a Lear who has driven away Cordelia and chosen Goneril and Regan instead. The double entendre the song

---

[16] Bradley, *Shakespearean Tragedy*, p. 287.

contains will soon induce a double nausea over ingratitude and sex in Lear. Perhaps the Fool's manner in these scenes is equivalent to that of Iago in the "temptation scene." Having heard out the song, Lear says to someone, or rather to himself:

> No, I will be the pattern of all patience.
> I will say nothing.

Thus arises the undercurrent of the "endurance" theme which runs through the latter part of the play. What is important in this context is that madness has already come very near to Lear. Soon after that, in fact, he declares, "My wits begin to turn" (3. 2. 66). The Fool still goes on singing:

> He that has and a little tiny wit,
> > With heigh-ho, the wind and the rain,
> Must make content with his fortune fit,
> > Though the rain it raineth every day.

> [3. 2. 73ff.]

Here appear "madness" and "endurance." The Fool seems to have prophesied Lear's destiny.

Thereupon Tom Bedlam (Edgar) enters. From this point, as Bradley says, Lear certainly plunges, as if down a declivity, into madness. I think, however, that Edgar is only a clue to the madness, a mere freak of fortune after all, while the Fool has been the instigator of madness. Long before Edgar enters, Lear's way to madness has been prepared. The madness has become ripe enough, and "Ripeness is all."

It may be thought that in the Fool's abuse and raillery there is an exorcising function appropriate to fools. According to Welsford, the belief was current that raillery is a protection against misfortune.

> When threatened with misfortune it is a good thing to provoke your neighbours in order that they may abuse you and thereby transfer the bad luck from you to themselves. But why rest contented with an occasional transference of this kind, why not employ a permanent scapegoat whose official duty it is to jeer continually at his superiors in order

to bear their ill-luck on his own unimportant shoulders? Who better fitted for such a post than a misshapen dwarf or fool?[17]

In later ages, however, the fools need not have been actually misshapen. Instead, the parti-colored coat, the cap with a bell, the grotesquely shaped stick must have been invented as symbols and uniform for the fool. And at this point the fool's role as mascot or scapegoat began. From this point of view, Lear's Fool fulfills the traditional magic role fools had been playing for well over a millenium. The true meaning of the anonymous gentleman's witness —"None but the Fool; who labours to out-jest / His heart-strook injuries" (3. 1. 16–17)—may be read in this way.

Granted all these things, however, I would contend nonetheless that the Fool's essential function is equivalent to that of the Vice, because Lear is never so much exorcised from madness as possessed at last with a madness induced by the Fool. In other words, the Fool's function has been to make a "Fool" of Lear himself. He prophesied early to Lear, "Yes, indeed; thou would make a good Fool" (1. 5. 36). That is to say, in my opinion Lear's Fool is not so much a common noun as an allegorical proper noun. As the Vice "Avarice," for example, corrupts *Mankind* or *Everyman* and makes an "Avarice" of him, so the Fool *corrupts* Lear and makes a "Fool" of him. "When we are born, we cry that we are come / To this great stage of fools" (4. 6. 180–81). This is also the ultimate recognition that Lear gained through madness. In a word, Lear's Fool is the same as Touchstone (a criterion for the qualities of others) and Feste (a feast), as that name suggests. *King Lear* possesses some remarkable allegorical properties. Why not, then, call the Fool an allegorical character?

We must not, then, find a too delicate and tender character in the Fool and sentimentalize him. It is D. G. James who rightly lays great emphasis on the allegorical quality of *King Lear*. But even he takes the Fool to be the image of "helpless and suffering love"[18] and deals with him in the same category as Cordelia and Edgar. Even though

---

[17] Welsford, *The Fool*, p. 74.
[18] D. G. James, *The Dream of Learning* (Oxford, 1951), p. 116.

the image of "helpless and suffering love" holds true for the Fool, however, can we talk about him on a level with Cordelia and Edgar? While they conform to the typical pattern of goodness, there is never such clean definition to the pattern of the Fool's "suffering love." His "suffering love" is one with far more complex nuances. The thing differentiating him from the knave is that he does not run away but stays with Lear.

> The knave turns fool that runs away;
> The fool no knave, perdy.
>
> [2. 4. 80–81]

This meaningful ambiguity of "handy-dandy" between the fool and the knave decisively rules out the interpretation of the Fool as a delicate and gentle-hearted man, let alone "a boy."

There does not exist for the Fool such a convenient standard of good and evil by which he can simply declare the knave to be evil. I regret that I cannot dwell upon the relationship between the fool and the knave in Elizabethan drama. But we should remember that they both originated from the Vice during the later development of the Morality play. This means that the fool and knave are, so to speak, half-brothers. Their common mother is, of course, the Vice. Who, then, are their fathers? The father of the fool is, I think, the spiritual tradition of the fool exemplified by Erasmus and More. And the father of the knave is Machiavelli, or rather the new *Zeitgeist* that gave rise to Machiavellianism. The development of the fool from Speed and Launcelot Gobbo, through Touchstone and Feste, to Lear's Fool neatly parallels the development of the knave from Aaron and Don John (*Much Ado*), through Iago, to Edmund. The brothers have matured, as it were, hand in hand. Now, in the tempestuous wilderness, the brothers, the Fool and Edmund, meet face to face. Shakespeare, who created these half-brothers in *King Lear*, must also have been standing amidst the sound and fury of an age in which the ideas of Erasmus and Machiavelli coexisted. It is no wonder, then, that the Fool who quits the knave should also be the man who knows evil to the bottom.

But what should be remembered here is that Lear's Fool, although he stands in the spiritual tradition of the fool, inherits more of the blood of his mother, and that his dramatic function is directly taken over from the Vice. Among Shakespearean fools there is no other fool with so strong an element of the Vice as Lear's minion. Conversely, John Falstaff—that lovable, fat drunkard—may be said to be a character who, although he stands in the tradition of Vice, draws more heavily on the tradition of the fool. Having created Falstaff, Touchstone, Feste, and Lear's Fool, Shakespeare exhausted the gamut between the Vice and the Fool.

After such a long detour, I now return to the subject of the Fool's exit from the play. If his function is equivalent to the Vice's dramatic role, to know how the Vice makes his exit from the Morality play must give a decisive clue to the enigma of the Fool's exit.

There are several types of exits by the Vice. According to Cushman's classification, they consist of the following: (1) the Vice simply leaves the stage; (2) the Vice takes formal leave of the audience; (3) the Vice is led away to punishment (to prison, the gallows, or the like); (4) the Vice is carried off by the devil (in only one play, *Like Will to Like*).[19] The key point here is that no matter which mode of exit he takes, the Vice leaves the stage before "Mankind" corrupted by his temptation is converted again to good. This is natural, for there is no need for the Vice to remain after Mankind's conversion.

In early Moralities the first type of exit was usually used, whereas in later Moralities the technical problem of how to make the Vice leave the stage seems to have gradually become the matter of greatest interest to the authors. Surely we can safely say that the success of the technique determines the success of the play in the later Moralities. Inclination, the Vice in *The Trial of Treasure* (1567), for example, is led away to prison, still uttering abuse: "Well, yet I will rebel, yea, and rebel again, / And though a thousand times you shouldest me restrain." This scene is one that might remind us somewhat of Iago's last moment. If the Vice stays to the last, as in this instance, it is the inevitable logic of the Morality that he must be punished. Ill

[19] L. W. Cushman, *The Devil and the Vice in the English Dramatic Literature Before Shakespeare, Studien zur englishen Philologie herausgegeben von Lorenz Maisbach*, 6 (Halle, a.S., 1900): 120 ff.

Report, the Vice in *The Most Virtuous and Godly Susanna* (1578), is actually executed on stage. Let us examine a more famous instance, the end of John Falstaff. It seems very reasonable and natural that Falstaff, a metamorphosed Vice, is treated at last in such a merciless way. His final fate must have appeared neither brutal nor merciless to the author and his audience. But the problem is that he is too charming to be declared a mere Vice—hence the endless discussions about his banishment. The responsibility for this lies wholly in Shakespeare's genius for humor in creating a flesh-and-blood figure despite his original intention to create a Vice.

To speak frankly, however, is not the punishment of the Vice fundamentally absurd? The Vice is essentially an allegorical being which should be an unchanging universal principle beyond time. This granted, it seems inconsistent that such a creature should be punished in some way, in other words, should suffer some change. We may be thankful that Lust is put in prison or is executed on the gallows, for instance, but it is against the reality of *Mankind* or *Everyman*—for Lust ought to harass Mankind since Adam and Eve and ever after. If Lust should be completely liquidated, there would be no foundation for the Christian dogma of continuing original sin. It seems that the authors in the early Moralities must have known better in choosing the most simple mode of the Vice's exit—to let him leave simply during the course of the play as soon as he has corrupted Mankind. This means that the principle of allegory was faithfully observed. Therefore, the fact that the type or mode of the Vice's exit in the later Moralities came to be more complex in punishment and execution is one aspect of the general phenomenon of the decline of allegory. In a word, by this I mean the humanizing of the Vice. My reasoning is as follows: punishment or execution can make sense only when the object is a human being, viz., a mortal being; whereas when punishment is imposed on the Vice, who is, as it were, an immortal being essentially beyond time, he must be considered on a level with mortal beings. In this connection, the punishment of Falstaff may be said to be the punishment of the timeless by time, i. e. History. He is the timeless Vice lost in the world of history (the historical play). His doom was inevitable. The humanizing of the

Vice in the later Moralities is, of course, not irrelevant to the fact that the Vice gradually turned out to be the central figure in the play as allegory declined. The audience must have had a purely dramatic interest in finding out the fate of this master character. In addition to this, the Calvinistic sentiment strong in the later Moralities dared even to violate the dramatic principle of allegory and tried forcibly to direct the audience's eyes to the punishment and condemnation of evil and sin. Such a demand for religious teaching also contributed, to a great extent, to the humanizing of the Vice.

The humanizing of the Vice does not always assume the form of punishment. There are also Vices who stay to the end of the play without suffering any punishment and vanish somewhere, after taking an obscure last leave of the audience. Ambidexter in *King Cambises* and Revenge in *Horestes* are good examples. Having finished the duty their proper allegory allotted to them, they go on another journey seeking a new master. They are humanized in that they look very much like the free lance, or the hobo in the Western. This mode of exit perhaps testifies to their immortality as allegory, for their mode of exit bars us from predicting when and where they will come up next, and whom they will possess and throw into the familiar tragic plight.

In this connection, it seems very significant that Iago, a direct descendant of the Vice, was not killed by Othello. Realizing at last that everything was Iago's trick, Othello also realizes that he will not be satisfied even if he cuts Iago to pieces. He merely says:

I look down towards his feet: but that's a fable:
If that thou be'st a devil, I cannot kill thee.

[5. 2. 288–89]

It is mere "fable" that the Devil has a cleft foot. Although Iago has no cloven foot, he is a devil, and if he is the devil, he must be immortal. So Othello says, "I cannot kill thee." At this moment the stage direction says that Othello "*wounds* Iago." Iago offers only abuse: "I bleed, sir, but not killed."

Now, finally, we hasten back to our Fool. The Fool's exit, according to Cushman's classification, belongs to the first type, although it may belong to the second if we take his last speech—"And I'll go to bed at noon"—as his farewell address to the audience. It is a matter of no concern here to which type the Fool's exit conforms. What is important is that by the time he exits the corruption of Lear, the hero, has already been completed. As I have said above, Lear has been drastically changed by the Fool. What is, then, the essence of the Fool's corruption? It is "madness," a falling from kingship to foolery. Once Lear himself has turned fool, there is no need for the Fool to stay. Truly Lear's speech after the Fool's exit is nothing but foolishness. Is it not the Fool's complete victory over Lear? His corruption has been perfectly carried out. And corrupted perfectly into "madness," as a "fool," Lear—"every inch a king"—can for the first time look through the reality of the world and the cosmos, in other words, through "the thing itself" and see the irony of all things. "Madness," that is, degeneration into a fool, was the only path to Lear's enlightenment. In this lies, I believe, the deep paradox of the Fool as Vice, as instigator. The dramatic irony of Shakespeare's creation of the Fool consists in the fact that the Vice performs the work of leading the hero into spiritual awakening. At all events, once the paradox is completed, it no longer matters where the Fool has gone. That is why Shakespeare chose the simplest and the most artless type of exit for his Fool. Or rather, only this simple and awkward mode of exit is fitting for the Fool, for if his destiny should be thoughtfully, or thoughtlessly, explained away, the very subtlety of his being would be sacrificed. Did not Shakespeare secretly try to preserve the allegoricality of the Fool by adopting the old mode of exit proper to the Vice in the early Morality play? The Fool is beyond time: he is a character free from the time restraints of the world in this play.

It is certainly foolish to try to calculate the Fool's age. And it would also be nonsense to ask whether he is dead or alive, because he is necessarily alive, and because he is invulnerable and immortal, in principle. It is through the creation of this immortal being that Shakespeare succeeded for the first time in keeping his balance in the midst of the tempestuous conflict between two natures—the benignant nature of Lear, Cordelia, and Edgar and the malignant nature of Goneril, Regan, and Edmund[20]—and in enduring the chaos of *absurdity* since *Hamlet*. If this is so, the Fool lives first of all within Shakespeare himself, as a figure not subject to death.

[20] Cf. Danby, *Doctrine of Nature,* part 1. Although Danby takes a very negative attitude toward the Fool's "handy-dandy," I am positive. But this would require another essay.

The Decadence of John
Ford's Tragedies

Takashi Sasayama

Thonere is probably no other major dramatist in English on whom
critical opinion has been so widely divided as John Ford. As
early as the first quarter of the last century, Charles Lamb and
William Hazlitt were irreconcilably opposed to each other in their
appraisal of the final act of *The Broken Heart*.[1] There has since been
a long series of arguments on the merits of his work. Some critics
have insisted upon a "modernity" exemplified in his daring exploration of the human psyche, while others have refused to see in his
plays more than an ingenious apparatus designed for sensationalism
and the evocation of pity. It is quite unlikely that there will ever be
agreement between these two extremes of opinion.

In addition, there has been, since the puritanical attacks on Ford
by American critics in the first decade of this century, an animated
controversy within the pro-Fordian camp as to whether the morality
revealed in his plays was in line with the accepted religio-ethical
code of his time. For instance, in their latest book-length studies of
Ford's works, H. J. Oliver and Clifford Leech attempted to cor-
roborate the existence in Ford of a traditional Christian faith, refuting
the thesis advanced by S. P. Sherman and later by Sensabaugh that
Ford "throws down the gauntlet to orthodox morality."[2] The
opinions expressed on both sides have tended to be arbitrary, how-

---

[1] Charles Lamb, *Specimens of English Dramatic Poets* (London, 1900), p. 228; and
William Hazlitt, *The Collected Works*, 12 vols. (London, 1902), 5: 273.

[2] H. J. Oliver, *The Problem of John Ford* (Melbourne, 1955); Clifford Leech, *John
Ford and the Drama of His Time* (London, 1957); S. P. Sherman, "Introduction" to
'*Tis Pity She's a Whore and The Broken Heart*, Belles-Lettres ser. (Boston, 1915), p.
xxvii; G. F. Sensabaugh, *The Tragic Muse of John Ford* (Stanford, 1944).

ever, since they are based more or less on the assumption that a playwright's ideas, either moral or philosophical, never fail to find direct expression in the speeches of certain characters in his plays.

A dramatist may entertain various points of view which, reinforcing or qualifying one another, incorporate themselves into a coherent moral vision. Informed as it is by such a vision, his play is a far more complex thing than it appears to a casual reader. It is a self-contained organism, each component part of which is carefully integrated into the total pattern. The raison d'être of a character or an incident, therefore, must be determined on the basis of the meaning of the play as a whole. To try to explain the character of Cleopatra, for instance, from her action and speeches alone would be to lose sight of her magnificent stature and reduce her to a mere royal whore. Every scene in which she does *not* appear, every character with whom she has *no* connection on the story level, is also instrumental in building up in our minds a dramatic image of her. Similarly, it would be quite beside the point to comment on Cordelia's "pride and sullenness"[3] on the sole basis of certain speeches assigned to her in the play. A play is not "decadent," therefore, simply because it deals with an immoral theme, or because certain characters in it might be regarded as morally reprehensible in real life. The problem of "decadence" should be discussed only in relation to the full moral texture of the play.

In considering the tragedies of John Ford, it is wise to bear these points in mind, because most of his critics have hitherto seemed to be concerned with particular characters or situations rather than with their relationships to the play. Such a climactic scene as the banquet in *'Tis Pity She's a Whore* (5. 6) or Calantha's dance in *The Broken Heart* (5. 2) used to be discussed independently, as if the value of the entire play hung upon a single scene.[4] It was also customary with these critics to censure cruelty and violence in the former tragedy as indicative of a lapse of taste and to praise the treatment of

---

[3] *Coleridge's Shakespearean Criticism*, ed. T. M. Raysor, 2 vols. (Cambridge, Mass., 1930), 1: 60.

[4] Ford references here and throughout the essay are to act and scene in *John Ford*, ed. Havelock Ellis, "Mermaid Series," reset ed. (London, 1960).

suppressed passion in the latter as a most effective use of dramatic technique.

Cruelty and violence, however, are no uncommon things on the Elizabethan stage and as such may hardly be called signs of decadence. What matters is not so much whether or not they are kept within certain bounds as whether or not they are integrally incorporated into the whole artistic design. Waxen corpses, the dance of madmen, the strangling rope round the heroine's neck—all these macabre elements may indeed horrify the audience of *The Duchess of Malfi*, but they are dramatically significant in that they bring into relief the heroic self-assertion of a free ego unshackled by the frailty of the flesh, which constitutes the central motif of Websterian tragedy. The ringed finger cut off the hand of the dead body leads the amoral Beatrice-Joanna to awaken for the first time to the moral implications of her own deed, a process that is closely related to the theme of *The Changeling*.

What, then, is the dramatic function of Giovanni's entry with his sister's heart upon his dagger? Or of the stabbing by Orgilus of Ithocles, entrapped immovably in a mechanical contrivance? Do these scenes contribute in any way to the expression of a coherent meaning? The answer must be negative. The only function of such scenes on the stage is the "theatrical" one of externalizing Giovanni's and Orgilus's passion, which never achieves literal expression. What actually happens here is that we are prompted to fill in the gaps between the speeches which are so restrained and the actions which are so abnormal by projecting some imaginary feelings into the characters, until we get so deeply immersed in an empathic state of mind as to disenable ourselves to question the cause and the meaning of these abnormalities. We cease at this moment to be conscious of incest or revenge as a moral issue, and, half-automatically, we take them for granted. Moreover, the fact that neither Giovanni nor Orgilus is conceived, as Macbeth and Flamineo *are*, in relation to the act of sin, and that their moral position is, as it were, "neutral," facilitates such psychological responses on the part of the audience. Probably for the same reason, the mental processes by which these protagonists reach their final decisions are purposely obscured or left unexplained. Thus, in *The Broken Heart*, quite contrary to the dramatic convention of the time, we are not made privy to Orgilus's design of vengeance until the last moment, although his speech in an earlier scene adumbrates his sinister intention against Ithocles.

We ought to approach in similar fashion the psychological effect aimed at in the dance scene of *The Broken Heart*. Since Lamb's extravagant commendation, the descriptions of Calantha in this and the next scene have generally been considered the highest achievement of the author's craftsmanship. We must ask afresh, however, whether or not the emotions that are expected to be evoked there really make for an ordered dramatic experience of the tragedy. And this may lead us to note that the would-be stoicism of Calantha can only be a stagey form of self-pity. Perhaps the author expects us to indulge in masochistic pleasure through the vicarious suffering of the heroine's inner pain, so much so that the meaningless artificiality of the mask that conceals it will escape us.

Love's Sacrifice also abounds in situations in which false sentiments predominate. To cite the most remarkable instance, there is a scene in act 2 where Bianca, the young and beautiful Duchess of Pavy, comes into the bedroom of Fernando, her secret lover, in a "night-mantle" with disheveled hair and, apparently surrendering herself, declares that she will take her own life if she becomes unfaithful to her husband, who went against custom in marrying beneath his rank. Fernando accepts this curious form of responsibility for her chastity, and they restrain themselves to the end. Here, we are offered an alluring concoction of eroticism, pseudo-puritanism, and pathos, but the author gives us no frame of reference in which to grasp the moral implications of her conduct. The sentiments are there simply to be enjoyed for their own sake.

It is to Ford's credit, however, that in such scenes as this he apparently does not aim at prurient provocation, as Beaumont and Fletcher do without fail when they deal with female characters on their wedding night in *The Maid's Tragedy*, *A Wife for a Month*, and similar tragi-comedies. Ford's treatment of amorous situations is far more restrained than might well be expected from the themes he treats. Yet, in another respect, his treatment has the same conspicuous demerit as that of Fletcher. The feelings that animate it are, for the most part, generalized and so completely lacking in immediacy and pressure from within that no more than certain stock responses can possibly be produced in our minds. To Ford, poetry and drama appear to be two separate substances to be combined to make "poetic drama." As T. S. Eliot points out, Ford's is "good poetry and good drama, but it is poetry and drama of the surface."[5] Comparing Vendice's address to the skull in *The Revenger's Tragedy* and a speech from Ford's *Lover's Melancholy* on the same subject, Theodore Spencer writes:

> [In Ford's speech] Tourneur's ethical intensity, like Webster's bitterness, is missing; the truth is described as a general truth, unrelated to moral indignation or moral value. . . . It is significant that Tourneur's speech is an essential part of the structure of his play, whereas Ford's is relatively incidental; the reflection is used for ornament, it does not bind the play together.[6]

The point might be illustrated in another way by comparing Giovanni's speech to Annabella in the wooing scene in *'Tis Pity* (1. 3) with De Flores's speech to Beatrice-Joanna at their first meeting after Alonzo's murder in *The Changeling* (3. 4). The vigor and directness with which the galvanizing truth is forced upon Beatrice helps to make this scene one of the most intense moments of tragic *anagnorisis*, while the flat and but generally relevant description of Annabella's beauty by her incestuous brother fails to produce a sense of tragic inevitability.

Critics have emphasized Ford's interest in psychological problems. Una Ellis-Fermor has good reason for viewing Ford as a true successor to Middleton because of his "close analysis of hitherto disregarded or less fully examined movements of the mind."[7] There is, however, a basic difference between the two. Behind Middleton's cold,

---

[5] T. S. Eliot, *Selected Essays*, new ed. (New York, 1950), p. 172.

[6] Theodore Spencer, *Death and Elizabethan Tragedy* (Cambridge, Mass., 1936), pp. 260–61.

[7] Una Ellis-Fermor, *The Jacobean Drama*, rev. ed. (London, 1953), p. 228.

apathetic anatomy of man's inmost nature, we are always aware of a moral eye no less stern and ironical than Marston's, whereas Ford seems to have no objective standard of judgment of any sort. Neither in action nor in characterization is his angle of vision made known to us. His characters constantly remain, as it were, in a morally neutral zone, all ties to the conventional divisions of good and evil having been lost.

Ford's primary concern is obviously with making the most of the audience's psychological responses for an esthetic end. It seems that he envisages first of all some emotions which he wants to evoke in the mind of the audience and then proceeds to create characters and plots so that they may best contribute to the stimulation of these emotions. As a result, most of the main characters are reduced to incorporeal sensibilities, and their actions are given dramatic signifi-cance only insofar as they are affected and given shape by these sensibilities.

Henri Fluchère writes of Ford that "his tragedies anticipated in some sort Racine's stripping off of inessentials—they were moving towards that state of the drama in which exclusively the purity of human passions, irrespective of time and space, is responsible for their fate."[8] In fact, there is a certain affinity between the two: everything in their tragedy is focused on a single point where sublimated passion burns itself out in a white glow. But, after all, Ford is no English Racine. While Racine, taking advantage of "classical" restrictions, achieved a superb unity in tragedy, Ford was heavily handicapped in his attempt to organize action around certain intensified moments by those Elizabethan dramatic conventions which still had a con-siderable hold on him. The ability to construct compact and coherent plots was certainly not Ford's. The dramatic incidents are so casually introduced that they function only as so many incoherent *tableaux vivants*, the gaps between which the audience is called upon to fill in. Scattered here and there are situations apparently designed to generate such an isolated mood or emotion as the pathetic sense of loss and frustration, silent griefs over irrevocable wrongs, or calm

[8] Henri Fluchère, *Shakespeare and the Elizabethans*, trans. Guy Hamilton (New York, 1956), p. 73.

dignity in the face of imminent death. But there is no tragic sequence
of events throughout the play. Only a smooth pervasive rhythm of
lyric feelings gives it a tonal unity:

> And 'twere a comely music when in parts
> One sung another's knell.[9]

In *The Broken Heart*, for instance, our sympathy goes alternately to
Penthea, to Ithocles, and to Calantha, so that our dramatic experience
of the play can never be more than an aggregate of our separate
emotional responses to the four different types of "frozen passions."

The subplot of *'Tis Pity* has often been severely criticized for
introducing unnecessary characters and incidents. What must come
into question here, however, is not the extravaganza of subsidiary
characters but whether the action on this lower level is organically
related to that on the upper level. The point will become clear if we
compare *'Tis Pity* with Middleton's *Women Beware Women*. The
Annabella-Donado-Bergetto-Poggio plot in the former play closely
resembles the Isabella-Guardiano-the Ward-Sordido plot in the
latter. Yet, while Middleton's subplot forms an integral part of the
artistic whole by functioning as a comic parody of the serious main
plot, of which mercenary bargaining and the subsequent degradation
of the soul form the theme, Ford's is mere "comic relief"; Bergetto's
transference of his affection from Annabella to Philotis and his somewhat pathetic death at the hands of the mistaken murderers do not
give us a point of departure from which the serious main plot about
incest can be approached. It might be noted furthermore, as M. C.
Bradbrook suggests, that the masque of Hippolita is "only a make-
weight," while that of Livia in Middleton's play "is linked with the
rest of the play through contrasts of characters and feelings."[10] It is
evident from the Prologue to *The Lover's Melancholy* that Ford himself regarded the subplot as quite distinct from the main plot.[11]

The lack of internal unity is also noticeable in characterization.

[9] Penthea's speech in *The Broken Heart*, 4. 2.

[10] M. C. Bradbrook, *Themes and Conventions of Elizabethan Tragedy* (Cambridge,
1952), p. 256.

[11] "Yet you will please, that as you meet with strains / Of lighter mixture, but to
cast your eye / Rather upon the *main* than on the *by*" (14–16).

We find some of his characters' actions quite puzzling, even un-expected, not because the psychological motives that animate them are, as many pro-Fordian critics assert, too complex to be put into obviously consistent actions, but because these characters are for the most part split within themselves. No doubt, the "split character" is in itself fairly common in Jacobean drama. Vendice in *The Revenger's Tragedy* is often referred to as a "double personage." So is Hamlet, to a certain extent, duality constituting the core of the much discussed mystery of his dramatic personality. With Vendice or Hamlet, however, these double aspects are never irrelevant to each other, since the moral intensity of the informing vision has caused the "splitting" per se to be invested with a meaning which is to be translated into dramatic terms. But the equivocality of the motives and actions of Ford's characters is a sign of complete moral dis-orientation on the part of the author.

The case of Bianca in *Love's Sacrifice* offers a striking example. Her earlier puritanical restraint and her later bold profession of the physical attraction of Fernando have no relation to each other. Here are two irreconcilable characters glued into one for the mere purpose of bringing into existence a series of piquant situations. And the whole tragic action revolves around the falsely conceived character of the heroine—hence the total loss of catharsis on the part of the audience. Equally disjunct is the character of the hero of *The Lady's Trial*. The splitting of Auria into the trustful and affectionate husband before leaving for the adventurous campaign and the obstinately jealous one after his return is a mere expedient for introducing a sequence of pathetic scenes, in which the wronged Spinella, his faithful wife, passes through three different stages of distress: the initial sorrowful lamentation, the later heroic perseverance, and the final impassioned outburst "Auria, unkind, unkind!" As for Spinella herself, no plausible reason exists for keeping her so long from seeing her misguided husband, to plead her innocence against the charge of adultery. The ambiguity of her motive for restraint here is necessary as a means of lengthening the span of her agony as well as of arousing our pity for Auria, who is deprived of the only means of learning the truth, so that the psychological tension may reach its climax when the two are at long last brought together and reconciled in the final scene.

Many other Fordian characters show this sort of inconsistency. Conspicuous among them is Orgilus, who appears to be not so much a dramatic character as a stage *objet* designed to strike whatever emotional note the situation demands for the esthetic satisfaction of the audience, doing now the soft and sensitive, now the ironical and pseudo-stoic, in accordance with the character with whom he is brought into contact. Nearly every Fordian character is a lonely inhabitant of an isolated world of his own, exchanging, as it were, monologues with other characters and acting totally within his own scale of values, which is never challenged but remains absolute throughout the course of the play. In Shakespeare's tragedies, each value represented by a character or an incident is constantly placed in juxtaposition with a counterbalancing value: opposite Lear there is the Fool; opposite Othello there is Emilia; and so on. And to each of the latter set of characters is assigned the role of a bold exposer of the true meaning of the acts committed by each of the former set of characters in his self-deceptive exaltation. In *Antony and Cleopatra*, Rome is an indispensable background against which Egypt must be seen; it is only in contrast with the values Caesar stands for that the love of Antony and Cleopatra takes on its significance. In Ford's plays, however, the movements of the dramatic characters do not inevitably involve conflicts of values. Nor is anything offered in the form of either character or action that might give us a clue to the issues raised in the play. With all his extravagant, aberrant passion, Giovanni is made to appear neither ludicrous nor disgusting; rather, his passion is allowed to burn itself out in self-intoxication, giving occasion to inflated speeches not quite unworthy of our sympathy.

It is true that Tecnicus, the Philosopher, in *The Broken Heart* and Friar Bonaventura in *'Tis Pity* deliver lengthy speeches on moral or religious themes. Both these speeches, however, unlike Ulysses's famous speech on order in *Troilus and Cressida*, are ineffective in striking an ethical keynote so as to give us a sure angle of vision from which we can view the values presented in the plays: the Philosopher preaching the ideal of honor based on knowledge stands too aloof from the drama itself, while the Friar's attitude to the question of incest is so expedient that we are unable to decide whether he is set as a champion of orthodox faith against Giovanni's egocentric rationalism, or is a dummy employed for the purpose of satirizing the inadequacy of conventional, revealed religion.

T. B. Tomlinson says that "Ford's plays are irresponsibly written in the sense that the governing emotional patterns . . . are never brought up in a social or intellectual context which could test, probe, and modify them."[12] Moral problems are never squarely faced; they are exploited for the sake of theatrical emotionalism. Even such a social taboo as incest seems to carry no more serious import than does, say, a family feud in *Romeo and Juliet*. In *Love's Sacrifice*, love and chastity—which ought to be treated as the central theme of the play—appear to be false values, inasmuch as the author himself is not quite certain about the moral nature of the heroine's action. Having once sworn herself to a platonic relationship with Fernando, Bianca later boldly makes love to him, willing to renounce "The outside of my titles" "To purchase one night's rest with thee." Nevertheless, both Fernando and the Duke accept her as a "spotless wife" and call her death "martyrdom." (Does the fact that she is forestalled by the entrance of the Duke's band from going beyond kissing prove her virtuousness?) As a result, the Duke's fury at Fernando in the last scene lacks moral fervor, and his sacrifice of himself at her tomb may appear to the audience to be no more than a meaningless suicide.

Ford seems to have no awareness of moral evil. Behind the tortured figures he depicts with such an abundance of pathos, we cannot feel his moral involvement. Those doubts, fears, and misgivings about man, about society, and about the universe with which most other Jacobean playwrights were more or less preoccupied cannot be found in his tragedies. In them there is no persistent quest for the meaning of life; he has reduced life to a mere "noble sufferance" which is rounded off by death. Consequently, death becomes a welcome liberator from life's ennui and horrors. The whole action of a play leads up to the moment of death when the courage and the

---

[12] T. B. Tomlinson, *A Study of Elizabethan and Jacobean Tragedy* (Cambridge, 1964), pp. 275–76.

dignity of the hero or heroine are demonstrated in the most touching manner. But the question why man must suffer and die never seems to inform his tragedies.

One might object that what is at the core of Fordian tragedy is an irreconcilable conflict between the established standards of religion and morality on the one hand and man's inborn desires on the other. From this point of view, the incest between Giovanni and Annabella would be the most shocking form of challenge to those traditional values which apparently have lost their validity through the corruption and incompetency of a church represented by the Cardinal and the Friar. Viewed in the same light, all four tragic characters in *The Broken Heart* might well be called victims, either direct or indirect, of the outdated aristocratic code to which they find themselves subject. However, this is not how we feel in our immediate dramatic experience of these tragedies. Our minds are so fully engrossed by the independent emotions aroused in the sequence of disparate situations that the underlying story needed to afford a logical interconnection among them almost escapes us. In other words, emotions are given a free hand to liberate themselves somehow from their "narrative" contexts. Penthea and Calantha, for instance, are two different emotive beings, each contributing separately to the esthetic patterning of emotions in which Fordian tragedy consists. These characters are, therefore, located on different planes and can hardly be related *dramatically* to each other through the story or through any underlying theme of the whole play.

It must also be noted that Ford frustrates once and for all our quest for the play's meaning by placing in the concluding scene an ethically ambiguous character in the role of one entrusted with the duty of restoring civic or moral order. Bassanes, the jealous husband of Penthea in *The Broken Heart*, is not only forgiven by Orgilus but is appointed "Sparta's marshal" by the dying Calantha, to fill the post of honor after the death of all the other tragic figures. In *'Tis Pity*, it is to none other than the Cardinal, who has during the course of the play been made to represent the degeneration of ecclesiastical power, that the role of an administrator of justice and preacher of morals is assigned at the end of the play. Again, in *Love's Sacrifice*, the usual scheme of poetic justice is overturned without any integral meaning when in the final scene the Duke, having every reason to seek revenge, kills himself in an act of self-imposed punishment for his sin against his wife, while Fiormonda, his lustful sister, who has so far been the most repulsive character in the play, is left behind as the only living character of princely blood, whereupon of her own accord she appoints the new duke and offers to marry him herself.

When all this is taken into consideration, it seems quite natural for Eliot to blame Ford for what he calls "the absence of purpose."[13] However, if a certain lack of seriousness is implied by "the absence of purpose," Ford's is not of the same kind as that of Beaumont, Fletcher, or Shirley. In the most fantastic of situations, there is none of that Fletcherian lightness of tone which comes from a smug assurance of the artificiality of the values presented. Nor does he try to beautify his characters by such melodramatic means as self-intoxicating idealization or counterfeit heroics. None of his tragic characters is unconscious of the true nature of what is driving him. Giovanni is never blind to the moral obliquity of his own passion, nor does Bianca hide the fact that her love for Fernando rests on her carnal desire.

It should also be noted that Ford never allows a comic touch to come into the serious action. It would be pleasant, as Robert Ornstein suggests, to think that the last scene of *Love's Sacrifice* is intended as a burlesque of romantic melodrama.[14] But here Ford is as earnest as can be, and he calls upon the audience to take everything seriously. Middleton might have made the Duke a comic figure in an attempt to expose a pattern of grotesque irony involved in his suicide, after the fashion of his chess-game scene in *Women Beware Women*, or Shakespeare's Dover Cliff scene in *King Lear*. Indeed, the finest Elizabethan and Jacobean drama had something in its nature that forced its audience to draw back from the play and see it in a per-spective that would make clear to them the wider patterns of the action and its general implications. The ritualistic nature of its setting and performance as well as the inherited popular acceptance of the

[13] Eliot, *Selected Essays*, p. 180.
[14] Robert Ornstein, *The Moral Vision of Jacobean Tragedy* (Madison, 1960), p. 220.

stage as an epitome of the universe greatly contributed to the growth of this tendency, while expository characters, multiple plots, and ambivalent situations were the chief dramatic means employed by playwrights in their conscious attempts to promote psychological detachment on the part of the audience. Villains were often made to fulfill a sort of choric function: Edmund, Flamineo, Bosola, and De Flores are among the most acrimonious critics of human nature and boldest exposers of truth on the Elizabethan stage. Even soliloquies sometimes served to make the speaker more distant in the eyes of the audience.

These conventional methods of playwriting, however, were not employed by Ford. His characters seldom speak soliloquies; even Perkin Warbeck, the most enigmatic character of his creation, is not given a single soliloquy in which to reveal his real state of mind. His villains—such as Vasques and D'Avolos—are, indeed, typical machinators. But they are by no means such bitter commentators on things related to the themes of the plays as those Websterian malcontents. What is fatally missing in Ford's plays is a distance between the stage and the audience, or what Brecht called "alienation." All his tragic characters claim our sympathy and entice us to identify ourselves with them one after another. The kind of audience Ford had in mind is one that, to quote from Shirley's preface to his folio of Beaumont and Fletcher (1647), "shall not chuse but consent and go along with them [i.e., with 'passions raised to that excellent pitch'], finding yourself at last grown insensibly the very same person you read." In the attitude of an audience like this, there can be no more of that subtle balance between engagement and detachment on which alone depends the enjoyment of tragedy. Pity, the impulse to approach, gets the better of terror, the impulse to retreat, precluding the possibility of catharsis. When the audience is thus bereft of the sense of the incongruous and of ambivalence, in which the highest tragic awareness consists, the full richness of tragedy dissolves. Reduced to an experience of an esthetically patterned sequence of liquefying emotions, tragedy now comes to exist nowhere but within the heart of the audience.

This is the phase tragedy was entering with Ford. Most of his mature works belong to the Caroline period, when dissociation was gaining ground in many facets of intellectual activity, and when values were beginning to lose their hold on reality. Although his eyes were turned backward to the great writers of the preceding period, whom he tried to imitate, it is undeniable that he was totally given to a laxer spirit. "Decadence" in his tragedies is, therefore, not a simple matter of sensationalism or of a lapse in taste. It has to do with something far more fundamental, that is, with the author's uncertainty about his own values. It consists in a failure to provide an adequate frame of reference in which immoral behavior is given a moral significance so that a play can be experienced as a meaningful whole.

"Celestial Light": The Irradiating Ideas of *Paradise Lost*

Hiroichiro Doke

1. Man

Christianity assisted in redirecting human thought by making man the center of the universe. Bringing man to the front stage of world history, Christianity can be said to be anthropocentric. From this view, it might be questioned whether *Paradise Lost* is a human or, in my sense, Christian epic, for in it only two persons, Adam and Eve, appear, while all the other characters are superhuman beings. In order to answer this question I shall have to take a somewhat roundabout route.

In the first place, Aristotle begins his *Metaphysics* as follows:

> All men by nature desire to know. An indication of this is the delight we take in our senses; for even apart from their usefulness they are loved for themselves; and above all others the sense of sight. For not only with a view to action, but even when we are not going to do anything, we prefer seeing (one might say) to everything else. The reason is that this, most of all the senses, makes us know and brings to light many differences between things.[1]

Aristotle's intellectual contemplativeness is perhaps better represented here than anywhere else. He is, in short, a man who sees. His attention is attracted above all to the visible things of this world. So when he looks at human beings, he seems to be more concerned with their

[1] *The Works of Aristotle, Metaphysica*, trans. W. D. Ross (Oxford, 1948), VIII: 980a. Throughout this essay, all quotations from Milton are taken from *Paradise Lost and Selected Poetry and Prose*, ed. Northrop Frye (New York, 1951), numbers indicating book and line.

human natures than with their humanity itself—hence his interest in individual characters. It is not altogether coincidental that his disciple Theophrastus wrote the famous book titled *Characters*. Characters are the images of other people seen by the eye turned outward. Such characters are various and admit of being compared with each other. However, once the gaze is turned inward, it does not discover character.[2] What is discovered there is the inner conflict between good and evil, the fight against temptation, and the persistent desire to know what *humanity* is—there is no longer leisure for contemplation of *human nature*.

From such a point of view, the fact that only two human beings, Adam and Eve, appear in *Paradise Lost* cannot be the basis for concluding that it is not anthropocentric; on the contrary, I reach the opposite conclusion. Milton provides only two human beings in *Paradise Lost*—or rather, only one, since Eve is bone of Adam's bone, and flesh of Adam's flesh. They are not two individuals but one flesh—and yet Milton managed to write an epic of such length. This proves how seriously and completely he examined humanity through himself. The subtle complexities of human characters should not be sought in the poem. Milton's eye was turned to humanity, not to human nature; to personality, not to individuality. And yet Milton was blind; he was deprived of the sense of sight which according to Aristotle "brings to light many differences between things."

Nonetheless he was able to see "things invisible to mortal sight" and wished to communicate them to others. He could not help praying:

> So much the rather thou, Celestial Light,
> Shine inward, and the mind through all her powers
> Irradiate; there plant eyes; all mist from thence
> Purge and disperse, that I may see and tell
> Of things invisible to mortal sight.
>
> [3. 51–55]

[2] C. S. Lewis, *The Allegory of Love* (Oxford, 1953), p. 61: "No man is a 'character' to himself, and least of all while he thinks of good and evil . . . within he finds only . . . the passions and emotions which contend for mastery."

When he wrote this passage, it was not Aristotle but Plato who was in his mind, the Plato who believed that purest truth is invisible.

> Philosophy points out that the evidence of the eyes and of the ears and of the other organs of sense is thoroughly misleading and urges them [i.e., the souls] to withdraw from the use of the senses except when such use is inevitable. It encourages the soul to gather itself up into itself, all alone, and to put trust in nothing but itself—to trust only such realities as it may discern in their essential nature by its own essential nature; whatever it sees by the use of something else, things appearing variously *in various other things*, it should count in no way real. Such things are objects of sense and visible, while what the soul sees *by itself* is an object of thought and invisible.[3]

How subjective and existential Plato is in comparison with Aristotle! It is no wonder that the predominance of the soul in Milton's poetry should be recognized by Coleridge, who has been identified along with Kierkegaard as a typical philosopher of Christian existentialism by Basil Willey in his *Christianity Past and Present*.[4] Coleridge says:

> In all modern poetry in Christendom there is . . . a fleeting away of external things, the mind or subject greater than the object, the reflective character predominant. In the *Paradise Lost* the sublimest parts are the revelations of Milton's own mind, producing itself and evolving its own greatness.[5]

This helps to justify, in a way, Denis Saurat's opinion that the hero of *Paradise Lost* is neither Satan nor Adam but Milton himself. That truth is subjectivity seems inconceivable outside Christianity. Paul properly says, "the Spirit searcheth all things. . . . For what man knoweth the things of a man, save the spirit of man which is in him?" (1 Corinthians 2:10-11).

[3] *Plato's Phaedo*, trans. R. S. Bluck (London, 1955), pp. 82–83.
[4] Cf. Basil Willey, *Christianity Past and Present* (Cambridge, 1952), p. 134.
[5] S. T. Coleridge, "Milton," in *Milton Criticism*, ed. J. Thorpe (London, 1951), p. 96.

For that reason, knowledge is remembrance. The Adam and Eve whom Milton describes through his remembrance are, as T. S. Eliot puts it, "the original *Man* and *Woman*, not types, but prototypes."[6] And it is because they are prototypes that Milton could pursue the most fundamental problem, what man is, through Adam and Eve. They are introduced in *Paradise Lost* in the following way:

> Two of far nobler shape, erect and tall,
> God-like erect, with native honour clad
> In naked majesty, seemed lords of all,
> And worthy seemed; for in their looks divine
> The image of their glorious Maker shone,
> Truth, wisdom, sanctitude severe and pure—
> Severe, but in true filial freedom placed.
>
> [4. 288–94]

Thus Adam and Eve are given the dignity of man created in the image of God. "[Adam] is indeed the lord of creation, which exists entirely for him and for Eve; he has named the animals, and they sport for his entertainment; his dwelling is rich with all the beauty that flowers and trees can give. His very lack of external splendour only enhances his natural dignity."[7] Adam's life before the Fall appeals strongly to every man's nostalgic imagination as the embodiment of his heartfelt aspirations.

Milton has also given Eve much of his own deep admiration for womanhood. The mother of mankind is as preeminent in female beauty as her husband is in male. Milton suggests this beauty by comparisons with figures from Greek and Roman legend. "She is even, in her special circumstances, a good housewife; she prepares their dinner of 'savourie fruits,' and when Raphael joins them at it, she ministers to his and to Adam's wants and fills their cups. When Raphael discourses to Adam, she listens in respectful silence to the story of the war in Heaven and of the Creation, but when the talk turns to more disputable topics like the awkward comparison of the

---

[6] T. S. Eliot, "Milton II," in *On Poetry and Poets* (London, 1957), p. 155.
[7] C. M. Bowra, *From Virgil to Milton* (London, 1948), p. 200.

Ptolemaic and Copernican systems, she sees the studious look on her husband's face and retires

> With lowliness Majestic from her seat,
> And Grace that won who saw to wish her stay."[8]

[8. 42–43]

Or again:

> Yet went she not as not with such discourse
> Delighted, or not capable her ear
> Of what was high. Such pleasure she reserved,
> Adam relating, she sole auditress;
> Her husband the relater she preferred
> Before the Angel, and of him to ask
> Chose rather; he, she knew, would intermix
> Grateful digressions, and solve high dispute
> With conjugal caresses: from his lip
> Not words alone pleased her.

[8. 48–57]

Her graceful humility is beautifully described. The marriage of Adam and Eve is celebrated as an incomparable ideal.

We must not overlook, however, the idea of hierarchy on which their marriage is based. When he wrote this passage, Milton may possibly have thought of Paul, who said:

> Let your women keep silence in the churches: for it is not permitted unto them to speak; but *they are commanded* to be under obedience, as also saith the law.
>
> And if they will learn any thing, let them ask their husbands at home: for it is a shame for women to speak in the church.
>
> What! came the word of God out from you? or came it unto you only? [1 Corinthians 14: 34–36]

Behind this is Paul's key theme, that everything should submit to its superior authority, which is also expressed in 1 Corinthians 11: 1–16 and Ephesians 5: 22–23. This point is the most important key to

[8] Ibid., p. 203.

interpreting *Paradise Lost*. If Lucifer, Eve, and Adam had kept their places and sustained the proper order, the cosmos would have remained perfect; when they did not conform to order, the larger order of the world was itself affected.

In obedience to order, all the things in the universe are able to flourish and enjoy freedom, but in disobedience they lose freedom though seemingly enjoying it: this is the true meaning of Christian liberty. And this is also what Milton intends to express in *Paradise Lost*, when he begins with "Man's first disobedience" and ends by insisting on man's steadfast obedience to God.

Milton describes his ideal in Adam and Eve before the Fall, and their happy marriage is in striking contrast with his own unhappy marriage, reflections of which may be found here and there in *Paradise Lost*. The trauma that the failure of his marriage inflicted on his heart produced a lasting distrust of women. Yet the more disappointed he was in his own marriages, the greater blessing he gave to the ideal marriage of Adam and Eve. Here one can detect his consciousness of the sharp discrepancy between his lofty ideal and the actuality he met with; or in other words, dream and reality.

> Hail, wedded Love, mysterious law, true source
> Of human offspring, . . .
> By thee adulterous lust was driven from men
> Among the bestial herds to range; by thee,
> Founded in reason, loyal, just, and pure,
> Relations dear, and all the charities
> Of father, son, and brother, first were known.
> Far be it that I should write thee sin or blame,
> Or think thee unbefitting holiest place,
> Perpetual fountain of domestic sweets,
> Whose bed is undefiled and chaste pronounced,
> Present, or past, as saints and patriarchs used.
> Here Love his golden shafts employs, here lights
> His constant lamp, and waves his purple wings,
> Reigns here and revels; not in the bought smile
> Of harlots, loveless, joyless, unendeared,

Casual fruition; nor in court amours,
Mixed dance, or wanton mask, or midnight ball,
Or serenade, which the starved lover sings
To his proud fair, best quitted with disdain.
These, lulled by nightingales, embracing slept,
And on their naked limbs the flowery roof
Showered roses, which the morn repaired. Sleep on,
Blest pair! and, O! yet happiest, if ye seek
No happier state, and know to know no more!

[4. 750–75]

We observe the juxtaposition of his praise of natural, productive, and pastoral love with his curse of unnatural, unproductive, and artificial courtly love, or lust. The contrast reveals that, since lust seems so near to love, it must be repudiated as strongly as love is approved.

Milton is far from being a rigorous Puritan when he describes Eve in the following manner:

She, as a veil down to the slender waist,
Her unadorned golden tresses wore
Dishevelled, but in wanton ringlets waved
As the vine curls her tendrils, which implied
Subjection, but required with gentle sway,
And by her yielded, by him best received,
Yielded with coy submission, modest pride,
And sweet, reluctant, amorous delay.

[4. 304–11]

These few lines describing Eve's sweet hesitation also suggest that Adam's passion is stirred by it and that she intends to stir him. The subtlety of love between men and women is given concise but full expression. Every happy couple keeps a memory of their first meeting. When Eve speaks of her first meeting with Adam, she leans on him, half embracing, with eyes of conjugal attraction and meek surrender:

half her swelling breast

Naked met his, under the flowing gold
Of her loose tresses hid. He, in delight
Both of her beauty and submissive charms,
Smiled with superior love, as Jupiter
On Juno smiles when he impregns the clouds
That shed May flowers, and pressed her matron lip
With kisses pure.

[4. 495–502]

There is no sense of obscenity here: there are only the pure "rites /
Mysterious of connubial love" (4. 742–43) to be blessed. There is no
sense of sin; everything has the original approval and grace of God.
This is one affirmative or positive aspect of Christianity that has been
handed down these centuries, originating from Genesis and inherited
by Augustine and Thomas Aquinas. And Milton belongs to this
tradition. God says of Adam and the Angels:

I made him just and right, . . .
Such I created all th' ethereal Powers
And Spirits, . . .

[3. 98–101]

And Raphael also tells Adam:

one Almighty is, from whom
All things proceed, and up to him return,
If not depraved from good, created all
Such to perfection.

[5. 469–72]

Thus it is from the thought that all created things are good that the
approval of the flesh is derived, though of course the superiority of
the spirit over the flesh is indisputable. This is the order, but the flesh
can never be said to be evil because of its inferior place. As Cleanth
Brooks puts it,

Milton actually scandalized his Puritan contemporaries by
his stand on divorce and the view of sex expressed in his
Paradise Lost is in certain startling ways reminiscent of that of

D. H. Lawrence. For both men, sex is of central importance. Both deal with it frankly. Both affirm the flesh and its passions to be holy.[9]

It seems that Milton could not bear the idea of the spirit remaining immortal while the body dies away, for in that view the body is slighted. He seems to have felt that, if the mortality of the body is inevitable, the spirit should also be mortal. And the spirit will be resurrected with the body. The death until the resurrection is "a death like sleep, / A gentle wafting to immortal life" (12. 434–35). Milton receives modern support in the biblical interpretation provided by Oscar Cullman.[10]

Such a conclusion, that is, what has been called Milton's mortalism, comes not so much from the mere affirmation of the body as from its denial, or his particular spiritualism, his emphasis on motives rather than on acts. This emphasis comes from his belief as a Protestant. Considering that "the wages of sin *is* death" (Romans 6: 23), is it the spirit or the body that sins? Adam in *Paradise Lost* says in answer, "It was but breath / Of life that sinned: what dies but what had life / And sin? The body properly hath neither" (10. 789–91). Milton writes in his *De Doctrina Christiana*, "What could be more absurd than that the mind, which is the part principally offending, should escape the threatened death; and that the body alone . . . should pay the penalty of sin by undergoing death, though not implicated in the transgression?"[11] Milton's Adam says in conclusion, "All of me, then, shall die: let this appease / The doubt, since human reach no further knows" (10. 792–93).

It is this view of the body that enables Milton to describe the pure sexuality of Adam and Eve before the Fall and to praise connubial love. Augustine had different ideas, for, as C. S. Lewis points out, "for St. Augustine the unfallen sexuality is purely hypothetical:

---

[9] *Complete Poetry and Selected Prose of John Milton*, ed. Cleanth Brooks (New York, 1950), introduction, p. v.

[10] Oscar Cullmann, *Immortality of the Soul or Resurrection of the Dead?* (London, 1958). See especially ch. 4, "Those Who Sleep," pp. 48–57.

[11] *The Works of John Milton*, ed. Frank G. Patterson et al., 20 vols., 15 (New York, 1933): 219.

when he describes it he is describing what the act of generation *would have been* before the Fall, but he does not think it ever took place."[12] Saint Augustine came to defend and bless marriage with greater enthusiasm as he fought with the Manicheans and the Pelagians. However, he was once of the opinion, like some of the Fathers of the early Church, that there should have been a certain mysterious form of generation before the Fall different from marriage and that the generative form of the union of man and woman should have been brought about only by the Fall, which proved man's degradation.

He had enough reason to believe so in those passionate events of his life preceding his conversion.

> What had most worried Augustine until his conversion was the problem of sexual love. He was a premature, passionate person born in Africa. He knew a woman at the age of seventeen and had a child. . . . And yet he repeated the same mistakes when he was over thirty. It is beyond the bounds of imagination how long and how seriously he should have suffered from this problem. In his consciousness it had been taking the form of a fight against passion. It was only to passions he yielded and it was also passions that fettered him. That fetter of passions tortured him to the bones. Therefore, in his theology to carnal desire itself is attached the curse of a sin as old as the Original Sin.[13]

It is unlikely that he should think of the body or flesh without remembering his own sinful past. Thus he believed that the relationship between Adam and Eve before the Fall should never have been stained with sexuality.

On the other hand, Milton seems to have been free from agonizing memories of the past similar to Augustine's. Even the failure of his first marriage was a problem concerned only with the spirit, not with the flesh. Milton probably did not hesitate to accept the idea

---

[12] C. S. Lewis, *A Preface to Paradise Lost* (Oxford, 1967), p. 122.
[13] Takamasa Mitani, "Augustine," in *Mitani Takamasa Zenshu* [The Complete Works of Takamasa Mitani], I (Tokyo, 1965): 265–66 (my translation).

that Adam and Eve, born good, should have had the same kind of generative method that their descendants had, in carrying out the divine decree "Be fruitful, and multiply, and replenish the earth" (Genesis 1: 28), which was given to them before the Fall. It is natural that Milton should be quite different from Augustine in his way of dealing with unfallen sexuality between Adam and Eve.[14] Milton's Adam says that the body has no sin (see 10. 791). In Milton's mind, it was the spirit, the breath of life, that sinned, and not the flesh. What was wrong with his first marriage was the choice of a wife like Mary Powell and had nothing to do with his flesh. This is the ground on which Milton's special mortalism is conceived.

Here we should consider what kind of sin one is most seriously conscious and guilty of. Paul says, "Every sin that a man doeth is without the body; but he that committeth fornication sinneth against his own body" (1 Corinthians 6: 18). Unlike any other sin, that committed by carnal desire comes from within the flesh and therefore is felt to be so importunate and irresistible that a man helplessly bound by its fetters cannot help realizing the sinfulness of human existence. One must complain, as Paul does, "For the good that I would, I do not: but the evil which I would not, that I do" (Romans 7: 19). One finds oneself wholly corrupted by sin. In the extreme state of corruption, one can be led to the belief in the atonement of Jesus Christ, who is to deliver one from "the body of this death." Then the mystery of the Trinity is revealed to him as an expression of God's love for man.

Every reader of the *Confessions* knows that one of the strongest factors leading Augustine to the orthodox faith was the torture of the flesh. We can perceive some heterodox elements in Milton's faith and, further, we may observe that these elements have something in common with the thought of Pelagius, who was the theological opponent of Augustine. Milton's position naturally follows from his difference from Augustine in the view of spirit and flesh.

In the prefatory lines to the seventh book of *Paradise Lost*, Milton says:

[14] Cf. Bowra, *Virgil to Milton*, pp. 202–03.

> . . . I sing with mortal voice, unchanged
> To hoarse or mute, though fallen on evil days,
> On evil days though fallen, and evil tongues.
> In darkness, and with dangers compassed round,
> And solitude.
>
> [7. 24–28]

He prays to Urania for her protection and longs to find "fit audience . . . though few." If we look at Milton unsympathetically, he seems to be too aloof and arrogant; he speaks as if he were a pearl of clear water dropped into a puddle. Dante seems by comparison more humble and accessible, beginning the *Divine Comedy* with

> In the midway of this our mortal life,
> I found me in a gloomy wood, astray
> Gone from the path direct.[15]

Certainly Milton was proud, putting such trust in his own moral ability that he could not quite believe human nature was utterly corrupted through the Fall. He became estranged from those creeds maintaining man's utter corruption and the doctrine that to be Redeemer Jesus must be God Himself. The Holy Trinity rests on logic of this kind. Lacking such an urgent need, Milton came to cherish the Arian and Pelagian heresies in his mind. In such ways religious views are formed under the influence of our view of man.

2.   God

Discussing the theology of *Paradise Lost*, C. S. Lewis has written:

> . . . it is also Catholic in the sense of basing its poetry on con-
> ceptions that have been held "always and everywhere and
> by all." This Catholic quality is so predominant that it is the
> first impression any unbiased reader would receive. Heretical
> elements exist in it, but are only discoverable by search: any
> criticism which forces them into the foreground is mistaken,
> and ignores the fact that this poem was accepted as orthodox

---

[15] Dante, *The Vision of Dante Alighieri*, trans. H. F. Cary (London, 1910), p. 1.

by many generations of acute readers well grounded in theology.[16]

This view of C. S. Lewis's is confirmed by John Bailey:

> To the serious world it appeared to be a religious book and as such enjoyed the great advantage of being thought fit to be read on the only day in the week on which many people were accustomed to read at all. . . . When Sunday readers were tired of the Bible they were apt to turn to *Paradise Lost.*[17]

The discovery in 1823 of *De Doctrina Christiana*, which was written about the same time as *Paradise Lost*, threw a different light on Milton's thought in the poem and rendered certain hitherto ignored phrases conspicuous. The comparison between the two has proved that some lines in the poem are certainly heretically tinted. It was Denis Saurat who was the first to undertake a new approach to Milton by exploring this aspect of the poet. And Saurat's approach has been followed and modified by Arthur Sewell, Maurice Kelley, and others. As Takeo Iwahashi points out, however, "even Dr. Johnson, who would never have forgiven Milton if he had detected any kind of heresy in him, declares that the poet's departure from the Church of England only concerns forms of church politics and that it has nothing to do with heresy."[18] And so it may be concluded, with Lewis, that the essential doctrine of *Paradise Lost* is orthodox and that its heretical elements can be overlooked unless it is closely examined with the aid of external evidence.

Lewis insisted that the definitely heretical thoughts embodied in *Paradise Lost* are confined to two points: (1) the thought based on the *Zohar* that God is infinitely extended in space, and therefore that in order to create God must contract His infinite essence, and (2) the idea that God made the material universe not "out of nothing," but "out of Himself," and therefore that matter is a part of God.

[16] Lewis, *Preface to Paradise Lost*, p. 82.
[17] John Bailey, *Milton* (Oxford, 1950), p. 143.
[18] Takeo Iwahashi, *Shitsurakuen no Keijijogaku* [The Metaphysics of Paradise Lost] (Tokyo, 1933), p. 309.

Paying particular attention to Milton's subtleties, Lewis tried (pp. 87–90) to interpret these two points as not contradicting orthodoxy. It seems almost as if he sought to give a higher assessment to *Paradise Lost* as a Christian epic. However, this attempt of Lewis's by no means helps to clarify the reason Milton was inclined to entertain such heterodox thoughts. When he wrote *Paradise Lost*, Milton certainly had the general reader of his day in mind, but at the same time he was irresistibly conscious of the existence of various thoughts conflicting with each other in his own mind.[19] This tension resulted in the complexity of the poem. If, therefore, we must refrain from forcing the heretical elements into the foreground lest we should misread what Milton actually meant, Milton's inclination to heterodoxy, his ethos deeply hidden behind the expressed thought, must still be given proper attention.

We have already seen why Milton turned his back upon the Calvinistic belief that man is so utterly corrupted through the Fall that he can never be saved without the gratuitous grace of God. In Milton, instead of Calvinistic and Augustinian doctrines of the divine grace, instead of Christ's love as the Savior who is crucified for the atonement of mankind, the human, moral struggle of the Son as a model or teacher of mankind is pushed into the foreground. This image of the Son seems to find its expression in the Jesus of *Paradise Regained*. It also seems to be this view of Christ that gives some Arian bias to his idea of the Trinity.

Milton thought God the Father was "Omnipotent, / Immutable, Immortal, Infinite, / Eternal King . . . Author of all being" (3. 372–74). He is the fountain of light so dazzling that the flaming seraphim cannot approach Him, but must veil their eyes with their wings. It is very likely that this conception of God forbade Milton to represent God as a human being. So in *Paradise Lost* God never appears in any corporeal form except as a voice, and the work of creating heaven

---

[19] Cf. Bowra, *Virgil to Milton*, p. 213: "Milton lived in an age of religious change and dispute. He himself never remained for very long in any single set of beliefs." And L. A. Cormican, "Milton's Religious Verse," in *From Donne to Marvell*, ed. B. Ford (Harmondsworth, Mddx., 1956), p. 180: "*Paradise Lost* was probably written while he was exploring Christian doctrine to decide what he should believe. The poem is not, consequently, based on a finally settled creed such as we find in Dante or Bunyan."

and earth is left to the Son. The Son, in whom "all his Father shone /
Substantially expressed" (3. 139–40), is represented as follows:

> . . . Divine Similitude,
> In whose conspicuous countenance, without cloud
> Made visible, th' Almighty Father shines
> Whom else no creature can behold: on thee
> Impressed the effulgence of his glory abides;
> Transfused on thee his ample Spirit rests.
> He Heaven of Heavens, and all the Powers therein,
> By thee created.
>
> [3. 384–91]

At the same time, however, the preceding lines, "Thee . . . of all
creation first, / Begotten Son" (3. 383–84), when they are compared
with chapter 5 of *De Doctrina Christiana*, titled "de Filio Dei," reveal
the poet's Arianism. The Son was born within the limits of time and
is consequently not eternal, as is the Father. In Milton's belief, the
Father is the one invisible God, and his offspring the only begotten,
visible Son. The divine attributes belong only to the Father; when
these are attributed to the Son, they are understood to be attributable
in their original and proper sense to the Father alone; whatever share
of divinity the Son possesses is assigned to him by gift of the Father;
in this way the Father is greater than the Son in all things. The Father
and the Son are clearly distinguished, one being infinite, invisible,
independent, absolute, and the other finite, visible, dependent, relative. Milton's attitude seems to derive from the characteristic Christian discrimination between the visible and the invisible. We, as well
as Milton, would reach his conclusions about the Trinity if we
followed the logic of *De Doctrina Christiana*. In fact, however, the
dogma of the Trinity is to be acquired not so much through rational
reasoning as through faith.

Thought to be the infinite, Milton's God should be, not a Creator
existing external to His creation, but the total and perfect Being who
includes in Himself the whole of space and the whole of time. Therefore, God must have made the world not "out of nothing" but "out
of Himself." This doctrine was directed against dualism—against the

idea that God was not the sole origin of things, but rather found Himself from the beginning faced with something other than Himself. What I have called materialism (i.e., the idea that matter is a part of God) and its consequent, the "mortalism" of the soul, are closely connected with the idea of creation that I have mentioned. Matter and spirit are not opposed to each other; in fact, the former, when refined, can be turned into the latter. Such hylozoism[20] and a deep-seated optimism regarding human nature underlie the idea of creation.

> . . . one Almighty is, from whom
> All things proceed, and up to him return,
> If not depraved from good, created all
> Such to perfection; one first matter all,
> Endued with various forms, various degrees
> Of substance, and, in things that live, of life;
> But more refined, more spirituous and pure,
> As nearer to him placed or nearer tending
> Each in their several active spheres assigned,
> Till body up to spirit work, in bounds
> Proportioned to each kind.
>
> [5. 469–79]

We observe heresy in the process as well as in the basic matter of creation. Saurat observes the *Zohar's* influence in Milton's idea of creation through God's retirement:

> . . . ride forth, and bid the Deep
> Within appointed bounds be heaven and earth.
> Boundless the Deep, because I am who fill
> Infinitude; nor vacuous the space,
> Though I, uncircumscribed, myself retire,
> And put not forth my goodness, which is free
> To act or not.
>
> [7. 166–72]

[20] Expressions of an idea of this sort can be cited from *Paradise Lost*: "And God said, 'Let the waters generate / Reptile with spawn abundant, living soul' " (7. 387–88); and " 'Let th' Earth bring forth soul living in her kind, / Cattle, and creeping things, and beast of the earth, / Each in their kind!' " (7. 451–53).

In the *Zohar*, God is infinitely extended in space (like ether), and therefore in order to create—to make room for anything to exist which is not simply Himself—He must contract his infinite essence. The theory of God's omnipresence is perfectly orthodox, but it is heresy to make God present in space in the way in which a body is present. Because the *Zohar* does not reduce all to spatial matters, we should refrain from crude picture-thinking. This said, the *Zohar* is still too materialistic for the orthodox in conceiving of God's creation, because its theory derives from the axiom that two bodies cannot occupy the same space at the same time.

Milton certainly follows the *Zohar* to some extent, but without abandoning ideas of his own. If he had been true to the *Zohar*, he should have let his God say, "The space *is* vacuous *because* I have withdrawn." But in fact God in *Paradise Lost* says, "The space is *not* vacuous, *although* I have withdrawn." Thus the retraction or withdrawal of Milton's God is never spatial. Milton's point is revealed in the line "And put not forth my goodness"; that is, God is not exercising His efficacy over parts of space, though He is still, in some undefined mode, present in them. In Lewis's opinion, Milton takes care not to be too far from orthodoxy, using a word like "uncircumscribed" which can be compared with Thomas Aquinas's theory of divine omnipresence. Milton is, then, never strikingly heretical. But, "in fine, from this highly poetical but philosophically obscure passage, the most we can draw is that Milton is perhaps following the *Zohar* where the *Zohar* is perhaps heretical."[21] Thus Lewis admits that Milton discloses his heterodoxical inclinations in his idea of divine retraction, as also in his belief that matter is a part of God.

What interests me above all, however, is why Milton makes God withdraw His efficacy in the process of creation, and what Milton intends by this. Clearly, he wishes to establish the freedom of man's will. Without this retraction of God's goodness, how could man have been disobedient to God? Without this doctrine, unfallen Adam and Eve would be deprived of the possibility of committing sin (for the Fall brought about sin). Without it, they could not wish to do

[21] Lewis, *Preface to Paradise Lost*, p. 89.

anything but good, and so the fact of "Man's first disobedience" could not be explained. So Milton needs this doctrine to give the possibility of committing sin to unfallen Adam and Eve and angels. At the beginning of book 5, Milton therefore also lets Eve dream an ominous dream and has Adam say:

> Evil into the mind of God or Man
> May come and go, so unapproved, and leave
> No spot or blame behind.

[5. 117–19]

Milton's heterodoxy provides his characters with the internal means for freedom of choice. As Grierson put it:

> At the centre of all Milton's thought lies the determination to establish the freedom of man's will as for him the sole ultimate vindication of the justice of God. . . . Milton's metaphysics are the endeavour to find a secure basis for this entire freedom.[22]

Through God's withdrawal of His efficacy, man was given absolutely free will and action—free from even God—freedom of and responsibility for rising and falling. God could have forced man's obedience to Him through His omnipotence, but He wishes for man's free and voluntary obedience:

> Freely they stood who stood, and fell who fell.
> Not free, what proof could they have given sincere
> Of true allegiance, constant faith, or love,
> Where only what they needs must do appeared,
> Not what they would? What praise could they receive,
> What pleasure I, from such obedience paid . . . ?

[3. 102–07]

Milton strove to reconcile man's freedom with God's predestination. Judging from his willingness to incline toward heterodoxy, it is natural that his strong insistence on man's freedom should be in conflict with the orthodox doctrine of God's predestination.

---

[22] H. J. C. Grierson, *Criticism and Creation* (London, 1949), p. 39.

This is one of those common problems that have occurred repeatedly in Christianity. As L. A. Cormican says:

> The problem of reconciling divine foreknowledge with human freedom is not a poetic but a religious one; Milton assumed (and expected his audience to assume) that it was one of the divine mysteries, discussible but not soluble.[23]

Such problems may indeed be insoluble. But the approach taken to them by an individual reveals the nature of his faith. We shall understand Milton better in the problem of free will and election by examining the contexts in which Calvin, Luther, and their forerunner, Augustine, emphasize the doctrine of predestination. All three have in common a deep sense of sin; they believe man has lost the inborn goodness of his nature through Adam's fall, contradicting the optimistic opinion of Pelagius in this respect. According to Pelagius, man has a natural capacity to reject evil and seek God; while to Augustine, "There is none righteous, no, not one: There is none that understandeth, there is none that seeketh after God" (Romans 3 : 10–11).

Augustine thinks man is not able to attain the least goodness by himself, without God's grace. Man is free to disobey God, but he is not able to return to God without His help. Therefore, Augustine's sincere prayer was, "Grant what Thou commandest."[24] Pelagius, on the other hand, divides man's moral power into *posse*, *velle*, and *esse*. Admitting the *posse* to be a divine gift, he maintains that *velle* and *esse* are man's to realize himself. In Augustine's belief, even the *velle* and the *esse*, or man's faith itself, are never man's accomplishments but blessings from God; everything good is in God Himself and man is utterly corrupt and helpless, and so must rely totally upon grace for salvation. From such faith in the omniscience and omnipotence of God is derived the doctrine of predestination.

[23] Cormican, "Milton's Religious Verse," in *From Donne to Marvell*, p. 183.
[24] Augustine, "De peccatorum meritis et remissione et de baptismo parvulorum," 2. 5, in Philip Schaff, ed., *A Select Library of the Nicene and Post-Nicene Fathers of the Christian Church*, vol. 5, *Saint Augustine's Anti-Pelagian Works*, trans. P. Holmes and R.E. Wallis, rev. B. B. Warfield (Grand Rapids, Mich., 1956), pp. 45–46; hereafter cited as *Fathers*.

134 The Irradiating Ideas of Paradise Lost

A familiar question arises here. What is the point of discussing what men should be or how men should behave themselves, if every action or happening of men is determined by God? In answer, Augustine says:

> *When we see a lame man who has the opportunity of being cured of his lameness, we of course have a right to say: "That man ought not to be lame; and if he ought, he is able."* And yet whenever he wishes he is not immediately able; but only after he has been cured by the application of the remedy, and the medicine has assisted his will. The same thing takes place in the inward man in relation to sin which is its lameness, by the grace of Him who "came not to call the righteous, but sinners"; since "the whole need not the physician, but only they that be sick."[25]

Such a vision of man as morally sick reminds one of Pascal and Luther. Paul's painful cry, "O wretched man that I am! who shall deliver me from the body of this death?" (Romans 7: 24) leads to salvation by God and the doctrine of predestination.

What did Milton think of fallen humanity? Had Milton the *Kranken-Optik* of those thinkers mentioned above, who believe in the doctrine of predestination? Of fallen man in spiritual death, Milton says:

> It cannot be denied, however, that some remnants of the divine image still exist in us, not wholly extinguished by this spiritual death. . . . These vestiges of original excellence are visible, first, in the understanding. . . . Secondly, the will is clearly not altogether inefficient in respect of good works, or at any rate of good endeavors.[26]

Man's "Renovation" is defined as a change whereby

> the natural mind and will of man being partially renewed by a divine impulse, are led to seek the knowledge of God, and for the time, at least, undergo an alteration for the better.[27]

[25] *Fathers*, "De perfectione justitiae hominis," 5: 160–61; italics added.
[26] "The Christian Doctrine," I. 12, in *Works of John Milton*, 15: 209–11.
[27] "The Christian Doctrine," I. 17, in ibid., pp. 353–55.

Milton had no consciousness of "the body of this death." Augustine and the others, who are keenly conscious of the original sin that prevents man from doing good, seek to die in the old Adam and to be brought to life in the new Adam. Such a strain of Calvinistic theology seemed to be alien to Milton. Because man is not utterly corrupted, so his renovation need only be partial. Change to a better life is accomplished by the pursuit of divine knowledge; hence the importance of study and education. The purpose of education, Milton says, is "to repair the ruines of our first Parents by regaining to know God aright, and out of that knowledge to love him, to imitate him, to be like him."[28] We observe that "knowledge" precedes "love," and this links Milton with Hooker and the Cambridge Platonists. In contrast to the voluntarism of Calvin and Luther, Milton put an emphasis on "reason" resembling that of the Schoolmen. This could be called the intellectualism of Milton.[29]

---

[28] "Of Education" in *Works of John Milton*, 4 (New York, 1941): 277.

[29] See Herschel Baker, *The Wars of Truth* (Cambridge, Mass., 1952), pp. 1–42. Luther's stand in the *Smalcald Articles* is as follows:

Here we must confess what St. Paul says in Rom. 5:12, namely, that sin had its origin in one man, Adam, through whose disobedience all men were made sinners and became subject to death and the devil. This is called original sin, or the root sin. . . .

This hereditary sin is so deep a corruption of nature that reason cannot understand it. It must be believed because of the revelation in the Scriptures. What the scholastic theologians taught concerning this article is therefore nothing but error and stupidity, namely:

1. That after the fall of Adam the natural powers of man have remained whole and uncorrupted, and that man by nature possesses a right understanding and a good will, as the philosophers teach.

2. Again, that man has a free will, either to do good and refrain from evil or to refrain from good and do evil.

3. Again, that man is able by his natural powers to observe and keep all the commandments of God.

4. Again, that man is able by his natural powers to love God above all things and his neighbor as himself.

5. Again, if man does what he can, God is certain to grant him his grace.

6. Again, when a man goes to the sacrament there is no need of a good intention to do what he ought, but it is enough that he does not have an evil intention to commit sin, for such is the goodness of man's nature and such is the power of the sacrament.

7. That it cannot be proved from the Scriptures that the Holy Spirit and his gifts are necessary for the performance of a good work.

Such and many similar notions have resulted from misunderstanding and

In this view, Milton's heretical doctrines seem not merely a theory to discuss but a matter of how to feel; they are, after all, derived from his pride and his belief in the natural dignity and virtue of man. Such trust comes from a humanism linking Milton with the early Renaissance. But for all his heretical and humanistic qualities, Milton is first and foremost supported by the spirit of the Reformation. Even his heretical elements can be regarded as resistance against the church and its medieval manner of forcing traditional teaching on its followers; it is a manifestation of that element in Protestantism which emphasizes a man's right to examine established doctrines, to accept those he approves and deny those he does not. This outlook of Protestantism has of course led to the large number of Protestant denominations. As for Milton, his determination to be true to himself could not do away with his deep-rooted trust in "the man within." Milton must have felt a keen loneliness in the knowledge that he had left orthodoxy. Nothing makes one feel so lonely as the discrepancy between the subject and the object, especially in matters of faith. In such a case, one can do nothing but cling to one's own sincerity. In his last pamphlet, *Of True Religion*, Milton expressed his Protestantism clearly.

> It is a human frailty to err, and no man is infallible here on earth. But so long as all these profess to set the Word of God only before them as the Rule of faith and obedience; and use all diligence and sincerity of heart, by reading, by learning, by study, by prayer for Illumination of the holy Spirit, to understand the Rule and obey it, they have done what man can do: God will assuredly pardon them, as he did the friends of Job, good and pious men, though much mistaken, as there it appears, in some Points of Doctrine.[30]

---

ignorance concerning sin and concerning Christ, our Saviour. They are thoroughly pagan doctrines, and we cannot tolerate them. If such teachings were true, Christ would have died in vain, for there would be no defect or sin in man for which he would have had to die. [*The Book of Concord: The Confession of the Evangelical Lutheran Church*, trans. and ed. Theodore G. Pappert (Philadelphia, 1959), pp. 302–03]

[30] "Of True Religion" in *Works of John Milton*, 6 (New York, 1932): 168.

Milton's view of God and of man carries a degree of optimism, even when the subject is the Fall.

3.   Fall and Redemption

I wish now to examine that fundamental aspect of *Paradise Lost* implied by its opening phrase, "Of Man's first disobedience." Following this line and the interconnections between my earlier topics, man and God, we may best concern ourselves with the disobedience of man, not that of the angels, nor that of Satan. Because of his overwhelming presence in books 1 and 2, Satan at first may deceive us into viewing him as the hero of this epic. But from the time of his appearance until his disappearance in book 10 as a serpent chewing dust and bitter ashes, the Father of Lies follows a single course of decline, embodying no complex struggle. Pursuing his hostile course, Satan never wavers for long, unlike Adam and Eve—particularly unlike Adam. Satan says:

> To do aught good never will be our task,
> But ever to do ill our sole delight,
> As being the contrary to his high will
> Whom we resist. If then his providence
> Out of our evil seek to bring forth good,
> Our labour must be to pervert that end,
> And out of good still to find means of evil.
>
> [1. 159–65]

His sole aim is perversion of good, not facing choices and resolving inner conflict. This fact and the opening line makes it clear that Adam and Eve are the heroes of the poem.

To fill the loss of the fallen angels, God created the earth and Adam and Eve to live on it, commanding their free obedience. He forbade them to taste the fruit of the tree of knowledge, as "The pledge of thy obedience and thy faith" (8. 325). If they had remained obedient, loving God, their bodies would have turned to spirit and ascended to enjoy a free life in Heaven. God's prohibition was "that sole command, / So easily obeyed" (7. 47–48). But Satan, who aimed at the ruin of mankind as revenge on God, deceived credulous Eve:

> . . . her rash hand in evil hour
> Forth-reaching to the fruit, she plucked, she eat.
> Earth felt the wound, and Nature from her seat,
> Sighing through all her works, gave signs of woe
> That all was lost.
>
> [9. 780–84]

Sir Walter Raleigh, who regarded Satan as the hero of *Paradise Lost*, saw the climax or crisis in this fall of Eve. Her fall implies Satan's success and certainly marks a dark change of the plot, as Raleigh suggested. But from the point of view of a reader who regards Adam and Eve as the heroes of the poem, a different conclusion can be drawn. Tillyard sees the climax of the poem in the repentance and reconciliation of Adam and Eve. This reading is of course inconsistent with the title, *Paradise Lost* (though Tillyard interprets this as Milton's irony). Their penitence, reconciliation, and humility are the results that the dramatic crisis has brought about. Although their repentance and reconciliation are inseparably connected with their fall, the dramatic crisis is, as C. M. Bowra asserts, to be found in man's fall itself, particularly in Adam's fall. Eve was deceived and was deprived of the power of choice, while Adam could have chosen either to eat the fruit brought by Eve, so sharing her bitter lot, or to perfect his obedience to God by rejecting the fruit. Adam even knows the meaning of what Eve has done, and that "the wages of sin is death":

> How art thou lost! how on a sudden lost,
> Defaced, deflowered, and now to death devote!
>
> [9. 900–01]

Adam's reason persuades him to obey God, while his passion urges him to love Eve. Whether Adam falls or not depends on his free will: man faces the kind of choice that Satan has ignored. The problems of free will and predestination, or of freedom and servitude, are conclusively expressed in Adam's self-confrontation, and in this sense the crisis of *Paradise Lost* can be justifiably found in his conflict.

To me, therefore, the essential character of the poem consists of man's free subjectivity, which is contained by God's foreknowledge, and the whole dramatic development connected with the Fall. If, on the contrary, man's repentance and reconciliation are stressed, as in Tillyard's view, man's conflicting feelings and the tragic quality of human existence are slighted, and it is as if man had been caught like an automaton in God's trap.

Adam cannot live without Eve, and, when he knows Eve is doomed to die, he chooses to die with her. Few lines could express man's tormented mind so pathetically as those lines in book 9 (896–959). Adam finds himself unseparably tied and united to Eve, calling her "flesh of my flesh, / Bone of my bone" (9. 914–15), saying also, "I feel / The link of nature draw me" (9. 913–14) and "I feel / The bond of Nature draw me" (9. 955–56). Yet how vain is Adam's reasoning in the lines between these two declarations! On the other hand after taking the forbidden fruit, Eve is terrified, saying to herself,

> Then I shall be no more;
> And Adam, wedded to another Eve,
> Shall live with her enjoying, I extinct!
> A death to think!
>
> [9. 827–30]

Hoping that Adam will die with her, she tempts him to share the same fate with her, her persuasive words concealing her anxiety. When Eve, hearing Adam's resolution, holds him with tears of joy, the pathos is intense. And nature herself falls with man.

> Earth trembled from her entrails, as again
> In pangs, and Nature gave a second groan;
> Sky loured, and, muttering thunder, some
>   sad drops

> Wept at completing of the mortal sin
> Original.
>
> [9. 1000–04]

This idea is derived from Romans 8: 19–22; since medieval times it had been held that nature fell with man. Some—Bacon and the Cambridge Platonists, for example—believed in the incorruptible order and harmony of nature as God's Works as well as in the Bible as His Word. It seems that Milton belongs to the medieval tradition and that he resists the optimism of Bacon and the Cambridge Platonists. Although in a context of error, Adam's idea of nature is that held by Christians for many centuries.

> Us, his prime creatures, dignified so high,
> Set over all his works; which, in our fall,
> For us created, needs with us must fail,
> Dependent made.
>
> [9. 940–43]

The next question to be asked is what impact the Fall has on Adam and Eve. After their Fall, they must suffer disorder and loss of freedom.

> Since thy original lapse, true liberty
> Is lost, which always with right reason dwells
> Twinned, and from her hath no dividual being.
> Reason in Man obscured, or not obeyed,
> Immediately inordinate desires
> And upstart passions catch the government
> From Reason, and to servitude reduce
> Man, till then free.
>
> [12. 83–90]

Inside and out there are "high passions—anger, hate, / Mistrust, suspicion, discord" (9. 1123–24). The duality of reason and liberty on one hand and of passion and servitude on the other is a key pattern underlying Milton's works.

What does reason mean to Milton? Grierson notes the difference between reason and reasonings in *Samson Agonistes* (line 322), asserting that reason is a prophetic, intuitive insight corresponding to what Pascal calls *l'esprit de finesse*.[31] Similar distinctions can be found in *Paradise Lost*. In the scientific discourse at the beginning of book 8, Raphael criticizes Adam's way of thinking:

> . . . when they come to model heaven,
> And calculate the stars; how they will wield
> The mighty frame; how build, unbuild, contrive
> To save appearances; how gird the sphere
> With centric and eccentric scribbled o'er,
> Cycle and epicycle, orb in orb.
> Already by thy reasoning this I guess.
>
> [8. 79–85]

"Reasoning" here is not intuitive but discursive and possibly resembles Pascal's *l'esprit de géométrie*. The well-known passage in book 5 where Raphael discourses on monism of mind and matter proves that Milton is acquainted with distinctions like that between *l'esprit de finesse* and *l'esprit de géométrie*. Reason is given by Milton a much higher function than understanding, not to mention sense and fancy:

> . . . the Soul
> Reason receives, and Reason is her being,
> Discursive, or intuitive: discourse
> Is oftest yours, the latter most is ours,
> Differing but in degree, of kind the same.
>
> [5. 486–90]

Discursive reason is supposed to belong to man and intuitive reason to angels: the former is reasoning, the latter reason. Grierson sought a prophet's logic in reason; this might be called "the logic of faith" or "the logic of feeling."

In *Paradise Regained* Satan insists that Greek philosophers should be as highly assessed as Hebrew prophets, since "The Gentiles also know, and write, and teach / To admiration, led by nature's light" (*P.R.*, 4.227–28). But Jesus, resolutely denying Satan's opinion, says:

[31] H. J. C. Grierson, *Milton and Wordsworth, Poets and Prophets* (London, 1950), pp. 11–12.

> he who receives
> Light from above, from the fountain of light,
> No other doctrine needs, though granted true;
> But these are false, or little else but dreams,
> Conjectures, fancies, built on nothing firm.
>
> [*P.R.*, 4. 288–92]

The contrast between "nature's light" and "Light from above, from the fountain of light" should not be overlooked. "Nature's light" is what scholastics called *lumen rationis naturale*, and "Light from above" is *lumen gratiae supranaturalis*. In scholasticism, metaphysics by *lumen naturale* is the supreme branch of human knowledge and it is thought to be consonant with faith. However, in *Paradise Lost*, Milton's Son of God vehemently denies such rational metaphysics as false, emphasizing *sola fide*. As a result Milton's reason is not *lumen rationis naturale*, but *lumen gratiae supranaturalis*. Nor is it merely theoretical understanding; it is also a guide to action.

> . . . many lesser faculties . . . serve
> Reason as chief.
>
> [5. 101–02]

> Reason . . . frames
> All what we affirm or what deny, and call
> Our knowledge or opinion.
>
> [5. 106–08]

> . . . God left free the Will; for what obeys
> Reason is free; and Reason he made right,
> But bid her well beware, and still erect,
> Lest, by some fair appearing good surprised,
> She dictate false, and misinform the Will
> To do what God expressly hath forbid.
>
> [9. 351–56]

In Benjamin Whichcote's words, "To go against Reason, is to go against God . . . Reason is the Divine Governor of Man's Life; it is the very Voice of God."[32] Reason of this sort could justifiably be called "practical reason," in Kantian terminology.

---

[32] Benjamin Whichcote, cited in Douglas Bush, *Paradise Lost in our Time* (Gloucester, Mass., 1957), p. 38.

Basil Willey strongly insists that Milton's reason has a great deal in common with that of the Cambridge Platonists.[33] In the Cambridge Platonists' view, however, reason is *communes notitiae*, which can be found universally in heathens like Plato, Cicero, and Plotinus, as well as in Christians. In this sense their reason has more affinity with scholastic *lumen naturale*, which is quite distinct from Milton's reason, as has already been seen in the lines from *Paradise Regained* quoted above. On the one hand, Milton shares the same view with the scholastics and the Cambridge Platonists in admitting that man is possessed of the light of reason even after the Fall. On the other hand, he has more in common with reformers like Luther and Calvin in his understanding of the nature of reason. Thus both the medieval and the modern are mixed in Milton's idea of reason. As L. A. Cormican points out, "Milton lived and worked in three worlds which were in conflict along various fronts: the medieval, the Renaissance, and the Puritan."[34]

What is to be remembered in this connection is the powerful, confident eloquence with which Adam talks of the magnificence of nature. Tillyard describes it as one of the two main ways of access to God, that is, "through the contemplation of natural things (*per speculum creaturarum*)."[35] (He is comparing *Paradise Lost* with Dryden's operatic version, *The State of Innocence*.) In book 8 Milton makes Adam tell Raphael the story of his own creation. Adam's first conscious act was to turn his wondering eyes toward heaven. He then scanned the landscape and found he could name the things he saw there. He asked the natural objects around him, "Tell, if ye saw, how came I thus, how here?" (8. 277). Then, immediately answering the question himself, he concluded:

> Not of myself; by some greater Maker then,
> In goodness and in power pre-eminent.

> [8. 278–79]

On the other hand the first words of Dryden's Adam are:

[33] Cf. Willey, *Christianity Past and Present*, p. 88.
[34] Cormican, "Milton's Religious Verse," in *Donne to Marvell*, p. 191.
[35] E. M. W. Tillyard, *Studies in Milton* (London, 1951), p. 155.

> What am I? or from whence? for that I am
> I know, because I think.

Tillyard sums up the difference:

> Now Milton's Adam attains to his belief in a creator through
> the approved age-long process of seeing him through crea-
> tion, *per speculum creaturarum.* Dryden's Adam, on the con-
> trary, begins from within himself, from the doctrine that
> thought proves existence, according to the then novel phi-
> losophy of Descartes.[36]

Tillyard detects this propensity of Milton also in the morning prayer
of Adam and Eve (5. 153–208).

Is this the case, however? To the Schoolmen, the first cause or the
first mover was deduced from all things in nature, including man,
by means of the light of natural reason, which is after all the meaning
of *per speculum creaturarum.* But Milton's Adam starts with the question of *his own* existence first and foremost and then addresses himself to the natural things around him to ask about his own creation.
He never inquires into the cause of creation in general. Milton lets
Raphael and Adam follow the same attitude in the dialogue preceding Adam's speech on his own creation quoted above. To Milton,
scholastic inquiries are "intricacies" and "perplexing thoughts / To
interrupt the sweet of life" (8. 182–84). And Raphael exhorts Adam
as follows:

> Solicit not thy thoughts with matters hid;
> Leave them to God above; him serve and fear.
> . . . Heaven is for thee too high
> To know what passes there. Be lowly wise;
> Think only what concerns thee and thy being.
>
> [8. 167–74]

Adam replies:

> That not to know at large of things remote
> From use, obscure and subtle, but to know

[36] Ibid., p. 138.

That which before us lies in daily life,
Is the prime wisdom: what is more is fume,
Or emptiness, or fond impertinence,
And renders us in things that most concern
Unpractised, unprepared, and still to seek.

[8. 191–97]

What is expressed here with simple persuasive power is the entire denial of scholastic intellectualism and the deep approval of Protestant voluntarism, which grows out of human anthropocentrism.

It has already been seen that Milton's reason is distinct from scholastic reason in its connotation. Adam's "consciousness of self," the first working of his reason, seems to be more than a product of traditional ways of thinking. If it is less scholastic, Adam and Eve's morning prayer and the description of paradise, in which Milton praises nature's diversity, fertility, harmony, and glory, require another approach. It must be remembered that Protestants have not been satisfied with Roman Catholic standardization, comparing Catholicism to a geometrical, artificial garden, and that they have been ready to see immensely rich variety in a universe yet harmonious in its order. This mental attitude was given a philosophical ground by Kant in his "Third Critique." The faculty of judgment made Kant rediscover the beauty of nature, that is, "natürliche Zweckmässigkeit." It was indeed the stars shining in the sky that led him to increased reverence.

The morning prayer of Adam and Eve is based on Psalm 148, which is a song in praise of God springing spontaneously from an instinctive apprehension depending on the more prototypical Hebrew revelation. In this it differs completely from the Thomist or Aristotelian theoretical proof of God's existence. This kind of approach to God is often seen in the Old Testament, particularly in the books of Job and Psalms, in which, we recall, Milton took special pleasure. Rejecting the novelties of Cartesianism and modifying other ways of thinking, Milton built a theory firm enough to win Kant's approval.

4.   Free Will versus Love

The accomplishment of the Fall and man's consequent servitude to evil imply the impossibility of freedom until he is set free from evil, now that he has lost freedom, of his own free will. This is easily understood if one is versed in the rhetoric of the Pauline Epistles, where the Apostle preaches on faith, using the master and the slave as metaphors. When man is a slave to God, he receives perfect freedom, because God is free. On the contrary, when man is free from God, he virtually becomes a slave to himself, or to anything else except God; he is after all deprived of freedom, enslaving himself to evil. To become a slave to God is to become a master.

Christianity, taking a further step, asserts, however, that man should be God's child and that their relationship should be, not the legal one between master and slave, but the affectionate one between parent and child. God is not a fond, indulgent mother but a strict, just father. Seeking to save His beloved and enslaved child, the Father delivered the eldest Son to death, so that His justice and mercy could be accomplished. The atonement so conceived is talked about in book 3; the dialogue between the Father and the Son and the angels' hymn praising it speak of not only the atonement but also the resurrection and the promise of the new world. In book 12, Michael discourses on the meaning of law and also freedom from the law through Christ's redemption. Despite some Arianism, Milton's idea of the atonement is basically orthodox.

These passages on the atonement may well displease the reader. The greatest difficulty is that in book 3 God speaks just like man. This would be permissible in a miracle play, but in *Paradise Lost* it is by no means proper that God should explain and justify His own decrees. He even strikes us as a school divine, as Pope put it. For His tendency to earnest theological discourse and didactics comes to the surface so often that His divine love and mysterious ecstasy are overshadowed. For instance, God foresees man's Fall, which He declares is not designed by God but determined by man himself:

. . . They, therefore, as to right belonged,

> So were created, nor can justly accuse
> Their Maker, or their making, or their fate,
> As if predestination overruled
> Their will, disposed by absolute decree
> Or high foreknowledge. They themselves decreed
> Their own revolt, not I.
>
> [3. 111–17]

God is perfectly right in this reasoning, but because of our frail sensibility we are left forlorn and helpless. We naturally seek what saves us from our forsaken state, words of love that mitigate the severity of such declarations. And we hear them from the Son:

> Behold me, then: me for him, life for life,
> I offer; on me let thine anger fall;
> Account me Man: I for his sake will leave
> Thy bosom, and this glory next to thee
> Freely put off, and for him lastly die
> Well pleased; on me let Death wreak all his rage.
>
> [3. 236–41]

The Son gives Himself up for man who, "once dead in sins and lost," is not able to bring either "atonement for himself, or offering meet" (3. 233–34). And yet we are not fully satisfied with the Son in this scene; we feel too much restraint in His attitude. He is more vivid when He is in war, filled with anger and strength. This is due to the fact that the setting of book 3 is not suitable for describing Him vividly. In book 12, however, the setting (386–419) is quite suitable for it, for Michael talks to Adam about the fight between Christ and Satan and Christ's Redemption and Passion. In spite of that, as Tillyard lamented, "what is surprising is that he recounts this, the culminating scene in the great Puritan drama, with so comparatively little energy and passion. As passionate writing, the lines on Christian liberty a little before and the lines on the world's decay a little after quite overshadow the account of Redemption."[37] Tillyard also asked, "Is it not . . . possible that Milton came to be uneasy about the

[37] Ibid., p. 163.

form in which he had received the doctrine of the Redemption and yet was unable to get away from it, so powerfully had it been stamped into his mind in boyhood?"[38]

Redemption by the Son is an indispensable element in *Paradise Lost* from a structural point of view, and so it is sufficiently stated. Yet it lacks something of the strong feeling with which it should be depicted, giving the reader a legalistic impression. This deficiency is due not only to the inappropriateness of setting but also to Milton's special view of God. His inability to maintain Trinitarianism inevitably led to a heterodox conception of the Redemption. It is no wonder that the kind of ecstatic meditation on the cross that William Cowper, Richard Crashaw,[39] or Thomas Traherne[40] cherished should not be found in Milton. Milton's lack of love and his firm self-confidence, often noted by critics, are, after all, reflections of this tendency in his thought. As Grierson put it:

> . . . as a fact he [i.e., Milton] seems to lay small stress on grace as communicated directly or through the mediation of sacraments. Man's will is free, and on himself it depends whether tempted he falls like Adam, or overcomes every temptation like Christ, or falling repents and sincerely repenting recovers his freedom like Samson.[41]

So conceived, Milton reminds us of Pelagius, who emphasized Christ as an example or teacher rather than as Christ on the cross, calling Him *resurgentium forma* and Adam *morientium forma*. It is an interesting coincidence that Pelagius was also an English gentleman of firm morality, cool mind, and strong will, born in a northern country. And it is said with justice that the mystery of the Trinity is the dogma of love.

5.   Reason and Experience

Even C. M. Bowra, who considers Milton's Christianity to be

[38] Ibid., p. 162.
[39] Grierson, *Milton and Wordsworth*, p. 100.
[40] Tillyard, *Studies in Milton* (London, 1951), p. 280.
[41] Grierson, *Milton and Wordsworth*, p. 101.

utterly orthodox, says, interestingly enough, "Despite the Christian setting Milton concludes his crisis in the Greek spirit."[42] Grierson remarks, in the same manner, "*Paradise Lost . . .* seems to many people to-day imperfectly Christian in spirit."[43] Walter Raleigh's words are: "The central mystery of the Christian religion occupied very little space in Milton's scheme of religion and thought."[44] These comments are certainly valid, but Milton's faith, needless to say, is not limited to a Pelagian intellectual rationalism. In spite of Milton's professed belief, we are not satisfied with the legalistic expressions with which he describes the climax of the Christian epic, and we are tempted to seek the heterodoxy hidden behind this solid front.

I would like, then, to turn to the more positive aspect of Milton's Christian faith. I have already mentioned, referring to lines in *Paradise Regained*, that Milton's reason is different from the *lumen naturale* or *communes notitiae* in the scholastics or the Cambridge Platonists, because it is a direct light from Heaven. Those who are blessed with it need no other doctrine. Anti-intellectualism of this kind, though found in several places in *Paradise Lost*, is the main subject of books 11 and 12. When Michael reveals to Adam the history of the world to come, Adam says:

> Henceforth I learn that to obey is best,
> And love with fear the only God, to walk
> As in his presence, ever to observe
> His providence, and on him sole depend,
> Merciful over all his works, with good
> Still overcoming evil, and by small
> Accomplishing great things—by things deemed weak
> Subverting worldly-strong, and worldly-wise
> By simply meek; that suffering for Truth's sake
> Is fortitude to highest victory,
> And to the faithful death the gate of life—
> Taught this by his example whom I now

---

[42] Bowra, *Virgil to Milton*, p. 209.
[43] Grierson, *Milton and Wordsworth*, p. 99.
[44] Walter Raleigh, *Milton* (London, 1900), p. 164.

Acknowledge my Redeemer ever blest.

[12. 561–73]

In these calmly uttered words is hidden a passion that equals Satan's defiance in book 1. Those who remember Milton's proud character and his defiant figure as a pamphleteer during the interregnum can appreciate the distance he had walked to reach this humility. Here Adam's attitude is completely opposed to that of Satan, who whispers, "to be weak is miserable, / Doing or suffering" (1. 157–58). To be weak is to be strong. If the point is developed, life and death exchange their former places and values to the faithful. This is accomplished unconsciously by Adam and Eve in the concrete, dramatic action of the poem. As Tillyard concludes, this part "is true to the fundamental simplicities of human nature and composes one of the most moving dramatic episodes in literature."[45]

Adam learns through his own experience and Michael's revelation that obedience to God and humility are the ultimate values. Adam says,

Greatly instructed I shall hence depart,
Greatly in peace of thought, and have my fill
Of knowledge, what this vessel can contain;
Beyond which was my folly to aspire.

[12. 557–60]

And Michael's response:

This having learned, thou hast attained the sum
Of wisdom.

[12. 575–76]

This is the proper human wisdom. Man transgresses when he dares to explore the infinity of God with his limited knowledge, indulging himself in reckless fancy. Even if he prided himself on his accomplishment, on looking back, he would discern nothing but "fume, / Or emptiness, or fond impertinence" (8. 194–95). Besides this, he would find himself left immature and unprepared with regard to

[45] E. M. W. Tillyard, *Milton* (London, 1952), pp. 28–29.

what concerns him most. And all this comes from the Divine Wisdom, for

> God, to remove his ways from human sense,
> Placed Heaven from Earth so far, that earthly sight,
> If it presume, might err in things too high,
> And no advantage gain.
>
> [8. 119–22]

So Raphael's advice is that Adam

> . . . beyond abstain
> To ask, nor let thine own inventions hope
> Things not revealed, which th' invisible King,
> Only omniscient, hath suppressed in night,
> To none communicable in Earth or Heaven.
>
> [7. 120–24]

After his creation, Adam spoke to God with humility, affection, and
respect:

> . . . To attain
> The height and depth of thy eternal ways
> All human thoughts come short, Supreme of
>   things!
> Thou in thyself are perfect, and in thee
> Is no deficience found.
>
> [8. 412–16]

Milton's God wishes man to approach Him not intellectually but
with personal trust.

In the *Divine Comedy* there are lines (in canto 28, *Paradiso*) that sing
about the highest, purest, and holiest glory and blessing of the Ninth
Heaven, praising the cloudless happiness of brilliant angels assembled
there:

> And all
> Are blessed, even as their sight descends
> Deeper into the Truth, wherein rest is
> For every mind. Thus happiness hath root

> In seeing, not in loving, which of sight
> Is aftergrowth. [46]

What he means by "seeing" is intellectual contemplation in the Aristotelian sense. The *Divine Comedy* is in its theological construction subject to the orthodox theology of the age: it is represented and synthesized by Thomas Aquinas's system. And the framework of Thomism is the philosophy of Aristotle, based on Greek intellectualism. That is why in Dante intellect is superior to love.

In *Paradise Lost*, on the contrary, Milton stresses love; when the Son calls God "my Father" or "your Father," he means that the relationship between God and man should not be that of the intellect but that of love. Christ attacked Pharisees and scholars for their impersonal grasp of God through the intellect only and insisted that man should approach God simply, wholeheartedly, and directly, like a child, to receive His grace. In short, love should precede intellect. Our mental attitude, in consequence, should not be passive and contemplative, but active and willing. In the Protestant churches Luther and Calvin were extremely subjective and active in their religious attitude, trusting everything to God and not inquiring too much. While Greek philosophers, relying on human intellect, believed the existing world was knowable, those Protestant reformers thought things-in-themselves lay beyond human comprehension. It is through this realization that the practice of deep, great, devoted love has come to be valued more highly than anything else.

Max Weber brought out this point in *The Protestant Ethic and the Spirit of Capitalism*:

> Take for instance the end of the *Divine Comedy*, where the poet in Paradise stands speechless in his passive contemplation of the secrets of God, and compare it with the poem which has come to be called the *Divine Comedy of Puritanism*. Milton closes the last song of *Paradise Lost* after describing the expulsion from paradise as follows:
> Of Paradise, so late their happy seat,
> Waved over by that flaming brand; the gate

[46] Dante, *Vision*, p. 420.

With dreadful faces thronged and fiery arms.
Some natural tears they dropped, but wiped them
    soon:
The world was all before them, where to choose
Their place of rest, and Providence their guide.
They, hand in hand, with wandering steps and slow,
Through Eden took their solitary way.

[12. 641–49]

And only a little before Michael had said to Adam:
                                                Only add
Deeds to thy knowledge answerable; add faith;
Add virtue, patience, temperance; add love,
By name to come called Charity, the soul
Of all the rest: then wilt thou not be loth
To leave this Paradise, but shall possess
A Paradise within thee, happier far.

[12. 581–87]

One feels at once that this powerful expression of the
Puritan's serious attention to this world, his acceptance of his
life in the world as a task, could not possibly have come from
the pen of a medieval writer.[47]

Let me quote the end of the *Divine Comedy*, following Max Weber's
suggestion:

But yet the will roll'd onward, like a wheel
In even motion, by the Love impell'd,
That moves the sun in Heaven and all the stars.[48]

Compared with Dante's perfect circle of contemplation, Milton's
Puritan figure is an oval full of contradictions and tension. In front
of Adam spreads an immense prospect of secular life punctuated with
violent struggles against Satan.[49]

---

[47] Max Weber, *The Protestant Ethic and the Spirit of Capitalism*, trans. Talcott
Parsons (New York, 1958), pp. 87–88.

[48] Dante, *Vision*, p. 443.

[49] Cf. Hisao Otsuka, *Shukyo Kaikaku to Kindai Shakai* [The Reformation and
Modern Society] (Tokyo, 1956), p. 24.

Adam weeps, remembering the paradise from which Eve and he
have been driven, and fearing a strange life now begun; but at the
same time new hope, expectation, and courage are aroused in him.
When he was not able to lift up his head, he was addressed and
offered clothing by God. God promises that His only Son will be
born from the line of Adam and Eve, so to atone for the sin of
Adam. The promise includes Adam's descendants: those who believe
in God shall be justified, purged, sanctified, and admitted to the new
world. Adam looks up with his eyes full of tears to see the divine
light, proclaiming divine love in its seven-colored arch. "And hereby
we know that we are of the truth, and shall assure our hearts before
him. For if our heart condemn us, God is greater than our heart, and
knoweth all things" (1 John 3: 19–20). If man returns to God in
repentance,

> Undoubtedly he will relent, and turn
> From his displeasure, in whose look serene,
> When angry most he seemed and most severe,
> What else but favour, grace, and mercy shone?
>
> [10. 1093–96]

It is because, as God says,

> Man falls, deceived
> . . . Man, therefore, shall find grace;
> . . . In mercy and justice both,
> Through Heaven and Earth, so shall my glory excel;
> But mercy, first and last, shall brightest shine.
>
> [3. 130–34]

Adam is almost at a loss for any words but those of praise.

> O Goodness infinite, Goodness immense,
> That all this good of evil shall produce,
> And evil turn to good—more wonderful
> Than that which by creation first brought forth
> Light out of darkness! Full of doubt I stand,
> Whether I should repent me now of sin
> By me done and occasioned, or rejoice

Much more that much more good thereof shall
spring—
To God more glory, more good-will to men
From God—and over wrath grace shall abound.

[12. 469-78]

It is a pleasure for Adam to obey God, and through this obedience "works of Faith" (12. 536) are to be done. The observance of not the law of works but the law of faith (cf. Romans 3 : 27) becomes his blessed privilege. The essential thing, however, is obedience. The origin of obedience is the Latin *obēdīre*, meaning to hear. The German *Gehorsam* is derived from *hören*. In Japanese also *kiku*, to hear, means to obey, as in the expression *yoku yu koto o kiku* (to listen to what one is told, or to do as one is told). The Bible says, "faith *cometh* by hearing, and hearing by the word of God" (Romans 10: 17).

This apostolic assertion reminds us of the primitive Christian roots of Milton's Protestantism. And to remind ourselves of the contemporaneity of Milton's ideas, we may recall that Ernst Jünger stood in the ruins of a bombed, destroyed cathedral, spontaneously praying, his hands closed. Then the light of the rising moon fell on him and threw his shadow on the ground.

Von allen Domen bleibt nur noch jener, der durch die Kuppel der gefalteten Hände gebildet wird. In ihm allein ist Sicherheit.[50]

---

[50] "Of all the cathedrals, the only one that remains is that with a spire formed by clasped hands. Certainty can be found in this alone" (Ernst Jünger, *Strahlungen* [Tübingen 1949,] p. 463).

George Etherege and the Destiny
of Restoration Comedy

Tetsuo Kishi

We tend to forget that the earliest Restoration comedies, when they were first produced, were not "Restoration comedies" at all, but simply "comedies." Such was no doubt the case with Sir George Etherege's *The Comical Revenge; or, Love in a Tub*. The play was produced in 1664, twelve years before *The Man of Mode* appeared and seven years before Wycherley made his debut with *Love in a Wood*. This was the year Vanbrugh was born, and six years before Congreve's birth. In other words, the genre we now refer to as "Restoration comedy" was virtually nonexistent in 1664.

This obvious point needs some emphasis, since it makes clear in what spiritual climate Etherege started his artistic career. Although in *The Comical Revenge* he made use of certain techniques that eventually were to become the basic conventions of "comedy of wit," Etherege, unlike Congreve, for instance, had no tradition to rely upon and could not have been aware of the significance of his work in the history of English drama. It can be somewhat misleading and may deprive the play of its immediacy and novelty to discuss it only in connection with the later development of the genre.

It would be similarly dangerous to deal with it merely in the light of pre-Restoration comedies, even though their influence on it is undeniable. The earliest writers of Restoration comedies, Etherege among them, had at least one unique experience that the dramatists of the previous age did not have. That, of course, was the experience of the Puritan Revolution, and that upheaval will give us a viewpoint from which we can understand the play's meaning without too much historical bias.

The Puritan Revolution must have been a most serious and decisive experience for the dramatists of Etherege's generation, because it
probably had an impact as great, if not greater, on drama as it had on
politics. For about eighteen years it was practically impossible to
produce a legitimate play without fear of interference from the
Puritan authorities. The fact that such a situation lasted for only
eighteen years is of less importance. What is vital is the realization on
the part of the dramatists that theater, just like monarchy, could (and
really did) one day stop existing.

It may be relevant to this discussion to note that the Restoration
was not exactly a *restoration* so far as theater was concerned. I am not
thinking simply of technical innovations, such as the advent of ac-
tresses. The most important point is that Restoration drama, unlike
Elizabethan drama, was almost exclusively aristocratic, catering to
and supported by an aristocratic audience. In this sense the drama of
the new age was strongly class conscious.

The aristocracy was by no means *the* ruling class of contemporary
English society. It is true that the monarchy was restored, but nobody
could deny the economic (and political) power of the newly rising
bourgeoisie. Drama, more than any other form of art, was closely
related to the class consciousness and crisis of an aristocracy that had
just recovered from, and was still in danger of, an attack from the
bourgeoisie. In other words, there was a deep-rooted sense of decline,
even imminent end, in what was apparently stable.

This will suggest to us what the gay, witty Restoration comedies
in fact were. It cannot be mere chance that many of the aristocratic
characters in, as well as the writers of, Restoration comedies are
highly self-conscious and almost painfully self-critical. For instance,
Etherege in the prologue to *The Comical Revenge* complains:

> . . . such our Fortune is this barren Age,
> That Faction now, not Wit, supports the Stage:
> Wit has, like Painting, had her happy flights,
> And in peculiar Ages reach'd her heights,
> Though now declin'd. . . .

And he concludes by saying:

> . . . Gallants, as for you, talk loud i'th' Pit,
> Divert your selves and Friends with your own Wit;
> Observe the Ladies, and neglect the Play;
> Or else 'tis fear'd we are undone to day.[1]

Was he being modest as playwrights frequently were in their prologues? No doubt he was. But is it likely that he was *simply* being modest? The answer must be found in the play itself.

Almost all critics have been extremely hostile to *The Comical Revenge* as a piece of dramatic writing. It has been criticized for its lack of unity. Ostensibly there is no logical relation between the heroic, pseudo-tragic portion and the comic portion. However, we should examine the structure of the play in some detail before we decide whether this criticism is justified.

The first plot centers around the household of Lord Bevill, who has a son, Lovis, and two daughters, Graciana and Aurelia. Colonel Bruce, a Cavalier friend of Lovis, has been trying to win Graciana's heart but, after he is released from imprisonment by the Puritans, he learns to his grief that Graciana is in love with another Cavalier named Lord Beaufort, with whom he decides to fight a duel. However, just as they are ready to fight, several Puritans attack Bruce and Lord Beaufort rescues him. Because of this, Bruce hesitates to fight the duel. When they do fight, Beaufort beats Bruce but spares his life. Bruce then tries to kill himself and is seriously injured. Graciana, hearing the news, decides not to marry Beaufort, while Aurelia, who has secretly loved Bruce, confesses her love, which Bruce swears to return. Bruce miraculously recovers and is united with Aurelia, upon which Graciana and Beaufort marry each other. This is the kind of plot we would expect (except for the happy ending) in a heroic tragedy, but as we shall see later, it fails at several points to be really "heroic."

The second and probably the central plot concerns an intrigue of love between a witty gallant, Sir Frederick Frollick, and a wealthy widow, Mrs. Rich. Sir Frederick learns from Lord Beaufort (who is

---

[1] *The Dramatic Works of Sir George Etherege*, ed. H. F. B. Brett-Smith, 2 vols. (Oxford, 1927), 1: 4.

his cousin) that Mrs. Rich (who is Lord Bevill's sister) loves him, and he immediately begins courting her. Mrs. Rich, however, does not readily reveal her mind, since she fears it could be fatal to her plan of enticing Sir Frederick into marriage. After using a couple of wiles, Sir Frederick succeeds in making the widow confess her love, but she in turn gets him to promise to marry her. Sir Frederick belongs to that long line of witty heroes in Restoration comedy which includes Dorimant, Horner, and Mirabell, and the plot depends primarily on verbal wit for effect.

The third plot is also comic, though in a less subtle way. Two city rogues, Wheadle and Palmer, swindle a considerable sum of money out of a foolish country squire, Sir Nicholas Cully, by playing at dice. The rogues then introduce Sir Nicholas to Wheadle's mistress, whom they pretend is Mrs. Rich. Sir Frederick eventually detects their trick and forces the rogues and Sir Nicholas to marry three women with whom he has had more or less intimate relationships. The comic effect of the plot is created by disguises and subsequent misunderstandings.

The last plot, which is entirely farcical, deals with the misfortunes of Sir Frederick's French valet, Dufoy. His outlandish English, with its heavy French accent, and allusions to his "French" disease would perhaps have appealed to the less sophisticated members of the audience.

Thus the four plots are remarkably different in mood and tone. Furthermore, they have little organic relation with one another. Facts like Lord Beaufort's being Sir Frederick's cousin or Mrs. Rich's being Lord Bevill's sister are no doubt traces of Etherege's rather compulsory effort to "unite" the separate plots. But the argument, which most critics support, that the play is lacking in unity *because* the moods of the plots are different seems to me somewhat too simplistic. If the difference is so very remarkable, perhaps Etherege intended it that way. Are we not to search for a key to unity in the difference itself, rather than in the not-too-obvious similarity of the plots?

The most obvious "difference" is in the style. The scenes concerning Lord Bevill's household are written mostly in verse—many of them in extremely regular heroic couplets. The other scenes are in prose. But Etherege has inserted speeches in heroic couplets even into the scenes written largely in prose. Here is one such example, in which Lord Beaufort explains, in answer to a question from Sir Frederick, his relationship with Graciana:

> SIR FREDERICK: . . . But pray, my Lord, how thrive you in
> your more honourable adventures? Is harvest near? When
> is the Sickle to be put i' th' Corn?
> LORD BEAUFORT: I have been hitherto so prosperous,
> My happiness has still out-flown my faith:
> Nothing remains but Ceremonial Charms,
> *Graciana*'s fix'd i' th' circle of my Arms.
>
> [1.2][2]

Another example occurs in a scene following the entrance of Sir Frederick with fiddlers and linkboys. They come to Mrs. Rich's house and the noise awakens the widow, who asks:

> WIDOW: Whose insolence is this, that dares affront me
> thus?
> SIR FREDERICK [*in a Canting Tone*]:
> If there be insolence in Love, 'tis I
> Have done you this unwilling injury.
> WIDOW: What pitiful rhyming fellow's that? he speaks as
> if he were prompted by the Fidlers.
> SIR FREDERICK: Alas, what pains I take thus to unclose
> Those pretty eye-lids which lock'd up my Foes!
>
> [3.2][3]

The reason for such an abrupt appearance of heroic couplets is, in the first example, that Lord Beaufort is talking about his love for Graciana. It is not that he is primarily a verse-speaking character, as Bruce and Graciana are. He has been using prose up to this point in his conversation with Sir Frederick. Nor is it that to Lord Beaufort "love" is something that deserves treatment in verse. It is only his

---

[2] Ibid., 1: 7; reference in text is to act and scene.
[3] Ibid., 1: 31.

love for Graciana (and Graciana's for him) that makes him aware of a necessity to talk in heroic couplets.

This awareness is more obvious in the second example. There used to be an extrinsic norm according to which a noble love was to be dealt with in heroic couplets. To Sir Frederick his love for Mrs. Rich is noble, or at least he has to pretend it is. Therefore he suddenly changes his style, but at the same time he is aware that this norm is only superficial and can be comic when followed without natural motivation. This is why he uses an unnatural, artificial "Canting Tone." Mrs. Rich is aware of the comic effect, too, as she reveals when she calls Sir Frederick "pitiful." It hardly needs saying that Etherege himself was more than aware of the absurdity of this scene.

Beneath this comedy is the underlying conviction that the style of heroic tragedy can sometimes sound extremely funny. But it is not merely the style that is being ridiculed. In the first example we should pay attention to Sir Frederick's expression "more honourable adventures," which of course refers to Beaufort's amorous adventures. Normally, however, "honour" is one of the basic concepts of a heroic tragedy and, as a public principle, is opposed to the private principle "love," thus causing a dramatic conflict.

This identification of "honour" with "love" somewhat debases, in the play's context, the idea of "honour" itself and the related "heroic" virtues and it is certainly relevant to the various similarities between the plots, which we can find on a more or less symbolic level. For instance, both the first and the third plots contain a duel scene. Colonel Bruce challenges Lord Beaufort in order to solve the eternal triangle. Sir Nicholas Cully is challenged to fight Palmer when the former refuses to pay the sum of money he owes. When they are supposed to fight, Bruce, out of a sense of obligation, and Sir Nicholas, out of cowardice, do not dare to do so. In both cases, the people attending them try hard to force the hesitant fighters to draw their swords. When their efforts go beyond a certain point, they lose their meaning, as in the following speech by Beaufort addressed to his rival, Bruce:

Has nothing pow'r, too backward man, to move

Thy Courage? Think on thy neglected Love:
Think on the beauteous *Graciana*'s Eyes;
'Tis I have robb'd thee of that glorious prize.

to which Bruce answers:

There are such charms in *Graciana*'s Name,
                              [*Strips hastily*]
My scrup'lous Honour must obey my Flame:
My lazy Courage I with shame condemn:
No thoughts have power streams of blood to stem.

[4.4][4]

The absurdity of this exchange lies in the fact that the duel, which is nothing more than a means to solve the conflict, is pursued as if it were itself the end.

Bruce fights but fails to be killed. Then he tries but fails to kill himself. Then Lovis, Bruce's second, struck by his friend's deed, *"offers to fall on his Sword, but is hindered by Sir Frederick"* (Beaufort's second), who says, "Forbear, Sir; the Frollick's not to go round, as I take it."[5] Over and over again the situation draws very close to tragedy, but it never completes itself as one. In other words, the pseudo-tragic situations miss their climax and end up becoming a "Frollick."

It is significant that nobody dies in this play. Just once does a corpse appear on the stage—or, more precisely a man who plays the role of a corpse laid on a bier. This trick is used by Sir Frederick in act 4, scene 7, where he tests the widow's heart by pretending to be dead. Between this scene and the duel scene (4.4) are two others, in the first of which Graciana and Aurelia lament their destiny, believing Bruce to be dead. Then there is a short scene where Mrs. Rich's waiting-woman puts the anesthetized Dufoy into a tub to revenge his slander. The appearance after this of a corpse followed by a funeral procession will naturally make the audience connect it with the duel in the earlier scene. It is only after a mourner starts telling

[4] Ibid., 1: 54.
[5] Ibid., 1: 55; Etherege's italics.

the widow of Sir Frederick's "death" that we know the procession is in fact a fake. Sir Frederick's trick almost succeeds, when Dufoy, thinking his master is dead, bursts onto the stage and the sight of him changes the scene of lament into pure farce. Symbolically speaking, by playing the role of a corpse, Sir Frederick accomplishes the death that Bruce fails to achieve. And Dufoy, who cannot free himself from the tub, is a parody of the motionless Sir Frederick on the bier.

Sir Frederick's role playing in this scene makes him a kind of substitute for Bruce. But more than that, Dufoy functions as his master's substitute. It is interesting that the relationship between Sir Frederick and Mrs. Rich parallels that between Dufoy and Mrs. Rich's waiting-woman. Dufoy's disease, which is referred to quite often, relates him to certain aspects of his master's life. It is rather unfair that the witty heroes of Restoration comedies, including Sir Frederick, seldom suffer from this unpleasant disease in spite of their debauchery. It is always the characters of lower classes who are the victims. Dufoy gets caught in a tub and perspires: a treatment believed to be effective in curing venereal disease. This turns him into a kind of scapegoat and draws our attention to those hidden, dark aspects of his master's life which might otherwise be left unnoticed.

But it is Sir Nicholas Cully who is even more closely connected (symbolically speaking, that is) with Sir Frederick. Wheadle and Palmer introduce him to Wheadle's mistress, Grace, who, they tell him, is Mrs. Rich. In the scene of their encounter, Palmer disguises himself as Lord Bevill and Sir Nicholas dresses himself as a witty gallant—one like Sir Frederick. Of course the costume does not fit him well, making him a mere parody of Sir Frederick, just as Palmer is a parody of Lord Bevill and Grace, of Mrs. Rich. Needless to say, Sir Nicholas's rough and indecent style of courtship is a debased version of Sir Frederick's more elegant way of courting Mrs. Rich. Finally, Sir Nicholas marries a woman whom he believes to be Sir Frederick's sister but who is in fact one of his ex-mistresses, thus putting him in the position of the very person he had been aping.

It is almost amazing that Sir Nicholas appears as his own self hardly more than sporadically throughout the play. He is really a Puritan country squire; but, now that the political climate has

changed, in London he behaves as if he were a Cavalier knight—
someone like Sir Frederick. Wheadle persuades him to join in a ruse
to swindle money out of a foolish countryman (the role played by
Palmer in disguise), who is in fact exactly like Sir Nicholas himself,
though of course he thinks he is cleverer. In other words, Sir Nicholas
assumes the role of a city rogue more or less like Wheadle and Palmer.
When he gets drunk or courts a woman, he consciously plays the
role of a city gallant. His identity is to be found only in these attempts
to be somebody other than himself.

The attempt to annihilate oneself, the tendency toward role playing, is particularly noticeable in Sir Nicholas. This is because he is
subject to restraint by an extrinsic norm of behavior proper to a
"gallant." We can detect the same kind of restraint at work on Bruce
and other characters of the first plot. What is important to them is
their idea of what a "heroic" character ought to be. Strangely
enough, the most fundamental concept in both the first and the third
plots is "honour." Of course, its meaning varies from place to place:
not only "heroic" deeds but also love, violence, and even lewdness
are often understood by many of the characters to be "honourable."

We have already referred to the speech of Sir Frederick in which
he calls Beaufort's love for Graciana "more honourable adventures."
A little before that, there is an exchange between Sir Frederick and
Grace's maidservant concerning his "Heroic actions" of the previous
night. The maidservant says they are the "most honourable achievements, such as will be registered to your eternal Fame." What actually did he do? He got drunk, came to Grace's lodging, cried "a harsh
word or two" such as "*Whore* . . . or something to that purpose,"
"wag'd a bloody war with the Constable; and having vanquish'd
that dreadful enemy . . . committed a general massacre on the glass-
windows."[6] Obviously, words like "heroic" or "honourable" in
this exchange have ironic overtones. What is interesting is that Sir
Frederick's actions are described in the terminology of warfare as if
they belonged to the world of heroic tragedy where the basic principle is "honour."

[6] Ibid., 1: 6.

We can quote other examples of the same metaphor. Graciana in her tête-à-tête with Lord Beaufort says:

> Our weaker Sex glories in a Surprize,
> We boast the sudden Conquests of our Eyes;
> But men esteem a Foe that dares contend,
> One that with noble Courage does defend
> A wounded Heart; the Victories they gain
> They prize by their own hazard and their pain.
>
> [2.2][7]

There is a more straightforward example in Sir Frederick's words when he is ready to act as Beaufort's second at the place of the promised duel:

> I have not fenc'd of late, unless it were with my
>   Widows Maids; and they are e'en too hard for me at my
>   own weapon.
>
> [4.1][8]

Throughout the play, love and sex are described in the language of war. This metaphor in itself is hardly original. What is original in the play is that the metaphor is frequently accompanied by a distorted, ironic concept of "honour."

This leads us to be suspicious about the quality of the first, apparently "heroic," plot itself. Normally, the central character of a heroic tragedy suffers from a dilemma caused by a conflict between "love" (or a private principle, in general) and "honour" (or a public principle, in general), and the play deals with the process of his reaching a decision about which to choose. The fact that a play dealing with this process can be written at all implies that both of the principles are valid enough and that the choice, either way, will involve a serious sacrifice on the part of the hero.

But do the characters of the "heroic" plot in *The Comical Revenge*

---

[7] Ibid., 1: 17.
[8] Ibid., 1: 47.

really suffer from any such dilemma? Colonel Bruce's love for Graciana originally grew out of his friendship for Lovis, which is a "heroic" and "honourable" feeling by any standard. His marriage to Graciana would mean a fulfillment of both public and private principles. His giving up Graciana, on the other hand, is entirely pointless and would gain him nothing. There is actually no love-honour conflict in his situation. It is only after he is rescued from the Puritans by Beaufort that he has to face the necessity of choice. Graciana would fulfill the public principle, if she were to obey her brother Lovis and marry the noble soldier Bruce. But Beaufort is also a Cavalier, and he is in no way inferior to Bruce, even if we ignore Beaufort's skill as a fencer. The dilemma of Beaufort is not too serious, either. Aurelia's case may be somewhat different, but even then the conflict is lacking in tension. What is certain is that no character is in danger of death or complete ruin if he (or she) chooses the course which his (or her) private feelings dictate. This makes the situation quite different from that of an authentic heroic tragedy, such as that of Antony and Cleopatra in Dryden's *All for Love*.

Thus the first plot in this comedy is only superficially similar to the plot of a heroic tragedy. There are critics who judge this as proof of Etherege's failure, but a different interpretation will show the play in a better light. The four plots are various versions of "honourable, heroic actions." In fact they are closely connected with one another and draw our attention to aspects of the play that might otherwise be neglected. The result is that none of the four worlds is free from criticism. If there is a lack of unity on the realistic level, that lack of unity is itself a proof of unity on the symbolic level.

What looks like a discrepancy in the play no doubt shows the ambivalent attitude of the author toward the idea of heroic virtues as a whole and toward heroic tragedy as its artistic expression. We too must assume an ambivalent attitude and think of the possibility of a "tragedy" being comic, as one recent critic has done in the opening sentence of her essay on heroic tragedy: "It was characteristic of the Restoration, with its love of paradox, of contradiction and false faces, that it should have created a tragedy that was less serious than

its comedy."⁹ Another critic with a similar viewpoint says, "it is not
a little puzzling . . . that the rakes of Restoration London found
enjoyment in a stylized, exaggerated representation of ideal virtue.
One answer, and one that is not as foolish as it sounds, is that the
heroic drama, to some people at least, was a colossal joke. While
some writers and some people in the audience took it seriously,
possibly other members of the public saw the absurdity."¹⁰ Both
critics quote a passage from Dryden's *Essay of Dramatic Poesy*: "I have
observed that, in all our tragedies, the audience cannot forbear
laughing when the actors are to die; 'tis the most comic part of the
whole play."¹¹

It was in 1663, the year before *The Comical Revenge* was first produced, that the Duke of Buckingham and his collaborators started
writing *The Rehearsal*. In other words, when Etherege's play was
made public, the feeling was already shared by at least some members
of Charles II's court that the normal reaction to a heroic tragedy was
to laugh at it. It is impossible that Etherege knew nothing of this
feeling. I cannot agree with the critics whose judgment is that
Etherege failed to achieve unity in his play by taking in an element of
heroic tragedy. On the contrary, he very carefully distorted that element and ridiculed it from several viewpoints, achieving unity of the
play on the symbolic level.

Etherege's viewpoints may have been closest to those of Sir
Frederick, as he is the least criticized and least ridiculed character in
the comedy. He is free from the kind of dogmatic belief in the heroic
ideals that characters like Bruce and Graciana hold blindly. He is an
aristocrat and Cavalier and could well belong to the world of heroic
tragedy. The Revolution, however, has made him wiser. He is aware
that his social position ties him to the pre-Revolution world, whose

⁹ Anne Righter, "Heroic Tragedy," *Restoration Theatre*, Stratford-upon-Avon
Studies no. 6 (London, 1965), p. 135.
¹⁰ Norman N. Holland, *The First Modern Comedies* (Cambridge, Mass., 1959), p. 19.
¹¹ Dryden, *Of Dramatic Poesy and Other Critical Essays*, ed. George Watson, 2 vols.
(London, 1962), 1: 51. Since, however, the gist of this remark is later confuted by
Dryden's spokesman, Neander, there is no certainty that he himself held to the idea
in such simplistic terms.

ideals are not valid any more. Colonel Bruce or Lovis may be the kind of person he himself ought to be and could be, but to his sensibility their situation does not seem to be genuinely tragic. He cannot follow the norm of the "heroic" world and act like Bruce. Instead he can afford to laugh at Bruce and, unlike Bruce, who gets stiff when he is about to fight a duel, can make an obscene joke or two, or can cry, "Forbear, Sir; the Frollick's not to go round," to Lovis, who almost kills himself.

On the other hand Sir Frederick simply cannot behave like Sir Nicholas Cully. In that he tries to play the part of a "gallant," Sir Nicholas uncritically shares the absurdity of Bruce and others who foolishly play what they believe are tragic roles. Historically speaking, Sir Nicholas is a Puritan country squire, a member of the rising sector of society, and the future belongs to him. But to Sir Frederick, he is the epitome of what he ought not to be and cannot be. He is one of the earliest examples of those would-be wits who appear in Restoration comedies over and over again to be ridiculed both by the witty characters in the play and by the cultured members of the audience. It should be emphasized that the superiority of those who ridicule them is neither political nor economic—not even ethical—but simply and exclusively cultural and esthetic.

Although Sir Frederick is tied to the past, the Puritan revolution has given him insight into the future. His inaction is due to this contradiction in himself. Either way, his action has to be awkward and ludicrous. One possible solution is to refrain from action and remain in the position of a witty critic-esthete. In fact Sir Frederick does not easily commit himself to any decisive action; rather, he objectively criticizes what the other characters do. The parallelism between the Sir Frederick-Mrs. Rich plot and both the Sir Nicholas plot and the Dufoy plot implies that Sir Nicholas's and Dufoy's action is a compensation for Sir Frederick's inaction.

But of course Sir Frederick has to face the necessity of some kind of action in the end. He tries to objectify his own situation, too. His efforts to keep himself away from the apparently inevitable marriage signify something more than a rake's selfishness. What he must avoid is giving his existence one decisive form and restricting his otherwise liberated awareness. His marriage to Mrs. Rich, therefore, is a "revenge" on himself, as he himself admits. It is the revenge that reality takes on one who will not accept reality and choose an action. To those who share Sir Frederick's view it is tragic. To those who do not, it is "comical." This ambivalence is at the root of the esthetics of Restoration comedy, which is an artistic expression of the superiority of what is essentially inferior.

Who is Lucy?--On the Structure of Wordsworthian Imagination

Yasunari Takahashi

In the entire *œuvre* of Wordsworth, perhaps few poems can rival a group of five tiny poems in their simple charm and their unquestioned popularity. On the other hand, these poems have been one of the greatest victims (or lures, if you like) of biographical curiosity, attracting a host of mystery lovers (Japanese among them) around a riddle which seems perhaps only less enticing than the question, "Who is the Dark Lady?" What has been curiously lacking amid this tumult of futile passion is a serious discussion of the poems as independent literary works of art. Or perhaps it is taken for granted that they are too beautiful, their lyrical accomplishment too simple, too crystal clear and universal (they are among the favorite anthology pieces even in Japan), to demand analysis and interpretation. But are they really? Their simplicity and clarity seem to me to belie the complexity of their inner structure, and this complexity might finally be seen to lie at the heart of Wordsworth's poetic universe. We might wonder if it is not this rather than the simple lyricism that constitutes the universality, as well as the uniqueness, of his poetry.

The so-called Lucy poems seem, at first sight, rather exceptional and un-Wordsworthian, for they belong to "love poetry," a genre that is a rarity among Wordsworth's works. Without getting involved in psychoanalytical speculations about the reason for this, it would not be difficult to guess that love must have been a theme somehow constitutionally alien to this poet. Various contemporary witnesses seem to point to much the same impression, as in Coleridge's deeply felt remark that "he is a man of whom it might have been said,—'It is good for him to be alone,' "[1] as well as Shelley's sarcastic portrait of "a solemn and unsexual man"[2] and Keats's famous insight into "the wordsworthian or egotistical sublime."[3] The existence of *Vaudracour and Julia*, a full-length narrative about star-crossed lovers, is in fact no contradiction; this harassed outcome of that harassing Annette Vallon affair is a sad poetic failure, which serves only to stress the fact that this was the kind of subject to which Wordsworth's genius was fundamentally unsuited.

Such an unerotic genius seems to be an exception to the traditional rule that the artistic genius is by nature bisexual and hermaphroditic; "Of all the men I ever knew," Coleridge again testifies, "Wordsworth has the least femininity in his mind. He is all *man*."[4] And the Lucy poems are apparently an exception to this exception.

Again, the Lucy poems are un-Wordsworthian in that they are, though only partly, dramatic. "He never could," in Shelley's caricature, "Fancy another situation, / From which to dart his contemplation, / Than that wherein he stood."[5] His imagination was more reflective than dramatic, intent upon itself rather than fictionally creating an intensely human situation. And yet "Strange Fits of Passion Have I Known" describes a scene, somewhat Coleridgean in its psychological suspense, with the poet on horseback approaching Lucy's house, the sinking moon, and the sudden fear crossing his mind the moment the moon is gone behind the roof: "If Lucy should be dead!" Again, a sort of dramatic tension is created, at the end of "She Dwelt among the Untrodden Ways," by a pathetic sense of the gap separating the dead Lucy from the poet: "But she is in her grave, and, oh, / The difference to me!"

But are these poems really exceptional? Are they really "love

[1] S. T. Coleridge, *Table Talk and Omniana*, ed. and comp. T. Ashe (London, 1903), p. 339.

[2] P. B. Shelley, *Peter Bell the Third*, line 451. The text used here for Shelley is *The Complete Poetical Works*, ed. Thomas Hutchinson (London, 1956).

[3] Keats's letter to Woodhouse, October 27, 1818, in *The Letters of John Keats, 1814–1821*, ed. Hyder Edward Rollins, 2 vols. (Cambridge, Mass., 1958), 1: 387.

[4] Coleridge, *Table Talk and Omniana*, p. 339.

[5] Shelley, *Peter Bell the Third*, lines 299–302.

poems"? Are they really dramatic in structure? The titles of the five poems are:

1. "Strange Fits of Passion Have I Known"
2. "I Travelled among Unknown Men"
3. "She Dwelt among the Untrodden Ways"
4. "Three Years She Grew in Sun and Shower"
5. "A Slumber Did My Spirit Steal."

Of the five pieces the first two sound more like love poems than the others, but it is in fact the last three that, in their true excellence, form the core of the Lucy poems.

Approaching 3 and 4 as love poems, we are struck by the fact that the actual feeling of love, i.e., how it feels to be in love, is far from being the theme here, and that Lucy does not seem a real embraceable girl at all. At what point in the course of reading these poems do we become aware that she is the poet's love?

> The difference to me![6]

> She died, and left to me
> This heath, this calm, and quiet scene;
> The memory of what has been,
> And never more will be.[7]

Not until these last lines are we made to realize Lucy's relation to the poet. In other words, the girl who dominates ninety percent of the poem is not necessarily the poet's *beloved*; she looks just like other *girls* encountered in Wordsworth's poetry.

Who, then, is Lucy? Even those who refuse to be mystery addicts cannot bypass this question, so I may as well put forward my answer at once: she is not an object of what might be called either sensuous or spiritual love; she *is* indeed just like any other Wordsworthian girl. Or, to be more circumstantial, she is Lucy Gray's elder sister, a cousin of the Solitary Reaper and the Highland Girl; she is perhaps a

---

[6] "She Dwelt among the Untrodden Ways," line 12. The text used for Wordsworth is *The Poetical Works*, ed. E. de Selincourt and H. Darbishire, 5 vols. (Oxford, 1940–49).
[7] "Three Years She Grew in Sun and Shower," lines 39–42.

niece of the Leech-Gatherer and Michael, and possibly a distant relation of many others, including the Old Cumberland Beggar and the
dismissed Soldier (*The Prelude*, book 4). In a word, Lucy is no other
than a variant of the "Solitary," that characteristically Wordsworthian archetype.

Lucy is no less solitary, in a social sense, than her relatives. She
seems to have practically no commerce with the world, her existence
being devoted, not to any recognizably social activities, but solely to
itself—to the act of being there, pure and simple. She is indeed as
solitary as a violet or a star, and precisely as pure and total in her lack
of ulterior purposes as a violet or a star:

> A violet by a mossy stone
> Half hidden from the eye!
> —Fair as a star, when only one
> Is shining in the sky.[8]

There is at bottom nothing that separates this pretty image from the
bleak figure of the Leech-Gatherer, except that in the latter the
Solitary has suffered a terrifying "sea-change" into something "not
all alive nor dead," into "a huge stone . . . Couched on the bald top
of an eminence," and "a sea-beast crawled forth, that on a shelf / Of
rock or sand reposeth, there to sun itself." Of the original experience
that inspired this poetic portrait, we have the poet's own account:
" 'A lonely place, a Pond' 'by which an old man *was*, far from all
house or home'—not stood, not sat, but 'was'—the figure presented
in the most naked simplicity possible."[9] And it is as such, as a pure
being, as something inscrutable and silent that *is*, rather than by his
speech (which seems to be lost on the poet's ear—"The old Man still
stood talking by my side; / But now his voice to me was like a
stream / Scarce heard . . ."), that the Leech-Gatherer gives the despondent poet "apt admonishment."

A short but powerful portrait of another old man in a fragment

[8] "She Dwelt among the Untrodden Ways," lines 5-8.
[9] Letter to Sara Hutchinson, June 14, 1802, in *The Letters of William and Dorothy Wordsworth: The Early Years, 1787–1805*, ed. and comp. E. de Selincourt, 2d ed., rev. C. L. Shaver (Oxford, 1967), p. 366.

titled "Animal Tranquility and Decay" looks almost like a preliminary sketch for the Leech-Gatherer:

> he is one by whom
> All effort seems forgotten; one to whom
> Long patience hath such mild composure given,
> That patience now doth seem a thing of which
> He hath no need. He is by nature led
> To peace so perfect that the young behold
> With envy, what the Old Man hardly feels.

As John Jones has aptly instructed us,[10] the first published version of the poem had another six lines following the above, in which the old man said, in reply to the poet who asked whither he was bound: "Sir! I am going many miles to take / A last leave of my son, a mariner, / Who from a sea-fight has been brought to Falmouth, / And there is dying in a hospital." That Wordsworth finally omitted these is an immense credit to his capacity for self-criticism; he must have clearly seen that such a logical explanation of plausible human motivation did violence to the image of a profoundly self-sufficient being and thus was a betrayal of his own unique vision.

On the other hand, another portrait of an old man, the Old Cumberland Beggar, has failed, it seems to me, because the poetic force of "that vast solitude" to which the "tide of things has borne" this Solitary has been much adulterated by the poet's lengthy preaching against "Statesmen."

One of Wordsworth's greatest achievements lies in his creation of such a radical, primordial image of the Solitary. It is in the "vast solitude" which apparently can no longer be called "human" in any ordinary sense of the word that the highest, total mode of man's being exists—this paradoxical vision is what he struggled again and again to capture in verbal form. It may be said without too much exaggeration that it was a theme on which was spent the greater part (if not all, as we shall see) of his poetic exertions. A man who, neither "standing" nor "sitting," just simply "is," beyond every possible act

[10] John Jones, *The Egotistical Sublime: A History of Wordsworth's Imagination* (London, 1960), p. 63 (with a small correction made to his quotation from Wordsworth).

that is human—one could wonder if any other poet had ever been more obsessed with the verb "to BE," not a copulative in need of a complement but a full intransitive verb, independent and complete in itself. The poet who achieved what he had achieved was after all, contrary to T. S. Eliot's thesis, not wholly distinct from the man about whom it was said by his best analyst, "it is good for him to be alone."

All this is not to deny that, before reaching the *nonhuman* vision of the Solitary, Wordsworth had to go through many a *human* suffering, including his excitement and disillusionment over the French Revolution, the Annette Vallon affair with its probably traumatic scars on his conscience, the infatuation with Godwinianism, the consequent inner conflicts, and the doubts and wanderings evident in *The Borderers* and *Guilt and Sorrow*. Since I cannot here concern myself further with this aspect of the subject, let me briefly suggest my tentative view apropos of the Lucy poems: these poems seem to point to the kind of serenity that was finally arrived at through the poet's self-recovery or self-discovery after all those painfully human experiences. For the spiritual cycle whereby he found his true identity —the one that mattered most in making Wordsworth the poet we know him to be—was not, as the title of the eighth book of *The Prelude* would have it, "Love of Nature Leading to Love of Mankind," but the reverse, namely from politics, ethics, love, despair, in short from what Yeats called "All mere complexities / The fury and the mire of human veins,"[11] to a solitude in nature; the man entangled in the web of "relationships" grew to be a Solitary.

At all events, this self-sufficiency, so total in its solitariness and plenitude, seems to distinguish the Wordsworthian type of solitude from that of other Romantics. To the majority of Romantic poets, solitude was something bitter, forcing upon them an acute consciousness of privation and loss (which of course is not incompatible with the fact that they secretly loved that very bitterness and owed their creative energy to that very sense of loss). Solitude for Rousseau was, in spite of his narcissistic flair for it, an infinite provocation of long-

[11] W. B. Yeats, "Byzantium," lines 7–8, in *The Collected Poems* (New York, 1956), p. 243.

ings for human love, especially that of women: think of the repeated love affairs in his *Confessions*. (Wordsworth had only one, and the fact that it is not even mentioned in his autobiographical *Prelude* should not be interpreted as hypocritical concealment, as some critics suggest, exaggerating it; it means, rather, that Wordsworth came to realize that the affair had *not* been for him an experience of truly essential significance.) Kierkegaard posed the problem of solitude as, on one level, a prerequisite for love and, on another level, an existential springboard whereby to cast a man into the abyss of despair and bring him face to face with God. As for Coleridge, who confessed, "My nature requires another Nature for its support, & reposes only in another from the necessary Indigence of its Being,"[12] he was haunted by an unbearable anxiety arising from his sense of loneliness, and his painful life was both a long escape from it and a pathetic search for a happiness which was to have consisted either in communion with a kindred heart in the person of Wordsworth or Sara Hutchinson, or in merging with the Transcendent. There should be no need to mention such Romantic figures as Werther or Manfred.

In short, the one important verb for them was "to EXIST"—to live out there, tragically cast out, pathetically seeking to establish some moral contact with the "other," with people or a situation. By contrast, Wordsworth's Solitary, who just IS, is alien to a human or moral situation; almost nonhuman in his self-sufficient solitude, he lives in a world where tragedy and human drama are impossible and no desperate longings for human love can find their place.

Now where can this self-sufficiency come from? In my view, the source lies in a total communion with nature, which is exactly the reverse side of that total solitude in human terms. We do not feel, in the presence of Wordsworth's Solitary, such fear and pity as are our inescapable experience when we see Coleridge's Ancient Mariner gripped by the agony of a lonely hell. The Ancient Mariner leads an alien and estranged existence amidst the elements of nature, but the Leech-Gatherer is quite at one with nature, almost part of it. "A huge

[12] *The Notebooks of Samuel Taylor Coleridge*, ed. Kathleen Coburn, 2 vols. (New York, 1957–61), vol. 1 (text), entry no. 1679.

stone . . . on the bald top of an eminence" may be "solitary," but it is integrated into the landscape. There is established between the Solitary and nature a deep affinity, the most intimate communion possible. The Wordsworthian Solitary is, paradoxically, the least solitary of all men. The typically Romantic solitude, always imbued with the sadness of the *déraciné*, is something unknown to him. It must have been this self-sufficiency that attracted those comments from his contemporaries, who were very likely envying or even admiring as much as they were satirizing him.

Lucy, too, strikes us as a Solitary in perfect communion with nature, rather than as a woman in love. The most thoroughgoing and beautiful expression of this is "Three Years She Grew in Sun and Shower," in which Nature (the Wordsworthian "Dame Kind") decides to make of her a "Lady of [her] own" by nourishing her with all the good things of the natural world, which include not only such virtues of organic creatures as the sportiveness of a fawn but also "the silence and the calm / Of mute insensate things" (a stone on the bald top of a hill could perhaps be one of them). As the education, both sentimental and physical, nears its accomplishment, "beauty born of murmuring sound / Shall pass into her face" and "vital feelings of delight / [shall] Her virgin bosom swell." Lucy, thus presented, resembles "man naturalized" more closely than "nature humanized"; man has here become a metaphor, or even a pretext, for nature, and not vice versa, as is often the case with other Romantic poets. Wordsworth's attitude vis-à-vis nature seems diametrically opposed to the usual Romantic poetic which, anthropocentrically, treats nature as a metaphor for man, as *l'état d'âme* onto which is to be projected man's subjective feeling.[13]

We could go even further and say that Lucy was not even a pretext, but nature itself; she *was* a "violet by a mossy stone." If Words-

[13] Compare, e.g., Coleridge's remark: "In looking at objects of Nature while I am thinking, as at yonder moon dim-glimmering thro' the dewy window-pane, I seem rather to be seeking, as it were *asking*, a symbolical language for something within me that already and forever exists, than observing any thing new" (*The Notebooks*, vol. 2 [text], entry no. 2546). This sentence, which was later to fascinate Walter Pater in his inquiry into the nature of Romanticism, is indeed one of the best expressions of the Romantic *credo*.

worth's was a "literal" kind of imagination, as John Jones pointed out,[14] she might well *be* a violet, not *like* a violet; and the Leech-Gatherer could just as well have been, almost literally, a huge stone or a sea beast. While for Coleridge and Shelley everything was a symbol of something else, things *were* things for Wordsworth and had power to move him precisely because they were nothing but themselves. If in this sense the former were to be called "symbolists," our poet should certainly call for the label "realist." Indeed, some of Wordsworth's greatest lines, when I let them haunt my near subconscious, inarticulately but nonetheless powerfully, seem to me as if they consisted of some literal statements about things, almost tautological in syntactical structure, such as, "There was a stone," "A tree is a tree," or "I saw a stone which was a stone," and the like. And the irony is that, by the very same token, some of his dullest lines *do* consist of similar statements. Another unfortunate result of this *Sachlichkeit* is his notorious theory of "the real language of men," so rightly criticized by Coleridge, so easily parodied by many others.

If Lucy is nature, the reason for her premature death will become somewhat clear. Nature, for Wordsworth, is a *duration in change*, "decaying, never to be decayed," as the Alpine woods had revealed to him on the Simplon Pass. And death is no decisive event in the eternal cycle of perishing and regeneration. Lucy's death has nothing tragic about it in the order where she truly belongs. It was only proper that it should have been no more conspicuous and existential than her life had been—"She lived unknown, and few could know / When Lucy ceased to be." She has made only just a slight change in her mode of being; what is essential is *duration* rather than *change*. Lucy being nature incarnate, in that "She seemed a thing that could not feel / The touch of earthly years," was truer than the poet-lover apparently meant. Her death is indeed worthy of those two lines of the poem which Coleridge called "the sublime epitaph," the greatest verbal magic Wordsworth ever created:

> Rolled round in earth's diurnal course,

[14] Jones, *Egotistical Sublime*, p. 15.

With rocks, and stones, and trees.
["A Slumber Did My Spirit Seal"]

The profound sonority of this, clinching the whole series of these poems, almost convinces us that she has died as she must, that she has gone back where she must. The sorrow of the poet, so human and so negligibly small, is completely extinguished by the inevitability and the rightfulness of her death, which would seem rather odd, seeing that this is supposed to be the poet's complaint. And it is precisely here—in the virtual annihilation of the human by the nonhuman— that lies the crowning achievement of the Lucy poems, the astonishing triumph of Wordsworthian poetry.

Seen in this Wordsworthian context of nature, it is no mere rumor that another Lucy, Lucy Gray lost in the snow, is still to be seen tripping "upon the lonesome wild," singing "a solitary song"; we should realize, as "some maintain," that "to this day / She *is* a living child" (italics added). The same logic leads us to see that the girl who obstinately maintains that "We are seven" is, in the world of Wordsworth, a typical figure declaring a typical idea. Our Lucy is not the only one to die prematurely (prematurely from our conventional point of view); a boy ("There Was a Boy") who might well have been her younger brother also crosses the almost unnoticeable dividing line between a ten-year life spent in the bosom of nature and a death which seems completely natural. Dull would he be of soul who could remain unastonished by the description of the calmness of still another nature-child (the Danish Boy, who does not actually die): "Like a dead Boy he is serene." And yet this should in the last analysis be accepted as *le mot juste*.

Wordsworth may have come later to entertain a more orthodox Christian dualism in accordance with the decline of his "visionary gleam," as well as under the shock of the death of his brother John in 1805, which, as he confessed, made the evils and pains of this world seem to him inexplicable "except upon the supposition of *another and a better world.*"[15] But the height of his poetic activity was un-

---

[15] To Sir George Beaumont, March 12, 1805, in *Letters: Early Years*, p. 556.

doubtedly inseparable from the peculiar and powerful kind of monism we have seen.

Without going into discussions about the pantheistic or pagan character of Wordsworth's view of nature, what we should note here is that the boys and girls created by him all die too young to get involved in the process of moral education and the agonizing drama of human existence. The fact remains that Wordsworthian Solitaries are destined either to die in their childhood or to survive, the agonies of their lives left far behind, as hoary-haired old men "on the road," so old indeed that nobody can tell their age. The extremes meet.

In my engrossment in the figure of Lucy, I have so far left her poet-lover in oblivion. The attempt to redress the balance will lead me further into the structure of the Wordsworthian imagination, obliging me to recognize the one-sidedness of my whole argument in the section above. My starting point is once again the same question—Who is Lucy?

I will again give a straightforward answer: she is the boy Wordsworth. It is a commonplace that Wordsworth as a boy had a Lucy-like communion with nature, and it is easy enough to see that all his poetic boys and girls were so many glimpses of his alter ego, so many sketches for that self-portrait which was finally to find its completion in *The Prelude*. But I must hasten to point out that this common assumption tends to overlook a simple but crucial fact, namely, that the boy Wordsworth is *not* the poet Wordsworth and vice versa. It is one thing to *experience* and it is another to *express*. The boy's communion with nature was unself-conscious; in fact unself-consciousness is the essence of the boy—and of nature. On the other hand, the poet must willy-nilly be conscious, and the need to express, unknown to the boy-nature, is both his destiny and his raison d'être. The greatest paradox here is that only through the loss of his childhood, or only through the awareness of this loss, could the poet Wordsworth be born. The poet may complain of the disappearance of a "visionary gleam," but why write poetry at all if the "gleam" is still in possession?

Poor Susan suddenly sees the river of her country flow in Cheap-side. But the ecstatic vision soon vanishes: "She looks, and her heart is in heaven: but they fade, / The mist and the river, the hill and the shade: / The stream will not flow, and the hill will not rise, / And the colours have all passed away from her eyes!" The vision is to Susan essentially what the child is to the poet. The only difference is that unlike the poor beggar the poet can fix the fleeting vision in a verbal form—or perhaps the difference is a little greater, and we should say that he can not only recreate the vision itself but can also express its absence, that is, how it got lost and how it feels to lose it, just as he has done with Poor Susan's reverie.

Let us take another example which better illustrates the Words-worthian paradox of experience-loss-expression. "I Wandered Lonely as a Cloud" tells us that the wandering poet was deeply moved by a host of golden daffodils which met his eyes on a sudden. But the true meaning of the experience is not understood by him until it is re-created, after a long period of oblivion, by that "inward eye"—the re-creation being none other than this poem itself:

> I gazed—and gazed—but little thought
> What wealth the show to me had brought:
>
> For oft, when on my couch I lie
> In vacant or in pensive mood,
> They flash upon that inward eye
> Which is the bliss of solitude;
> And then my heart with pleasure fills,
> And dances with the daffodils.

What we see here is not the past experience alone but the process whereby the past becomes the present through the operation of the inward eye. This is a typical illustration of what might be called the double-exposure method by which the Wordsworthian imagination works.

The Prelude has at bottom a similar structure. We tend to forget the paradox, identifying the poet with the boy and assuming that each past episode has been captured at its actually lived moment. But the poem is really a record of significant moments like that of the daffodils experience—the moments for which Wordsworth coined his impressive phrase "spots of time."[16] It is more than a record, it is a story of how his life since childhood is shot through by so many "spots of time," how the past enriches the present and the present re-creates the past—in other words, how inner time, freed from the tyranny of clock and calendar, flows back and forth mystically.

It ought perhaps to be clear by now what I am trying to imply: *The Prelude* is a precurser of *A la recherche du temps perdu*, *The Portrait of the Artist as a Young Man*, and *Four Quartets*. What this poem on time, memory, and creative acts prophesied was possibly the kind of twentieth-century literature which Wyndham Lewis was to condemn summarily as "time-books," with Henri Bergson (Lewis's arch-enemy) as a presiding evil genius. It could be safely said at least that the honor of the first modern attempt at an inner autobiography might be claimed for *The Prelude*—unless perhaps one counts Rousseau's *Confessions* and *Rêveries du promeneur solitaire*.

We should note in this connection that Wordsworth himself was apparently well aware of the paradox we have been concerned with, as is shown by his critical utterances. The too well-known dictum that "poetry is the spontaneous overflow of powerful feelings" is one of the most flagrant untruths in the history of criticism, in that expression is never the same thing as experience, but the sentence that immediately follows is acute and appropriate: "it takes its origin from emotion recollected in tranquillity: the emotion is contemplated till by a species of reaction the tranquillity gradually disappears, and an emotion, similar to that which was before the subject of contemplation, is gradually produced, and does itself actually exist in the mind."[17] Although this obviously does not apply to the creative processes of all poets, or indeed not even always to Wordsworth—who saw his daffodils "*flash* upon that inward eye" instead of "gradually" recollecting them—yet it describes his own creative process with a remarkable appropriateness (which is probably no

[16] "There are in our existence spots of time, / That with distinct pre-eminence retain / A renovating virtue, whence . . . our minds / Are nourished and invisibly repaired" (*The Prelude*, ed. E. de Selincourt, 2d ed., rev. Helen Darbishire [Oxford, 1959], 12: 208–15 (text of 1850).

[17] *Lyrical Ballads*, ed. R. L. Brett and A. R. Jones (London, 1963), p. 266.

wonder, seeing that every critical theory put forward by a poet is his own justification, as, for instance is T. S. Eliot's "objective correlative" which Wordsworth's theory, rather unexpectedly, slightly resembles; his is no more and no less universally valid than Eliot's).

In any event, an "emotion recollected" presupposes forgetting and losing, just as the "time" one is "in search of" must be the time once lost. This is the paradox of memory on which hinge both the theories and the practices of Wordsworth. The reason *Tintern Abbey* and the *Immortality Ode* occupy such a central place in his *œuvre* is that the theme they struggle squarely with is none other than this paradox.

Now the *time* dimension of the "remembrance of things past" can be transposed into a *space* dimension where it becomes the question of the Solitary versus the Poet. Earlier I praised as one of Wordsworth's greatest achievements the creation of the figure of the Solitary, by which I am afraid I gave the impression that he himself was one of the Solitaries. Here I must correct such an impression and say definitely that he is *not* a Solitary—in just the same sense that the poet Wordsworth is not the boy Wordsworth.

It is true that, reading "Resolution and Independence," our eyes are inevitably riveted on that astonishing presence, the Leech-Gatherer. But we must not forget the "I," the poet watching the old man, for it is after all the poet's eye that makes the old man so astonishing, or, more precisely, what is really astonishing is that the poet's eye should have made such an old man so astonishing. Therefore, what the reader should do is to move back a little and put himself in a position to watch, from behind, the poet watching the Leech-Gatherer. The same applies to "We Are Seven" or "The Solitary Reaper." These, and similar poems, can only integrate their meaning when the reader takes full account of the situation which often remains implicit—the poet facing the girls with all too acute a sense of the gulf that separates him from these children-as-nature. This is a *spatial* version of the double-exposure technique that I examined earlier in *temporal* terms.

We must also modify the image of Wordsworth as a "realist" who makes a stone be a stone, a tree a tree, instead of a symbol of something else, and lets an old man just *be*. While Wordsworth "gazes and gazes," the stone and the old man remain themselves, or rather they reveal ever more truly their *stone-ness* and *old-man-ness*, but at the same time and by the same token, they begin to acquire a certain visionary character. This is the quintessential Wordsworth. For instance, in what I take to be the most haunting of all the "spots of time" in *The Prelude*, the boy visits by chance a place where in former times a murderer was hanged; he then sees "a naked pool," "the beacon on the summit" of a hill, and "a girl, who bore a pitcher on her head." These somehow combine to cause in him a most profound feeling: "It was, in truth, / An ordinary sight; but I should need / Colours and words that are unknown to man, / To paint the *visionary* dreariness / Which . . . invested" them.[18]

Certainly this is quite different from, say, the world of Shelley's imagination in which caves and rivers unhesitatingly become symbols of some sort. The pool, the beacon, the girl—there is nothing symbolic about them. And yet they *are* visionary. A. C. Bradley once described the Wordsworthian world thus: "Everything here is natural, but everything is apocalyptic."[19] One of the ways to describe such a poet would be to say that he was *both* a realist *and* a symbolist.

After what might seem a long detour, the structure of the Lucy poems should now be clear. Lucy embodies the most intimate communion possible with nature, she is almost nature incarnate; she confronts the poet as a thing lost; he mourns her death; for the death, though it may not mean any particular discontinuity for Lucy-as-nature, is an irrevocable event for the poet-as-man: "oh / The difference to me!" But it is only when she is lost that he realizes what she meant; at the same time he comes to realize what *he* means, an existence divorced from nature; he is now able to hear "the still, sad music of humanity." Furthermore, it is not until then that he discovers poetry, or finds it possible to write poetry; for poetry is precisely the re-creation of the lost Lucy in his memory. It seems as if we could say that the poet had to lose Lucy; we might even suggest, at the risk of carrying it too far, that it was the poet himself who *killed* Lucy,

[18] *The Prelude*, 12: 253–58 (text of 1850; italics added).
[19] *Oxford Lectures on Poetry* (London, 1909), p. 134.

along with those boys and girls, in order that he might be reborn as poet.

This is a new variation on the theme of the Fortunate Fall. Just as man acquired true humanity through the loss of Paradise, so Wordsworth became a poet through the loss of Lucy-as-childhood-as-nature-as-Paradise. In this he conforms to Schiller's famous category of the *sentimentalisch* poet as opposed to the *naïv* poet: the former must endeavor with excruciating self-consciousness to restore lost nature, whereas the latter can enjoy a nature with whose rhythm he is fundamentally at one.[20] All the Romantic poets, including Wordsworth and Schiller himself, were "sentimental" poets; perhaps Goethe was the only great exception to the modern role of *le poète maudit*. It may be that a common misunderstanding will insist on Wordsworth as the "naïve" poet, and it is true that he does look more naïve in Schiller's sense than such a typical "sentimental" poet as Coleridge. And yet, in spite of that self-sufficiency which I have stressed so much, he is far from Goethe's Olympian serenity. Goethe was never *hurt* by his countless love affairs, nor, as is well known, did he take any interest in the French Revolution (though he was not a young man then), while Wordsworth had to receive deep scars from his sensuous and political experiences alike. I must therefore modify somewhat, if not retract, my earlier statement about these experiences, that they were *not* of essential importance to him: they were, negatively, profoundly important insofar as they forced him to be aware of the loss of innocence through experience, to recognize the gulf between him and nature. In other words, the crucial thing was not so much the Annette-experience as the Lucy-experience.

As we have seen, what lies between Lucy and the poet is the void between the Leech-Gatherer and the poet, between the boy Wordsworth and the poet Wordsworth, between nature as an invulnerable whole and man as a tragic and fragmentary existence. It is also the distance between sensation and memory, between experience and expression. (Let me add in parentheses that it is also the difference between Dorothy and William, the sister being, in the brother's

[20] Cf. Friederich von Schiller, "Über naïve und sentimentalische Dichtung," in *Werke*, 42 vols. (Weimar, 1943–47), 20: 411–503.

words, "Nature's inmate,"[21] a "naïve" and happy soul, *die schöne Seele* as the German Romantics would have said, a zealous and minute observer of nature, in short a "realist," so that those biographers who would stick to Dorothy as Lucy's model are not, in this sense, too far wide of the mark.) And what dramatic tension there is in the Lucy poems, of which I spoke earlier in this essay, derives from an awareness of such gulf and distance.

The poetic zenith in Wordsworth's career was exactly a period when this awareness of the gulf most fruitfully stimulated his imagination, that is, when the double-exposure method worked most successfully. Conversely, his poetic decline would seem to have become inevitable when the awareness slackened and the double-exposure failed to work. Even in his heyday, the slackening and the failure entailed a lowered poetic quality. "Home at Grasmere" is a case in point; composed during the same period as *The Prelude*, it is a whole-hearted homage to the newly discovered happiness within the lovely confines of the Lake District. But the poet indulges in it so unashamedly and so single-mindedly (the poem is, as it were, a "spot of time" expanded to full poem length) that we miss the characteristic Wordsworthian charm and tension I have been defining. As Herbert Lindenberger suggests,[22] it may have been, in Wordsworth's own intention, a sort of *temps retrouvé* or a *Paradise Regained*, as contrasted with *The Prelude*-as-*Paradise Lost*, but in fact it may well become a sign of a regression into *L'Allegro* and *Il Penseroso*.

To put it differently, if his deep trust in that self-sufficiency of the Solitary which had been a cornerstone of his poetic universe should waver, and if the consequent uncertainty and anxiety should push him toward orthodox belief, then the obvious outcome would be a weakening, if not a collapse, of a poet who was not born a *religious* poet. Consider how boring the Solitary of *The Excursion* is. . . . But I must not overstep the bounds of this essay, the aim of which has been to suggest that the Lucy poems are a significant, if small, key to the structure of the Wordsworthian imagination.

[21] *The Prelude*, 11: 214 (text of 1805–06).
[22] Herbert Lindenberger, *On Wordsworth's Prelude* (Princeton, 1963), p. 165.

The Involuntary Memory as Discovered by Coleridge

Kimiyoshi Yura

In a chapter on Coleridge, René Wellek states that Coleridge's appeal to the unconscious "is simply the teaching of Schelling" and therefore concludes that it cannot be used as a claim for Coleridge's "greatness."[1] In this essay I propose to examine the justice of such an assertion. There appears in a volume of his manuscripts, compiled by Kathleen Coburn together with other published sources, a very striking account by Coleridge of the act of our involuntary memory and the mystery it involves.

I feel that there is a mystery in the sudden by-act-of-will-unaided, nay, more than that, frustrated, recollection of a Name. I was trying to recollect the name of a Bristol Friend, who had attended me in my illness at Mr. Wade's. I began with the letters of the Alphabet—ABC &c.—and I know not why, felt convinced that it began with H. I ran thro' all the vowels, aciouy, and with all the consonants to each—Hab, Heb, Hib, Hob, Hub, and so on—in vain. I then began other Letters—all in vain. Three minutes afterwards, having completely given it up, the name, Daniel, at once started up, perfectly insulated, without any the dimmest antecedent connection, as far as my consciousness extended. There is no explanation . . . of this fact, but by a full sharp distinction of Mind from Consciousness—the Consciousness being the narrow Neck of the Bottle. The name, Daniel, must have been a living

---

[1] René Wellek, *A History of Modern Criticism: 1750–1950*, 5 vols. (New Haven, 1955—), 2: 152.

Atom-thought in my mind, whose uneasy motions were the craving to recollect it—but the very craving led the mind to a reach [?] which each successive disappointment (=a tiny pain) tended to contract the orifice or *outlet* into Consciousness. Well—it is given up—and all is quiet—the Nerves are asleep, or off their guard—and then the Name pops up, makes its way, and there it is!—not assisted by any association, but the very contrary—by the suspension and *sedation* of all association.[2]

This notebook entry, whose significance has not previously been noted, furnishes us with a text in which, I believe, there is a great deal that is useful for a twentieth-century view of Coleridge. It is as if he were writing in the age of Freud and Jung, and, I may add, in the intellectual milieu of Marcel Proust.

There are, of course, not a few monographs on Coleridge's unusual interest in the unconscious workings of the mind and the role it plays in the creative artistic process. This has been assigned to the influence of the German *Natur Philosophie* of the first three decades of the nineteenth century, especially that of Schelling, not to mention the nascent influences of Neo-Platonic sources. There would seem to be so much to be said for all such ascriptions that they might be considered to have settled the matter. As the notebook entry clearly shows, however, Coleridge takes an entirely new point of departure, which is in no way found in his alleged sources or influences, in at least two points: a physical or topographical analysis of the unconscious, and the discovery of involuntary memory. Let us examine the first point in some detail.

In his widely noted book *The Unconscious before Freud*, Lancelot Law Whyte writes: "Like Goethe and Schelling he [Coleridge] recognizes the subtle interplay of conscious and unconscious in artistic creation":

---

[2] Kathleen Coburn, ed., *Inquiring Spirit: A New Presentation of Coleridge* (London, 1951), pp. 30–31.

In every work of art there is a reconcilement of the external
with the internal; the consciousness is so impressed on the
unconscious as to appear in it.

. . . that state of nascent existence in the twilight of the imagination and just on the vestibule of consciousness.

. . . the twilight realms of consciousness.[3]

Though learned and correct in his awareness of the general perspective, Whyte remains deplorably external in his treatment of
Coleridge. Goethe and Schiller, it is true, show a considerably acute
insight into the interplay of both in the act of creation. But it is
undeniable that the conscious or the unconscious remains a kind of
metaphysical assumption with them, from first to last. No observation is made in their massive *Werke* on the unconscious in physical,
not *meta*physical, terms. It is almost the same with Schelling. A
number of considerations establish a *prima facie* case that the earlier
works of Schelling were familiar to Coleridge, and that his general
idea of the unconscious must have been taken from Schelling. However, a glance at Schelling's works will show conclusively that he
worked out his conception of the unconscious on the same method-
ological postulates as Goethe, Carus, and Schubert. It will suffice to
quote here a few passages from Schelling:

. . . the work of art is . . . the document of philosophy, which
describes forever new what philosophy cannot hope to express.

. . . namely, the unconscious in artistic handling and productions, and its radical identity with the conscious as well.[4]

. . . the act of artistic genius, i.e., unpredictable reconciliation
of the conscious and the unconscious activity.[5]

Or again:

It has long been perceived that in the work of art not every-

---

[3] Lancelot Law Whyte, *The Unconscious before Freud* (London, 1960), p. 134.
[4] F. W. J. v. Schelling, "System der transzendentalen Idealismus," in *Schellings
Werke*, 3 vols. (Leipzig, 1907), 3 : 302 (my translations).
[5] Ibid., p. 298.

thing is worked out by consciousness: that an unconscious activity must be combined with the conscious activity; and that it is the perfect unity and mutual interpenetration of the two which give rise to the highest art; works which lack this seal of unconscious wisdom are recognized by the evident absence of life, a life which is self-supporting and independent of the artist himself.[6]

Because metaphysical and speculative thinking predominated among the German idealist philosophers and men of letters, there was little chance that more fruitful ideas and concepts of the unconscious would be fully developed. It is precisely at this point that Coleridge's new approach began, an attempt to deepen the speculation of contemporary German metaphysics by a subtle-minded psychology based on his concrete self-knowledge.

The quotation from Coleridge's manuscript with which I began is entitled by Kathleen Coburn "Mind Distinguished from Consciousness." As this apt title shows, Coleridge has at last discarded the traditional metaphysico-mystical assumptions. The conscious ceases to be, as such; the unconscious reappears as *under*-conscious or *below*-conscious in a fresh, topographical outline; and their dividing line as well as their dynamics are very subtly described.

The origin of the dichotomy may be traced as far back as the time when the word *conscious* was first coined. But the fully sharp distinction between the two, especially the image of the unconscious as constituted of many "living Atom-thoughts" craving ever to be re-collected, may be ascribed to Coleridge's initiative. With the publication of Freud's maiden work in 1889, or more precisely in 1913 with his famous pictorial diagram on a page of *Das Ich und das Es*, we are told, the first clear mental topography of this sort was drawn.[7] And as late as 1901 we find that Henri Bergson put much the same images and distinction in an address to L'Institut Général Psychologique. Here are some of the reasons Bergson gave for his claim:

[6] Schelling, "Über das Verhältniss der bildenden Künste zu der Natur," in W*erke*, 3: 396.
[7] Sigmund Freud, "Das Ich und das Es," in *Gesammelte Werke*, 17 vols. (Frankfurt am Main, 1940), 13: 252.

Our memories, at a given moment, form one solidary whole, a pyramid.

Suppose . . . I fall asleep. Then these repressed memories, feeling that I have set aside the obstacles, raised the trap door which held them back below the floor of consciousness, begin to stir. They rise and spread and perform in the night of the unconscious a wild *danse macabre*. They rush together to the door which has been left ajar.[8]

However deep and far back in our memory, memory-images are not inert and indifferent. They are active and almost attentive.[9]

Coleridge's anticipation of the Freud-Bergsonian phase and his break with the tradition of the German Natur Philosophie are, then, beyond doubt.

This brings us to the second point. Coleridge's manuscript entry clearly indicates that he, before Proust, had already coined as the English equivalent of "la mémoire involontaire" the expression "sudden by-act-of-will-unaided recollection" with all its significance, namely, a "mystery." These two points become all the more important when we realize that they are touched upon by Coleridge not casually, not as a mere *specifica*. They are some of the necessary fruits gathered on the very way to his establishing a new esthetics. Through his lifelong investigations into the acts of remembering and composition, he had obtained unusual insight into the inner fabric of the poetic process, in which they are inseparably connected. The actual experience of the involuntary memory thus vividly written down in the entry is, in my opinion, what Coleridge takes to be a solid foundation of a new poetics when he makes in passing an abrupt analogy in a passage in *Biographia Literaria*: "Now let a man watch his mind . . . while he is trying to recollect a name." The

---

[8] Henri Bergson, "L'énergie spirituelle," in *Oeuvres*, ed. André Robinet and Henri Gouhier (Paris, 1964), p. 886 (my translation).
[9] Ibid., p. 889.

analogy is made in the midst of one of the seminal passages of his writings, which starts from the destructive criticism of Hartleian associationist psychology and leads into the "intermediate faculty" of Imagination.

> Now let a man watch his mind while he is composing; or, to take a still more common case, while he is trying to recollect a name; and he will find the process completely analogous. Most of my readers will have observed a small water-insect on the surface of rivulets . . . and will have noticed, how the little animal *wins* its way up against the stream, by alternate pulses of active and passive motion, now resisting the current, and now yielding to it in order to gather strength and a momentary *fulcrum* for a further propulsion. This is no unapt emblem of the mind's self-experience in the act of thinking. There are evidently two powers at work, which relatively to each other are active and passive; and this is not possible without an intermediate faculty, which is at once both active and passive. (In philosophical language, we must denominate this intermediate faculty in all its degrees and determinations, the IMAGINATION.)[10]

This analogy between the act of writing and that of remembering and the incisive analysis of the act of involuntary memory will, if taken together, offer a sounder appreciation of what Coleridge had in mind when he was striving to discover a novel rhetorical device for penetrating the vast repertory of the human mind and for coming to final terms with his self-experience.

Students of Coleridge now accept without qualification the fact that Coleridge's theory of imagination was the product of his thoroughgoing critique of associationist theory. But just how his critique was thoroughgoing is the point still to be elaborated. To claim that Coleridge's theory of imagination is due to his rejection of associationism, i.e., to his rejection of such associationist postulates as "contemporaneity," "likeness," "contrasts," and so on, is not enough. Behind his refutation of the "passive fancy" and the

[10] J. Shawcross, ed., *Biographia Literaria*, 2 vols. (Oxford, 1907), I: 85–86.

"mechanical memory" there lies the affirmation of the mystery of involuntary memory as a factor "placing the whole before our view"[11] in the act of poetic creation. No wonder that in the notebook entry special attention is given to the "suspension and *sedation* of all association." His voice of triumph in 1801 over associationism—that he had "overthrown the doctrine of association as taught by Hartley" —or its reaffirmation in 1803—that "Hartley's system totters"—was really a shout of EUREKA, with the acceptance of the mystery of the involuntary memory as well as of the tentative description of it at its hidden center.

The acceptance is something to this effect: reality, whether inner or outer, never reveals itself in its totality by the mere act of rational comprehension. This is epitomized by the simple fact that the doctrine of David Hartley, the most comprehensive rationalist system available, had failed to explain the active phase of phenomena, such as the phenomenon of "the soul, the state of feeling" which creates the "breeze" running through the ideas and recalls "the trains of ideas" or "forgotten thoughts" from the deeper reality. Our springs of action, it is true, were sought out and to a large extent explained away in rational terms by association psychology, as far as the mechanical, habitual, superficial parts of the mind are concerned. But their psychology can never be applied to the creative, organic depth, for it is the theory of a "perfect Little-ist," of a "lazy looker-on of the external world." Through "the immediate Deduction" we should delve into the "twilight realms of consciousness," a realm freed from all the imperfections of objective perception; entrust ourselves with its "flux and reflux," now "resisting the current, and now yielding to it," and produce a life, a reality more perfect and real than that of the Little-ists. This is "the truest and the most binding realism."[12] The power and the existence of the involuntary memory, for one thing, will provide a breakthrough into it; and the feeling with which its reach is filled is the joy out of time and place.

[11] Ibid., 2: 15.
[12] Ibid., 1: 178.

Here I cannot resist the temptation to suggest a close resemblance between Coleridgean and Proustian esthetics. It has become a commonplace by now that the two cornerstones of the Proustian world are the idea of "mémoire involontaire" and that of "félicité" which is fully developed in the concluding volume of his *magnum opus*.

Scenes involving involuntary memory take place throughout *A la recherche du temps perdu*, some seventy-eight times, at first but dim anticipation, and at last turning into Marcel's growing conviction that the only real way of regaining lost time lies in this mystery. Stumbling on the uneven paving stones, he restores by the act of involuntary memory the sensation he once felt on the two uneven stones in the Baptistry of Saint Mark. And then the whole network of sensations experienced in Venice rises up out of the living catacombs. Venice recalled is far more real than the actual city. There, Marcel sees Venice in its essence, the regained time. The sound of a spoon knocked against a plate, of the hammer of a railway workman, the taste of some cakes and a glass of orangeade, the whiteness of a napkin, and again the sound of waterpipes—a whole series of events makes up an important undercurrent of feeling which ties these involuntary recollections together. Assisted, not by any willful associations, but by the "suspension and *sedation* of all association," Marcel realizes the mystery of involuntary memory. To this series of events making up the undercurrent of Marcel's feeling, the following comment by Coleridge will prove an accurate footnote from a century before Proust.

> I hold, that association depends in much greater degree on the recurrence of resembling states of Feeling, than on Trains of Ideas. . . . I almost think, that Ideas *never* recall Ideas, as far as they are Ideas—any more than leaves in a forest create each other's motion; Breeze it is that runs thro' them/it is the Soul, the state of Feeling.[13]
>
> . . . how imperishable Thoughts seem to be!—For what is Forgetfulness? Renew the state of affection or bodily Feeling,

[13] Earl Leslie Griggs, ed., *Collected Letters of Samuel Taylor Coleridge*, 4 vols. (Oxford, 1956–59), 2: 961.

same or similar—sometimes dimly similar/and instantly the trains of forgotten Thought rise from their living catacombs.[14]

And in the salon, at last, Marcel sees that youth and age are reconciled in the form of a young girl and becomes aware that a whole moment of his life has been brought into being and "freed from all the imperfections of objective perception," filling Marcel with "joy."[15] This leads him to the final affirmation that the vocation of the artist is to disclose a "thousand sealed jars, each filled with things of an absolutely different color, odor and temperature"[16] of our bygone years; to create a world "in which he could live and enjoy the essence of things, that is to say, entirely out of time";[17] to recapture "fragments of existence removed outside the realm of time."[18] Through these fragments the "moments bienheureux" or "félicité" can really be enjoyed. "This idea of joy," says Humphry House, "was a guiding principle of Coleridge's life."[19] His poetic space is filled with the sense of "joy" or "the deep delight." And it is the sense of joy he felt in a rare moment of elevation when he happened to be torn away from his regular, habitual self and immersed in the interior reality of the self. Paying tribute to Wordsworthian profundity Coleridge says: "it [the *Immortality Ode*] was intended for such readers only as had been accustomed to watch the flux and reflux of their inmost nature, to venture at times into the twilight realms of consciousness . . . to which they know that the attributes of time and space are inapplicable and alien,"[20] for, according to him, "the truth of nature" is given in terms of imagination by "awakening the mind's attention from the lethargy of custom."[21]

This again is what Proust discerned when he warned the artist not

[14] R. C. Bald, "Coleridge and *The Ancient Mariner*: Addenda to *The Road to Xanadu*," in *Nineteenth-Century Studies*, ed. Herbert Davis et al. (New York, 1940), p. 36.

[15] Marcel Proust, *Le temps rétrouvé*, in *A la recherche du temps perdu*, 3 vols. (Paris, 1953), 3 : 869.

[16] Ibid., p. 870.

[17] Ibid., p. 871.

[18] Ibid., p. 875.

[19] Humphry House, *Coleridge* (London, 1953), p. 138.

[20] Shawcross, 2 : 120.

[21] Ibid., p. 16.

to be beguiled by "habitude." "We have to bear in mind," he says, "that when we have attained reality, we shall not be able to express it and preserve it for all time unless we put aside all that is different from it and is being continually suggested to us by the haste that comes from habit."[22] Adducing Sainte-Beuve as a cautionary example, Proust speaks of the real work of art as a sort of depth gauge into the twilight realms.

> Real books must be the product, not of broad daylight . . . but of darkness and silence. Since art is a faithful recomposition of life, an atmosphere of poetry will always float around the truths that one has found at last within himself; there floats the sweetness of mystery, a trace of the twilight we have had to pass through. This is the measure of the profundity of a work of art indicated with precision as by a depth-gauge.[23]

From the very outset of his career, Proust took it as the task of the artist to make way back to life, shattering to the best of his ability "the ice of the habitual and the rational," finding a passage back to the "free waters."[24] This is something which the "romanciers matérialistment spiritualistes"[25] cannot dare to do, because they themselves cannot go beyond the world of outward appearances. As another "materialistically spiritualist" theorist, Coleridge would no doubt have cited the name of David Hartley. In the present context, even the abstruse doctrine of "the reconciliation of opposites" as cherished by Coleridge finds a distant and indirect echo in such an utterance by Proust. The only true relationship between the sensation and the memory, he says, lies in the effort of an artist "who must recapture it so that he may forever link together in his phrase reality's two discordant elements."[26]

We remember that Coleridge's "joy" is a joy with fearful symmetry, a joy felt momentarily at the summit of creative happiness but threatened to be lost forever. The theme of the lost Paradise

---

[22] Proust, *A la recherche du temps perdu*, 3 : 897.
[23] Ibid., p. 898 (my translation).
[24] Marcel Proust, *Contre Sainte-Beuve* (Paris, 1954), p. 303.
[25] Proust, *A la recherche du temps perdu*, 3 : 898.
[26] Ibid., p. 889.

recurs whenever he revives the moment of joy: "Could I revive within me that symphony and song..." Again we may be surprised to find that Proust shares quite the same lingering feeling.

> Yes! if thanks to our forgetfulness, a past recollection has been able to avoid any tie, any link with the present ... it suddenly brings us a breath of fresh air—refreshing precisely because we had breathed it once—of that purer air which the poets have vainly tried to establish in Paradise. Whereas it could not convey that profound sensation of renewal if it had not already been breathed, for the only true Paradise is always the Paradise we have lost.[27]

Like Kubla Khan's Pleasure Dome, his is also the lost Paradise of his heart's desire. Proustian "félicité" makes the same melodies of the "paradis artificiel" on the Coleridgean Eolian Harp which the breeze of involuntary memory at times strums through, winning the readers to "joy," a joy of being out of space, out of time. Their affinity is such that if we are allowed to replace Coleridge's "mackerel"[28] with Proust's "madeleine" sequence, then the dry pages of examination of the falseness of associationism will assume a twentieth century guise, and the theme of imagination will sound in the Proustian key.

Devoting two chapters to his very interesting study of Wordsworth's *Prelude*, Herbert Lindenberger demonstrates that Wordsworth's famous concept of "spots of time" may well be taken as an anticipation of Proustian time-consciousness.[29] If I am right in the foregoing analysis, Coleridge may be placed even closer to the Proustian milieu than Wordsworth. The achievement of the German philosophers of nature was characterized explicitly by Albert Béguin as "from pure psychology to metaphysics."[30] A sort

[27] Ibid., p. 870.
[28] Shawcross, *Biographia*, 1: 86.
[29] Herbert Lindenberger, *On Wordsworth's Prelude* (Princeton, 1963), pp. 131–204.
[30] Albert Béguin, *L'âme Romantique et le rêve* (Paris, 1946), pp. 145–47.

of phenomenological esthetics groped for in the Coleridgean darkness was, I should say, gained by dint of his initiative in switching off
"from metaphysics to modern psychology." The concepts of "joy"
and of the "involuntary memory" will cast no small amount of light
on the recent flood of theses on Coleridge, leading, hopefully, to a
better synthesized understanding of his criticism of associationist
theory, his existential strain, his doctrine of the unconscious, and his
idea of imagination.

Coleridge was never a plagiarist; his appeal to the unconscious was
not simply the teaching of Schelling. Even the passages that sound
almost like verbal echoes of other sources are, in fact, the voice of
the felt sensations of a "myriad-minded" poet ever shaping and
reshaping a more comprehensive theory of life. Thus, by way of
conclusion, let us say with R. P. Blackmur, in this the latter half of
the twentieth century, that "no one has finished mining Coleridge."[31]

---

[31] R. P. Blackmur, *The Lion and the Honeycomb* (New York, 1955), p. 184.

The Implications of *Dejection: An Ode*

Hisaaki Yamanouchi

1. The Dejection Throes

Among Coleridge's poetic works, *Dejection: An Ode* stands out as a direct presentation of a critical moment in the poet's mental history. In this poem the poet is deeply despondent, and he fears that he is losing his "shaping spirit of Imagination." From this we tend to assume that Coleridge's poetic genius is being jeopardized and that he is failing as a poet. The assumption may be correct up to a certain point, but imagination is not merely the power of writing a poem. It is the faculty, as the poet's later critical theory tells us, that intervenes as a mediator between mind and nature in the process of our perceiving the external world. In the present ode the poet, his faculty of imagination suspended, is alienated from nature. He feels himself a stranger to it and he attributes this to the numbing of his inner power of mind. The predicament in which the poet finds himself he terms "dejection."

From Coleridge's other poems we are familiar with that mental state which is more or less equivalent to dejection. For example, in consequence of his shooting the albatross, the Ancient Mariner is obliged to wander over the desertlike sea, alienated from nature and his shipmates. His lot on the ocean is described as "Life-in-Death," and only through his love for the water snakes is he able to restore his contact with the natural world and return to his native country. Again, Christabel, falling victim to the tempter Geraldine, becomes alienated from her father, her mother's spirit, and her lover. Finally, in "Kubla Khan" the splendor of Kubla's paradisal dome and garden is contrasted with the frustration of the poet, his inability to reproduce in his own work the splendor of Kubla's palace. Thus these three major poems provide instances of that mental disorientation which lies at the core of dejection. The sense of what may be designated the "dejection throes," or "dejection crisis," seems to pervade much of Coleridge's finest poetry.

Apart from Coleridge's poetry, a number of his notebook entries also describe his mental crisis. These were mostly written in the years from 1800 to 1803. The notebook entries prior to this period do not reveal so conspicuous a sense of crisis. Further, we have a comparatively small number of entries for the period when the poet was producing his major poems. Does it follow from this that dejection was a phenomenon alien to Coleridge when he was poetically productive? Hardly, for even in the themes of the major poems we can detect the dejection throes as I have outlined them. We may say that dejection haunted Coleridge from an early period to the end of his life. Then, can we not also say that, although Coleridge certainly experienced dejection at the time of writing *The Ancient Mariner*, he could relieve this emotion by sublimating it in poetic form, just as the Mariner himself can survive only by telling his story? To this extent poetic creativity or imagination may be a means for the poet to surmount the dejection crisis. When he cannot express it in poetic form, he records it in his private notebooks.

As noted above, three major poems testify to Coleridge's concern with dejection even before the *Ode*. The notebooks of the period offer some confirming evidence. When he notes how one may "inly agonize mid fruitless Joy,"[1] he describes a substratum of his consciousness, where some deep agony and intense but ephemeral joy coexist. Another entry in the Gutch Memorandum Book shows a symptom of the mental disorder: "the soul that is greatly vexed, that goeth stooping & feeble."[2] The symptom becomes more apparent around 1800, to which year the following entry belongs:

He knew not what to do—something, he felt, must be done—he rose, drew his writing-desk suddenly before him—sate

---

[1] *The Notebooks of Samuel Taylor Coleridge*, ed. Kathleen H. Coburn, 5 vols. (London, 1957—), 1: 266 G. 263 (conjectured by Coburn to have been written between September 22 and October 12, 1796).

[2] *Notebooks*, 1: 270 G. 267 (September 22–October 12, 1796).

down, took the pen—& found that he knew not what to do.[3]

The sense of disorientation revealed in this entry is further described in still another entry by means of the metaphor of a shipwreck, like that of the Mariner:

> Mind, shipwrecked by storms of doubt, now mastless, rudderless, shattered,—pulling in the dead swell of a dark & windless Sea.[4]

The significance of dejection may be further enlarged by reference to Coleridge's greatest poetic contemporary. One of Wordsworth's themes in *The Prelude* is "Imagination, how impaired and restored." In a similar way his *Ode: Intimations of Immortality from Recollections of Early Childhood*, which has in its origin some connection with Coleridge's *Ode*, runs thematically parallel to it. In his *Ode*, somewhat like Coleridge, Wordsworth laments the decline of the imaginative power he once had. Since the descriptions of despondency in the two odes resemble each other, we are tempted to surmise that the mental distress represented in these poems might be something universal to the Romantic poets, or at least common to these two poets, and that it has something to do with the essential quality of their imaginative activity. Wordsworth is fortunate enough to have his *Ode*. Might not this be the case with Coleridge too?

Coleridge's *Ode* is indeed a poem about "Dejection," but at the same time it puts forward his philosophy of "Joy." Being in the state of mind he describes in his *Ode*, Coleridge is perhaps incapable of sustaining joy as Wordsworth does in *The Prelude* and the *Immortality Ode*. But at least he wishes the "Lady" to be blessed with joy, and he knows very well what it is. Joy springs up from the fountain of the mind and enables man to attain to a beatific vision of that harmonious, organic universe where he is one with nature. This is exemplified by the phrase "the one Life within us and abroad" in "The Eolian Harp." The deprivation of this power of attaining a

---

[3] *Notebooks*, I: 834 4.117 (October 30, 1800).
[4] *Notebooks*, I: 932 6.16 (April–November 1801).

beatific vision through joy is what is meant by "Dejection." In this sense dejection is a matter not so much of inability to write a poem as of a disorientation in life, a failure to visualize a harmonious and organic universe in which one is settled securely. Joy, on the other hand, is one's sense of achievement of the beatific state in which mind and nature are harmoniously and securely unified. Moreover, joy and imagination work as complements to each other in visualizing this beatific vision. Viewed in this way, joy and dejection are of course understood to be antithetical elements; joy and imagination are complementary to each other; and in dejection the function of imagination is suspended.

Indeed, Coleridge achieves, or at least attempts to visualize, beatific visions in various forms. By means of Kubla's palace and garden he tries to represent some kind of paradisal splendor in "Kubla Khan," the imagery of which draws heavily on that of the paradisal scenery in Milton's *Paradise Lost*.[5] An aura of paradisal scenery is already latent in the setting of such earlier poems as "The Eolian Harp" and "Reflections on having left a Place of Retirement," even though in these the guise of familiarity and naturalness contrasts with the seemingly, if deceptively, supernatural atmosphere of "Kubla Khan." At the climactic moment of the Mariner's empathy with the water snakes, the poet succeeds in driving home the truth of "the one Life within us and abroad." But probably the Coleridge of the so-called conversation poems is most blest with visions of harmony and beatitude. Otherwise, ironically enough, these visions of harmony and beatitude are very often counterpoised by those of failure and frustration. The Mariner's blissful reunion with nature merely forms a counterbalance to the distressful alienation brought about by his offence against the albatross. Again, according to the projected plan of *Christabel*, the poem was intended to end in Christabel's reconciliation with her father and Geraldine's defeat by Christabel's betrothed, thus restoring harmony and redeeming the evil spirit through Christabel's innocence.[6] But Coleridge could not

---

[5] Cf. the long passage in *Paradise Lost*, 4. 131 ff.

[6] For the projected plan of the third part of *Christabel*, see James Gillman, *The Life of Samuel Taylor Coleridge* (London, 1838), pp. 301–02.

go beyond the second part; as it stands, the poem presents the picture
of innocent Christabel entrapped. Similarly, although some readers
of "Kubla Khan" think it concerns the consummation of poetic
creativity, others believe it to be a poem on frustration, on the inability of the poet to duplicate Kubla's paradisal splendor. Thus
throughout several of Coleridge's poems runs the antithesis between
the visions of harmony and beatitude on the one hand and those of
failure and frustration on the other, or, to return to Coleridge's
terms, the antithesis between "Joy" and "Dejection." What, then,
does this antithesis mean?

In the state of dejection the poet feels that he is deprived of the
inner power of joy and imagination; and life is felt to be life-in-
death, as in the case of the Mariner. There seems to be a certain
analogy between this state and that of the Fall of Man, although the
two states differ in that the Christian scheme is based on the triadic
relationships between God, nature, and soul, whereas the Coleridgean or Romantic scheme is based on the diadic relation between
nature (in which God is immanent) and mind.[7] In the Coleridgean or
Romantic scheme, mind is alienated from nature in the state of dejection; in the Christian scheme, man is alienated from God through
his disobedience or transgression. In both cases, life lapses into a living
death. The poet of Dejection: An Ode is living, yet his life is equivalent to the life-in-death of the Mariner. We find an archetype of the
Christian scheme in Milton's Adam, who has transgressed, has been
doomed to death, and is yet living, unrepentant, unredeemed by
Christ, and asking himself:

> Why am I mockt with death, and length'nd out
> To deathless pain? . . .
>   then in the Grave,
> Or in some other dismal place, who knows
> But I shall die a living Death?
>   [Paradise Lost, 10. 774–75; 786–88]

[7] For this schematization I am indebted to Meyer H. Abrams's lectures "Natural
Supernaturalism: Idea and Design in Romantic Poetry," delivered as the Alexander
Lectures at the University of Toronto on March 9–12, 1964.

In the Christian scheme, life is redeemed from the doom of death by Christ alone, so that for those saved the Fall turns into a fortunate fall. Thus Adam is allowed to regain

> New Heav'ns, new Earth, Ages of endless date
> Founded in righteousness and peace and love,
> To bring forth fruits Joy and eternal Bliss.
>
> [12. 549–51]

In Coleridge's scheme it is through the power of joy rather than redemption that the beatific visions come.

> Joy, Lady! is the spirit and the power,
> Which wedding Nature to us gives in dower
> A new Earth and new Heaven,
> Undreamt of by the sensual and the proud.
>
> [*Dejection: An Ode*, 67–70]

In terms of the archetypal pattern of paradisal bliss and fall, the whole body of Coleridge's poems would appear to comprise a coherent unity. However, instead of viewing Coleridge's poems in such a wide perspective, I will confine my discussion to *Dejection: An Ode*, examining in detail what is happening to Coleridge, as far as this is revealed in the poem, and trying to understand the meaning of "Joy" and "Dejection" specifically in the context of the *Ode*. Few would deny that this poem marks a critical moment in Coleridge's poetic creativity, and, more broadly speaking, in his creative view of life.

2. The Versions of the *Ode*

The following passage from Dorothy Wordsworth's *Journals* gives a clue to the discovery of the original version of the *Ode*:

April *21st, Wednesday*. William and I sauntered a little in the garden. Coleridge came to us, and repeated the verses he wrote to Sara. I was affected with them, and was on the whole, not being well, in miserable spirits. The sunshine, the green fields, and the fair sky made me sadder; even the little happy, sporting lambs seemed but sorrowful to me.[8]

As to these "verses" which Coleridge repeated to the Wordsworths, William Knight made a conjecture, as early as 1897, that they might be the original version of the Ode.[9] In 1929, Thomas Middleton Raysor mentioned Knight's conjecture and suggested the necessity of further research to confirm it, which he himself did not carry out at the time. Instead, by referring to Coleridge's then unpublished notebook manuscripts, he brought to light the important background of the Ode, that is, Coleridge's suppressed affection for Sara Hutchinson.[10] Then, in 1937, for the first time, Ernest de Selincourt published with commentary the text of the original version, a verse-letter addressed to Sara.[11]

---

[8] Dorothy Wordsworth, *Journals of Dorothy Wordsworth*, ed. Helen Darbishire (Oxford, 1958), pp. 147–48.

[9] Dorothy Wordsworth, *Journals of Dorothy Wordsworth*, ed. William Knight (London, 1930 [the first edition published in two volumes in 1897]), p. 110, footnote to the entry of Wednesday, April 21, 1802: "Can these 'Verses' have been the first draft of *Dejection, An Ode*, in its earliest and afterwards abandoned form? It is said to have been written on 2nd April 1802.—Ed."

[10] Thomas Middleton Raysor, "Coleridge and 'Asra,'" *Studies in Philology*, 26 (July 1929): 305–24. On Knight's conjecture, Raysor commented: "On April 21, 1802, the *Journal* contributes an item of the most extreme interest, when Dorothy speaks of Coleridge's repeating 'the verses he wrote to Sara. I was affected with them, and in miserable spirits.' The date corresponds with the known date of one of Coleridge's greatest poems, 'Dejection: an Ode,' which Coleridge himself dated April 4, 1802; and the subject-matter of the poem would surely have made Dorothy miserable, and for more than one reason. No other poem of Coleridge's fits either in date or subject-matter. This was pointed out by Professor William Knight in a footnote on this passage in Dorothy's *Journal*, but his suggestion has not been favored, because the first draft of the poem, if it is the first draft, is not only addressed to Wordsworth, but definitely refers to him in the text. This problem may, or may not, be settled by further research; for the present I merely wish to suggest the possibility that Professor Knight's conjecture may fit the known facts. The supposed first draft may in reality be a second draft, developing the poem and adapting to a different purpose in order to conceal its original application. At first thought, the poem seems naturally addressed only to Wordsworth, but Coleridge's thwarted love for Sara would give it an original equally probably" (pp. 309–10).

[11] Ernest de Selincourt, "Coleridge's Dejection: An Ode," *Essays and Studies by Members of the English Association*, collected by Helen Darbishire, 12 (1936): 7–25; reprinted in *Wordsworthian and Other Studies* (Oxford, 1957), pp. 57–76.

This verse-letter was written on April 4, 1802.[12] Then, to the *Morning Post* of October 4 of the same year, Coleridge contributed a poem, which was to be partly revised and included in *The Sibylline Leaves* of 1817, 1828, 1829, and 1834. For the sake of distinction let us call these three versions respectively (1) the letter version, (2) the *Morning Post* version,[13] and (3) the accepted version.[14]

The differences between the letter version and the other versions are major, and those between the versions other than the letter version are minor. The only noteworthy difference between the versions other than the letter version is that of the addressees, who are, respectively, (1) Sara; (2) Edmund, by which Coleridge means Wordsworth, while in those incomplete passages quoted in various letters Coleridge overtly addresses William or Wordsworth; and (3) the Lady. It was primarily in order to suppress his private affair that Coleridge changed the addressee from Sara to Wordsworth. At the same time, however, the difference in addressee changes the context of the poem, in which the key word "Joy" is used in relation to the person addressed. Certainly, the theme of joy concerns the universal

---

[12] The date of the composition of the *Ode* has a proximity to Wordsworth's *Immortality Ode*. From Dorothy Wordsworth's journal, the following is conjectured: on March 27, 1802, Wordsworth wrote part of his *Ode*; on March 28, the Wordsworths were with Coleridge, and Wordsworth might have recited his composition to Coleridge; on April 4, the original verse-letter was written by Coleridge. Thematically both odes are concerned with the decline of the poets' creative energy, although their final solutions to their plight are different. Apart from the thematic affinity, the two odes contain several verbal similarities that must have resulted from the two poets' mutual influences at the time. The following are the striking verbal similarities: (1) the symbolism of "light" as "glory"; (2) the reference to "Joy"; (3) Coleridge's line "there was a time when earth, and sea, and skies . . ." ("The Mad Monk," line 9) is echoed in Wordsworth's "There was a time when meadow, grove, and stream . . ." (line 1), and this in turn is re-echoed in Coleridge's "There was a time when, though my path was rough, etc." (line 76); (4) Wordsworth's "It is not now as it hath been of yore" corresponds to Coleridge's "They are not to me the Things, which once they were" (the letter version, line 295); (5) Wordsworth's "My head hath its coronal" (line 40) is echoed in Coleridge's "I too will crown me with a Coronal" (the letter version, line 136).

[13] *The Complete Poetical Works of Samuel Taylor Coleridge*, ed. Ernest Hartley Coleridge, 2 vols. (Oxford, 1912), vol. 2, app. 1, First Drafts, Early Versions, etc., pp. 1076–81.

[14] Much of parts of the *Ode* will also be found in various letters. See *Collected Letters of Samuel Taylor Coleridge*, ed. Earl Leslie Griggs, 6 vols. (Oxford, 1956), 2: 815–19, 831–32, 875, 970–72, 1008, 1201.

principle of life, but when it is used in relation to Wordsworth, it concerns a theme more relevant to a poet. By this token, in the *Morning Post* version, joy is described as already possessed by the poet Wordsworth, while in contrast Coleridge is failing as a poet and lamenting his loss of joy. In the letter version the poet laments the lack of joy on his part, but at the same time he hopes that Sara will be blessed with it. In the same way the poet's prayer that the Lady will always possess joy is repeated in the accepted version.

In comparing the versions, we ought to recall that for the past few decades we have been accustomed to the esthetic assumption that a poem has a life of its own, independent of the author. From this point of view, the accepted version of the *Ode* is in itself complete and the original letter version may seem full of personal triflings. This is the way most critics have assessed the poem.[15] A heretical position was taken by the late Humphry House, who asserted that the original version is more powerful than the finished, accepted version.[16] Instead of adjudicating this dispute, I shall limit my efforts to pointing out the differences between the two.

We have already considered one difference, in respect to the addressees. In connection with this, the tone of the original letter version is more consistent with its addressing Sara Hutchinson, whereas in the accepted version the less personal tone taken in addressing the Lady weakens the impression of real conversation. In the accepted version, some readers might wonder why the poet is addressing the Lady. This question is answered quite clearly in the original version: the poet's confession of his affection for Sara Hutchinson seems to have caused Sara both mental and physical suffering, and he is apologizing to her for it. Besides apologizing, he is wishing her joy. The poem turns on this fundamental theme and introduces other topics that we find in the accepted version as well. To this extent, the conversational tone flows more naturally and consistently. In the accepted version about two-thirds of the total

---

[15] For example, Stephen F. Fogle, "The Design of Coleridge's 'Dejection,'" *Studies in Philology*, 48 (1951): 49–55.
[16] Humphry House, *Coleridge: The Clark Lectures, 1951–52* (London, 1953), pp. 133–37.

lines of the original letter version are omitted and the remaining lines are arranged in a different order. As a result, the original consistency of one section with another is weakened. Or, at least, because of the inversion of the stanzaic divisions, the thematic emphasis has shifted.[17]

In simplified terms, the following structural and tonal differences may also be observed between the accepted version of the *Ode* and the letter version. The former omits the private references of the letter version; the "projective" view of nature and the definition of joy, which are placed toward the end of the letter version, occupy the middle and central part; the *Ode* as a whole is a poem, starting with the description of the weather outside, developing that of the mental landscape with its pinnacle in the "projective" view of nature and the definition of joy, returning to the weather outside, and ending with the poet's prayer for the "Lady." While the letter version is personal in tone, the accepted version is a less personal poem, which consists of a view of nature, a definition of joy, and a discussion of the relation between joy and imagination. The following discussion of the *Ode* will be based mainly on the accepted version, but from time to time reference will be made to other versions when significant differences are involved.

3. Symbols of Joy

The epigraph of the *Ode* (taken from the "Ballad of Sir Patrick Spence") uses the imagery of both the moon and the wind, which is carried over into the first stanza of the *Ode*. The image of the wind shows that the world outside and the poet's mental state run parallel to each other. The body of the poem is devoted to the latter, subjective concern, until, in the penultimate stanza, the poet turns to the world outside again. Anyone who is familiar with Coleridge's poems would be aware of the pervasive significance of wind symbolism in his writing. His symbols range from the disorienting tempest to the "correspondent breeze," from both of which extremes

---

[17] In the original version of this essay, a minute comparison of twenty major differences followed at this point.

the wind in the *Ode* seems to differ.[18] The winds that are blowing at
this moment are

> those which mould yon cloud in lazy flakes
> Or the dull sobbing draft, that moans and rakes
> Upon the strings of this Aeolian lute,
> Which better far were mute.
>
> [5–8]

The note that this wind brings forth is that of dullness, sterility,
"Life-in-Death."
The description of the wind is followed by that of the moon:

> For lo! the New-moon winter-bright!
> And overspread with phantom light,
> (With swimming phantom light o'erspread
> But rimmed and circled by a silver thread).
>
> [9–12]

The moon also differs from that in Coleridge's earlier poems, where
it is an image of fruitful poetic experience.[19] Just like the author of
the "Ballad of Sir Patrick Spence," the poet is predicting from this
dim moon the "coming-on of rain and squally blast"; furthermore,
curiously enough, he is even wishing for it:

> And oh! that even now the gust were swelling,
> And the slant night-shower driving loud and fast!
>
> [15–16]

---

[18] For a variety of wind symbolism in Coleridge's early poems, see "Dura Navis,"
"An Effusion at Evening," "Lines on an Autumnal Evening," "Lines" (1894), "The
Sigh," "Ode" ("Ye Gales . . ." 1792), etc. "The intellectual breeze" in "The Eolian
Harp" is equivalent to Wordsworth's "correspondent mild creative breeze" (*The
Prelude* [1805–06] line 43). Again, "the correspondent breeze," as expounded by Meyer
H. Abrams, is one of the Romantic poets' favorite images: the wind as the life-giving
power, which is "not only a property of the landscape, but also a vehicle for radical
changes in the poet's mind" ("The Correspondent Breeze: A Romantic Metaphor,"
in Abrams, ed., *English Romantic Poets* [New York, 1960], pp. 37–54). The wind in
The Ancient Mariner is ambivalent, working as both a benevolent and a malevolent
agent.

[19] In *The Ancient Mariner* the moon is associated with the benevolent power of
nature. For Coleridge's references to the moon in his prose, see: *Notebooks*, 2: 2402
21.567(b), 2453 17.27, 2988 11.57, and *Anima Poetae*, ed. E. H. Coleridge (London,
1895), p. 382.

Here a clear contrast is drawn between the two kinds of winds, the one being "the dull sobbing draft" that is blowing now, and the other the "squally blast" that formerly activated the poet's mind. He hopes that the gusts of this wind

> Might now perhaps their wonted impulse give,
> Might startle this dull pain, and make it move and live!
>
> [19–20]

From these lines we can see that in the opening stanza "the dull sobbing draft" and the poet's own mental state are identical. As the words "move" and "live" suggest, the mental state of dejection is the hindrance of movement or progression, or lifelessness in a metaphorical sense: the "Life-in-Death" of *The Ancient Mariner*.

The mental state of dejection, which is placed parallel to "the dull sobbing draft" in the first stanza, is described more explicitly in the second stanza:

> A grief without a pang, void, dark, and drear,
> A stifled, drowsy, unimpassioned grief,
> Which finds no natural outlet, no relief,
>   In word, or sight, or tear.
>
> [21–24]

The poet further describes this state as "this wan and heartless mood." He is gazing upon the yellowish green moonlit sky, but "with how blank an eye!" The crescent moon looks "as fixed as if it grew / In its own cloudless, starless lake of blue" (35–36). The situation is similar to that of the Ancient Mariner in part 4, where the Mariner, "in his loneliness and fixedness, . . . yearneth towards the journeying Moon, and the stars that still sojourn, yet still move onward." We may also remember an often quoted passage in the notebooks:

> In looking at objects of Nature while I am thinking, as at yonder moon dim-glimmering thro' the dewy windowpane, I seem rather to be seeking, as it were *asking*, a symbolical language for something within me that already and forever exists, than observing any thing new.[20]

---

[20] *Anima Poetae*, p. 136 (April 14, 1805); *Notebooks*, 2: 2546 17.104.

It is characteristic of Coleridge to see in nature the reflection of his own mind. Ironically, however, the poet's mind at this moment is dull and vacant. Although he cannot project anything into nature, nature itself is beautiful:

> I see them all so excellently fair,
> I see, not feel, how beautiful they are!
>
> [37–38]

Here the poet is afraid of his mental inertia and longs for the vital power of mind to perceive nature. This argument for the mind's vitality and initiative is continued into the next stanza:

> My genial spirits fail;
> And what can these avail
> To lift the smothering weight from off my breast?
> It were a vain endeavour,
> Though I should gaze for ever
> On that green light that lingers in the west:
> I may not hope from outward forms to win
> The passion and the life, whose fountains are within.
>
> [39–46]

The metaphor of the "fountain" used here to signify the mind's vitality may remind us of those used in Coleridge's earlier poems, the "gushing" of prayer from the Mariner's heart, the "fountain" in Kubla's garden, and so on, all of which represent mental energy.

In the letter version, after the description of the scenery outside and of the poet's mental inertia (stanzas 1, 2, and 3 of the *Ode*), there follow about 130 lines in which the poet's mind is occupied with the thought of Sara. Although Coleridge returns early in this section to the apparent lifelessness of nature owing to his own mental inertia, he is suddenly if feebly moved by the thought that Sara is gazing upon the same sky that extends before his indifferent eyes. This response to the sky reminds the poet of his childhood when he used to think that

> There does not live the Man so stripp'd of good affections
> As not to love to see a Maiden's quiet Eyes

Uprais'd, and linking on sweet Dreams by dim Connections
To Moon, or Evening Star, or glorious western Skies—
While yet a Boy, this Thought would so pursue me,
That often it became a kind of Vision to me!
[The letter version, 68–73]

The phrase "Moon, or Evening Star, or glorious western Skies" presents characteristic Coleridgean images.

This "Vision" is appropriately associated with Sara Hutchinson. But it is unrealizable under the present circumstances, except imaginatively. By means of imagination the poet draws a picture of Sara watching the crescent moon, sitting on a sod-built seat of camomile and hearing a beehive murmuring. In so fancying Sara, he feels his heart moved and filled with shared blessings:

Those dear mild Eyes, that see
Even now the Heaven, *I* see—
There is a Prayer in them! It is for *me*—
And *I*, dear Sara,—*I* am blessing *thee*!
[The letter version, 95–98]

The reverie extends not only spatially but also back in time. He recalls the time when Mary and Sara Hutchinson and he were together. At that time,

Such Joy I had, that I may truly say,
My Spirit was awe-stricken with the Excess
And trance-like Depth of it's brief Happiness.
[The letter version, 108–10]

In this case, just as in his earliest poems, memory produces the sense of Joy.[21]

Ah fair Remembrances, that so revive
The Heart, and fill it with a living Power,
Where were they, Sara?
[The letter version, 111–13]

---

[21] For Coleridge's references to "Memory" in his early poems, see, e.g., "An Effusion at Evening" (1792): "And Memory, with a Vestal's meek employ, / Unceasing feeds the lambent flame of Joy!" (53–54).

It was to preserve these "Remembrances" that the poet wrote the "Scroll," which, to his regret, "even to bodily Sickness bruis'd [Sara's] Soul" (116).

The poet's regret for having embarrassed Sara is repeatedly expressed. He regrets whatever turns Sara from "the Course / Of calm Well-being and Heart at rest" (131–32). This is not within his reach, but he wishes Sara to preserve it. Sara and his other close friends— William, Dorothy, and Mary—live happily together, and "I too will crown me with a Coronal"[22] (the letter version, 136). Here the poet compensates for his own deprivation with a wish for the welfare of someone else. This attitude is somewhat similar to that in "This Lime-Tree Bower my Prison," in which the poet imagines his friends' joyful tour of the valley while he himself is confined in one place because of an accident. Sara Hutchinson's importance in such a relationship is clear in the *Ode*:

> Be happy, and I need thee not in sight. . . .
> Where e'er I am, I shall be well content!
> Not Near thee, haply shall be more content!
> To all things I prefer the Permanent.
> And better seems it, for a heart, like mine,
> Always to *know*, than sometimes to behold,
>   *Their* Happiness and thine—
> For Change doth trouble me with pangs untold!
>   [The letter version, 144–54]

The poet tries to maintain tranquillity of mind by deliberately avoiding Sara's presence. This attitude is based on the paradox that deprivation is even better than changeable and transient possession:

> The transientness is Poison in the Wine,
> Eats out the pith of Joy, makes all Joy hollow,
> All Pleasure, a dim Dream of Pain to follow!
>   [The letter version, 160–62]

Once again we see the vicious circle of "alternate groups of Joy and

[22] For the relation of this line to the *Immortality Ode*, see n. 12, above.

Grief," shown in the early poems.[23] "Joy" is almost the illusion of
the vanishing Garden of Eden or of a Golden Age. It is so transient
that its presence is felt only through its loss. And one way to avoid
disillusionment over the loss of Paradise is to abstain from entering
it. In this passage, the poet resolves to abstain from participating in
the group formed by Wordsworth, Dorothy, Mary, and Sara.

> Wherefore, O wherefore! should I wish to be
> A wither'd branch upon a blossoming Tree?
> > [The letter version, 167–68]

The sharp contrast between life and lifelessness is drawn by means of
the characteristic Romantic metaphor of a tree.[24]

The ascetic attitude which the poet has so far maintained is reversed for a moment in the next stanza. He regrets that he cannot be
beside Sara when she is sick. After this momentary fit of emotion, the
poet pacifies himself by asking,

> Nay, wherefore did I let it haunt my Mind
> The dark distressful Dream!
> > [The letter version, 184–85]

In the letter version the poet's preoccupation with the thought of
Sara is followed by lines (184–215) equivalent to stanza 7 of the
accepted version. In the accepted version, the fourth stanza seems to
be an immediate development of the argument in the third stanza.

> I may not hope from outward forms to win
> The passion and the life, whose fountains are within.
>
> O Lady! we receive but what we give,
> And in our life alone does Nature live:
> Ours is her wedding garment, ours her shroud!
> > [45–49]

---

[23] Cf. "Lines: To a Friend in Answer to a Melancholy Letter" (1795), line 11.
[24] Not only in Coleridge's poetry, as for example, in "To Matilda Betham from a
Stranger," but also in his prose writings, the tree is used recurrently as a metaphor of
organic growth and unity. There is a detailed discussion of the subject in Frank
Kermode, *Romantic Image* (London, 1957), pp. 92–103.

The passage turns on the problem of knowledge, i.e., the relationship between mind and nature. To clarify this difficult matter, I
should like first to discuss Coleridge's general idea of the problem
and then to consider this passage in the context of such knowledge in
relation to joy.

In realizing Wordsworth's and Coleridge's objective of revitalizing nature, there are two alternatives: (1) to consider nature once
more alive; (2) to take the view that the mind has a vital power to
project itself into nature and enliven it. In Wordsworth's case, the
former is predominant, but the latter view may also be found, since
he vacillates between the two. Actually, the two alternatives complement each other in achieving their common objective. The
difference between the two is one not of kind but of degree. Coleridge's concept of "the one Life within us and abroad" is the manifestation of the view of vital or organic nature.[25] In the above passage
from the Ode he gives the initiative to the mind (or subject), which
projects itself into nature, in perceiving nature (or object). The
"wedding garment" in this context is an appropriate symbol of life,
and the "shroud" that of death or life-in-death. It depends upon the
mental state of the perceiver whether nature is alive or dead. To the
inactive mind, nature is merely "that inanimate cold world allowed /
To the poor loveless ever-anxious crowd" (51–52).

Coleridge goes on to describe this projective power of mind by
means of light symbolism:[26]

Ah! from the soul itself must issue forth
A light, a glory, a fair luminous cloud

[25] From this point of view Coleridge calls Locke "a perfect Little-ist" (Letter to
Thomas Poole, March 23, 1801, Collected Letters, 2: 709). In a similar way, in Newton's
system "mind is always passive—a lazy Looker-on on an external World" (ibid.).
About the time of this criticism of Locke and Newton, Coleridge also declares his
departure from David Hartley, in whose system, too, as he later expounds in Biographia Literaria, the soul is such a passive faculty that it "is present only to be pinched or
stroked, while the very sequels or purring are produced by an agency wholly independent and alien" (Biographia Literaria, ed. J. Shawcross, 2 vols. [London, 1954] 1:
81). As a result "our whole life would be divided between the despotism of outward
impressions, and that of senseless and passive memory" (ibid., p. 77).
[26] For the correspondence of the light symbolism used in the Ode to that used in the
Immortality Ode, see n. 12, above.

Enveloping the Earth.

[53-55]

Coleridge often associates light with the glory of God or with other symbolic glories implying subjective states.[27] The light mentioned in the present stanza is that of the setting sun, judging from the following lines in the letter version:[28]

> sweet Dreams by dim Connections
> To Moon, or Evening Star, or glorious western Skies.
> [The letter version, 70-71]

Coleridge follows this magnificent visual symbolism of light with aural symbolism:

> And from the soul itself must there be sent
> A sweet and potent voice, of its own birth,
> Of all sweet sound the life and element!
>
> [56-58]

The aural symbolism is carried over into the fifth stanza:

> O pure of heart! thou need'st not ask of me
> What this strong music in the soul may be!
>
> [59-60]

The connotation of this "strong music" is enriched if we recall

[27] See, for instance, *Notebooks*, 1: 209 G.205; 528 5.26; 581 5.128; and 713 21.63.
[28] This scenery also reminds us of that of *The Ancient Mariner* at the climactic moment of the Mariner's empathy with the water snakes in part 4 of the poem. Further, in a letter written a little later than *Dejection: An Ode*, Coleridge described the setting sun over Mount Skiddaw as follows:
> The Image now before my eyes—over Bassenthwaite the Sun is setting, in a glorious rich *brassy* Light—on the top of Skiddaw, & one third adown it, is a huge enormous Mountain of Cloud, with the outlines of a mountain—this is of a starchy Grey—but floating fast along it, & upon it, are various Patches of sack-like Clouds, bags and woolsacks, of a shade lighter than the brassy Light of the clouds that hide the setting Sun—a fine yellow-red somewhat more than sandy Light—and these the highest on this mountain-shaped cloud, & these the farthest from the Sun, are suffused with the darkness of a stormy Color. Marvellous creatures! how they pass along! [Letter to William Sotheby, July 19, 1802, in *Collected Letters*, 2: 819]
From this description of the cloud colored by the setting sun we can understand the phrase "a fair luminous cloud."

Coleridge's references to music in his earlier poems: music as the symbol of harmony in "The Eolian Harp," the heavenly music in *The Ancient Mariner*, Bard Bracy's "music sweet and loud" or "music strong and sweetly sung," the music played by the Abyssinian maid, by means of which the poet wishes to reconstruct Kubla's pleasure dome, and so on. And we might also recall Coleridge's references to music in his prose, especially to "the sense of musical delight" as the gift of imagination.[29]

The next step the poet takes is to combine the visual and aural metaphors.

> What, and wherein it [this strong music in the soul] doth
>   exist,
> This light, this glory, this fair luminous mist,
> This beautiful and beauty-making power.
>
> [61–63]

The dynamic power of the mind, which has so far been described by means of visual and aural symbols, is given only to the "pure" of heart "in their purest hour," and never to "that poor loveless ever-anxious crowd" (52). This statement corroborates the fact that joy requires purity and innocence, as we see in *The Ancient Mariner* and *Christabel*. Joy is here called "Life," "Life's effluence," "cloud"— that "luminous cloud"—and "shower," which is also an important symbol of a resuscitating power, as in the Mariner's release from his paralysis. Here again, the metaphor of "wedding" is repeated:

> Joy, Lady! is the spirit and the power,
> Which wedding Nature to us gives in dower
> A new Earth and new Heaven.
>
> [67–69]

The middle part of the accepted version is thus devoted to the definition of "Joy." The middle part of the letter version, on the

---

[29] In *Biographia Literaria*, Coleridge remarks that "the sense of musical delight, with the power of producing it, is a gift of imagination" (2:14). Elsewhere we find the following passage: "What is Music?—*Poetry* in its grand sense? Answer. Passion and order atun'd! Imperative Power in Obedience!" (*Notebooks*, 2: 3231 24.21).

other hand, is concerned with the state of "Dejection" itself, while its closing part is devoted to the definition of joy. In the letter version is found one additional aspect of joy—in this case, incarnate in children:

> My little Children are a Joy, a Love
> A good Gift from above!
>
> [The letter version, 272–73]

It is one of these children that Wordsworth had in mind when he described a joyful child in the seventh stanza of the *Immortality Ode*.[30] The definition of joy, whether it occupies the middle part of the poem as in the accepted version or is placed toward the end as in the letter version, is put forward so powerfully that for a moment we get the impression that the poem concerns not dejection but joy.

4. Dejection: "Natural Man" versus "Abstruse Research"

After presenting his definition of joy, the poet turns again to dejection, first recalling the past when joy was powerful enough to dispel distress:

> There was a time when, though my path was rough,
> This joy within me dallied with distress,

---

[30] Elsewhere Coleridge depicts his children as symbolizing joy in the following way:

> The wisdom & graciousness of God in the infancy of the human species—Its beauty, long continuance &c &c. ⟨Children in the wind—hair floating, tossing, a miniature of the agitated Trees, below which they play'd— the elder whirling for joy, the one in the petti-coats, a fat Baby, eddying half willingly, half by the force of the Gust—driven backward, struggling forward—both drunk with the pleasure, both shouting their hymn of Joy.⟩ [*Notebooks*, 1: 330 21.32]

There are several interesting expressions in this passage describing joy incarnate in children: first, the "hair floating" reminds us of the "floating hair" of the ecstatic poet in "Kubla Khan"; second, the children are appropriately compared to "Trees," which symbolize organic growth and unity (see n. 24, above); and finally, "whirling" and "eddying" are predominant metaphors for the state of joy, which will appear again in the final stanza of the *Ode*. In this connection see also *Notebooks*, 1: 1001 21.153, and the letter to John Thelwall, January 23, 1801, in *Collected Letters*, 2: 668.

And all misfortunes were but as the stuff
Whence Fancy made me dreams of happiness:
For hope grew round me, like the twining vine,
And fruits, and foliage, not my own, seemed mine.

[76–81]

This psychological process of surmounting distress by means of hope
is mentioned often in the early poems.[31]

But now afflictions bow me down to earth:
Nor care I that they rob me of my mirth;
But oh! each visitation
Suspends what nature gave me at my birth,
My shaping spirit of Imagination.

[82–86]

The passage seems to offer clues to our discussion: first, it is another
passage that delineates what is happening to Coleridge in the state of
dejection; second, it speaks of the state of dejection in terms of the
"shaping spirit of Imagination," which is certainly the central concept of Coleridge's critical theory. As to the first point, the poet
describes his state as "afflictions" bowing him down to earth. What
are these "afflictions"? From the biographical materials we know of
many factors that seem to be conducive to dejection: the ill-health,
laudanum, and the ensuing guilty conscience, domestic discord,
unfulfilled love for Sara Hutchinson. These are certainly "afflictions."
Does it follow from this that dejection means the sense of unhappi-
ness as a result of these "afflictions"? The answer is no. Let us consider the letter version in this connection.

In the letter version, instead of "afflictions," the passage in question reads "Ill tidings," which is in turn a substitute for "misfortunes," which was crossed out in the manuscript. The poet's vacilla-
tion between these phrases at least suggests the ambiguity of what
the poet was trying to represent. It may be that Coleridge tried to

[31] Cf. "Thus Fairy Hope can soothe distress and toil; . . ." ("Monody on a Tea-
Kettle," line 39); "Hope itself was all I knew of Pain!" ("An Effusion at Evening,"
line 20).

and yet could not define precisely what his "afflictions" were. For this purpose he starts by negating what appear to be afflictions:

> I speak not now of those habitual Ills
> That wear out Life, when two unequal Minds
> Meet in one House and two discordant Wills—
>   This leaves me, where it finds,
> Past Cure and past Complaint—a fate austere
> Too fix'd and hopeless to partake of Fear!
>   [The letter version, 243–48]

Although testifying to the existence of domestic discord, the poet does not think of the things listed in the passage as the afflictions that are bowing him down to earth. The discord is "too fix'd and hopeless to partake of Fear!" This is contrasted to the group of Sara, William, Dorothy, and Mary, who make up "a World of Hope and Fears for me" (252). What, then, is really afflicting Coleridge: the fixedness of his domestic life, or the contrast represented by his happy friends? There seems to be a certain inconsistency or at least confusion. Earlier in the *Ode*, the poet was complaining of his mental inertia, but here he is afraid of the stirring up of emotions. It appears that he fears human bonds and voluntarily withdraws from them. In the end, he cannot decide one way or another:

> Not that I mourn—O Friends, most dear! most true!
>   Methinks to weep with you
>   Were better far than to rejoice alone.
>   [The letter version, 255–57]

He then bursts again into complaint over his domestic life.

> But that my coarse domestic Life has known
> No Habits of heart-nursing Sympathy,
> No Griefs but such as dull and deaden me,
> No mutual mild Enjoyments of it's own,
> No Hopes of it's own Vintage, None, O! none—
> Whence when I mourn'd for you, my Heart might borrow
> Fair forms and living Motions for it's sorrow.
>   [The letter version, 258–64]

The poet is far from successful in suppressing his emotion and keeping sufficiently detached. As a result we see him wavering between a tendency to make emotional outbursts and a stoic, even ascetic, abstention from them. By thus tracing the development of the argument in the letter version, it now seems easier to see the logical location of the latter half of stanza 4: this section (265–71 in the letter version) immediately follows the passage we have been examining (249–64), but in the accepted version it is connected, after the omission of many lines, to the passage ending ". . . My shaping spirit of Imagination." In the context of the letter version, it is much easier to understand such much-discussed lines as "haply by abstruse research to steal / From my own nature all the natural man," which I shall examine in a moment.

We have been examining the meaning of the "afflictions" mentioned in the first half of the sixth stanza. From this we may proceed to examine Coleridge's concept of joy and dejection in more detail. In stanza 6, Coleridge says he does not care that "afflictions" rob him of "mirth." If we retrace for the moment the logical development of the preceding stanzas, we see that Coleridge first started with the description of the "dull pain" and "heartless mood"; then he stated that his "genial spirits fail"; at the next stage, he called his "genial spirits" "Joy" and gave ample description and definition. This "Joy" is not equivalent to "mirth" but is something more comprehensive than mere "mirth," and something vitally important. In this connection, E. H. Coleridge has written a significant passage:

> He called it joy, meaning thereby not mirth or high spirits, or even happiness, but a consciousness of entire and therefore well being, when the emotional and intellectual faculties are in equipoise.[32]

This statement seems to anticipate I. A. Richards's theory of a poetic activity as equipoise, equilibrium, or synthesis of the neural system.[33] Or again, the statement fits into Coleridge's own theory of

---

[32] Quoted by I. A. Richards, in *Coleridge on Imagination* (London, 1950), p. 150, n. 2.

[33] See I. A. Richards, *Principles of Literary Criticism* (London, 1926).

222 Implications of *Dejection: An Ode*

imagination as "the balance or reconciliation of opposite or discordant qualities" or "the whole soul of man" brought into activity.[34] But before running hastily to Coleridge's esthetic theory, it would be best to examine his references to his personal experiences.

In a passage such as the following we may perceive the critical moment of mental disintegration:

> Amid all these changes and humiliations and fears, the sense of the Eternal abides in me, and preserves unsubdued
> My chearful Faith that all which I endure
> Is full of Blessings!
> At times indeed I would fain be somewhat of a more tangible utility than I am, but so, I suppose, it is with all of us—one while cheerful, stirring, feeling in resistance nothing but a joy & a stimulus; another while drowsy, self-distrusting, prone to rest, loathing our Self-promises, withering our own Hopes, our Hopes, the vitality & cohesion of our Being![35]

For the integrity or equipoise implied by "the vitality & cohesion of our Being," Coleridge elsewhere uses the phrase "Quietness & Unity of Heart.[36] What matters is this sense of integral totality, not the physical afflictions themselves. Coleridge says something to this effect in several places:

> Pain is easily subdued compared with continual uncomfortableness—and the sense of stifled Power! . . .
> I work hard, I do the duties of common Life from morn to night, but verily 'I raise my limbs, like lifeless *Tools.*' The organs of motion and outward action perform their functions at the stimulus of a galvanic fluid applied by the *Will*, not by the spirit of Life that makes Soul and Body one.[37]
> . . . for my Case is a species of madness, only that it is a derangement, an utter impotence of the *Volition*, & not of the intellectual Faculties—[38]

---

[34] *Biographia Literaria*, 2: 12.
[35] Letter to Humphry Davy, December 2, 1800, *Collected Letters*, 1: 649.
[36] Letter to George Coleridge, October 2, 1803, ibid., 2: 1008.
[37] Coleridge, *Inquiring Spirit*, ed. Kathleen Coburn (London, 1951), no. 12, p. 37.
[38] Letter to Joseph Cottle, April 26, 1814, *Collected Letters*, 3: 477.

Illness never in the smallest degree affects my intellectual powers. I can *think* with all my ordinary vigour in the midst of pain: but I am beset with the most wretched and unmanning reluctance and shrinking from action. I could not upon such occasions take the pen in hand to write down my thoughts for all the wide world.[39]

In these passages Coleridge testifies to the fact that his physical sufferings are not destructive of thought. What is fatally destructive for him is the sense of disintegration of personality deriving from the suspension of will.

The *Ode* starts with a description of mental inertia, of deadening for the poet. What alone can animate nature is activity of mind, "Joy," or the sense of integral totality of mind, as dejection is the disintegration. Then Coleridge comes to speak of it in terms of imagination:

> But oh! each visitation
> Suspends what nature gave me at my birth,
> My shaping spirit of Imagination.
>
> [84–86]

The dejection crisis is nothing but the crisis of the imagination itself and to ask what dejection is, is at once to ask what imagination is. Fifteen years later Coleridge set forth a theory of imagination, but at least the rudimentary ideas are revealed in the *Ode*. The imagination is the power that perceives "the inanimate cold world" as vital and organic; to work it actively requires "the whole soul of man." It is, not merely the power of making a poem, but the power that covers the total activity of the poet's mind.

Those critics who read the *Ode* as the poet's farewell to his poetic power usually refer to the following lines:

> And haply by abstruse research to steal
> From my own nature all the natural man.
>
> [89–90]

---

[39] Coleridge, *The Table Talk and Omniana* (London, 1909), p. 140.

T. S. Eliot says of the lines:

> When I spoke of Coleridge as drugging himself with metaphysics I was thinking seriously of these his own words: "haply by abstruse research to steal from my own nature all the natural man." Coleridge was one of those unhappy persons—Donne, I suspect, was such another—of whom one might say, that if they had not been poets, they might have made something of their lives, might even have had a career; or conversely, that if they had not been interested in so many things, crossed by such diverse passions, they might have been great poets. It was better for Coleridge, as poet, to read books of travel and exploration than to read book of metaphysics and political economy.[40]

Did, then, Coleridge the metaphysician kill Coleridge the poet? Eliot seems inclined to say yes, and he might have found some justification in Coleridge's own remarks. About a year before the *Ode* appeared, Coleridge wrote to William Godwin:

> The Poet is dead in me—my imagination (or rather the Somewhat that had been imaginative) lies, like a Cold Snuff on the circular Rim of a Brass Candle-stick, without even a stink of Tallow to remind you that it was once cloathed & mitred with Flame.[41]

A few months after completing the *Ode* Coleridge wrote to Southey:

> As to myself, all my poetic Genius, if ever I really possessed any *Genius*, & it was not rather a mere general *aptitude* of Talent, & quickness in Imagination / is gone—and I have been fool enough to suffer deeply in my mind, regretting the loss—which I attribute to my long & exceedingly severe Metaphysical Investigations—& these partly to Ill-health, and partly to private afflictions which rendered any subject, immediately connected with Feeling, a source of pain & disquiet to me.[42]

[40] T. S. Eliot, *The Use of Poetry and the Use of Criticism* (London, 1933), p. 68.
[41] Letter to William Godwin, March 25, 1801, *Collected Letters*, 2: 714.
[42] Letter to Robert Southey, July 29, 1802, ibid., p. 831.

On the other hand, may we not suspect that in these passages Coleridge himself is confusing a causal with a temporal relation of "abstruse research" and the loss of poetic genius?

> I have been, during the last 3 months, undergoing a process of intellectual *exsiccation*. In my long Illness I had compelled into hours of Delight many a sleepless, painful hour of darkness by chasing down metaphysical Game—and since then I have continued the Hunt, till I found myself unaware at the Root of Pure Mathematics—and up that tall, smooth Tree, whose few poor Branches are all at it's very summit, am I climbing by pure adhesive strength of arms and thighs—still slipping down, still renewing my ascent.[43]

> After my return to Keswick I was, if possible, more miserable than before. . . . I found no comfort except in the driest speculations.[44]

The passages seem to me to imply that the "abstruse research" was not the cause of dejection, but rather a compensation Coleridge sought when he was already in the state of dejection, deprived of "Joy," of "vitality and cohesion of our Being," of "the Unity of Heart," of "volition," of "moral character," and so on. Even in such a state, Coleridge was at least capable of intellectual activity. But how painful it must have been to him we can imagine from this remark:

> . . . but all is vanity—I feel it more & more—all is vanity that does not lead to Quietness & Unity of Heart, and to the silent aweful idealess Watching of that living Spirit, & of that Life within us, which is the motion of that Spirit—that Life, which passeth all understanding.[45]

Eliot's remarks on lines 89–90 sound very authentic in giving a picture of Coleridge torn between metaphysical research and poetic creativity. But if we take a close look at the latter half of the sixth stanza, in which these lines are included, Eliot's remarks seem

[43] Letter to Godwin, March 25, 1801, ibid., pp. 713–14.
[44] Letter to Thomas Wedgwood, October 20, 1802, ibid., p. 875.
[45] Letters to George Coleridge, October 2, 1803, ibid., p. 1008.

strained. In the letter version, this section of the stanza does not continue directly from the preceding section. In between come six lines describing Coleridge's domestic misery and sixteen lines in which Coleridge addresses Sara Hutchinson as a comforter and mentions the lack of sympathy in his home. From this it may be assumed that the larger passage grew not so much from those abstract topics of a metaphysician inimical to a poet as from Coleridge's personal problem. Here the poet is trying to suppress, by absorbing himself in "abstruse research," his own affections as a "natural man" for Sara Hutchinson. There is a relevant notebook entry.

> A lively picture of a man, disappointed in marriage, & endeavouring to make a compensation to himself by virtuous & tender & brotherly friendship with an amiable Woman— the obstacles—the jealousies—the impossibility of it.—Best advice that he should as much as possible withdraw himself from pursuits of morals &c—& devote himself to abstract sciences.[46]

The complexities of "brotherly friendship with an amiable Woman" follow in the letter version. Its lines 184–85 read:

> Nay, wherefore did I let it haunt my Mind
> The dark distressful Dream!

These lines are preceded by a passage in which Coleridge mentions Sara's physical and mental sufferings, his wish to comfort her, and his lament over his inability to do so. Then he asks himself why he lets "the dark distressful Dream" haunt his mind. He changed this to:

> Hence, viper thoughts, that coil around my mind,
> Reality's dark dream!
>
> [94–95]

The significance of the metaphor "viper thoughts" emerges in a passage in one of Coleridge's later letters.

---

[46] *Notebooks*, 1: 1065 21.190 (December 1801). Similar patterns of a natural scene, withdrawal, and return may be found in numerous other poems. Cf. "The Eolian Harp," "To the Author of Poems," "Reflections on Having Left a Place of Retirement," "This Lime-Tree Bower My Prison," etc.

By the long long Habit of the accursed Poison my Volition (by which I mean the faculty *instrumental* to the Will, and by which alone the Will can realize itself—it's Hands, Legs, and Feet, as it were) was compleately deranged, at times frenzied, dissevered itself from the Will, & became an independent faculty: so that I was perpetually in the state, in which you may have seen paralytic Persons, who attempting to push a step forward in one direction are violently forced round to the opposite. I was sure that no ease, much less pleasure, would ensue: nay, was certain of an accumulation of pain. But tho' there was no prospect, no gleam of Light before, an indefinite indescribable Terror as with a scourge of ever restless, ever coiling and uncoiling Serpents, drove me on from behind.[47]

A similar terrible agitation may be found in the poet's address to the wind as a "mad Lutanist" making "Devil's yule," "Actor, perfect in all tragic sounds," and even "mighty Poet, e'en to frenzy bold!" The wind tells a story about

> the rushing of an host in rout,
> With groans, of trampled men, with smarting wounds—
> At once they groan with pain, and shudder with the cold!
>
> [111-13]

There comes, however, "a pause of deepest silence" followed by another kind of wind, which tells a different story, "the tender lay" of a child astray in the wilderness, "framed by Otway's self," or "by Edmund's self" as in the *Morning Post* version; "the tender lay" in the latter case being Wordsworth's "Lucy Gray," a poem that also treats disorientation.

In the final stanza of the accepted version, the poet turns to the Lady again. He entreats a good night's sleep for her and a cheerful morning:

> Joy lift her spirit, joy attune her voice;
> To her may all things live, from pole to pole,
> Their life the eddying of her living soul!
>
> [134-36]

[47] Letter to John J. Morgan, May 14, 1814, *Collected Letters*, 3: 489.

It is in terms of joy that the poet prays for her. The function of joy in attuning her voice is in keeping with the metaphor of music applied to joy in stanza 5. "Eddying" too is one of Coleridge's metaphors for joy, which we have already touched upon in relation to the description of joy incarnate in his children.[48]

5. The Aftermath

The dejection crisis reappears in some of Coleridge's later poems such as "Work without Hope" (1825) and "The Garden of Boccaccio" (1828). Also, as Kathleen Coburn remarks, "the emotional conflicts of 1802 emerge [in the notebooks] before and after Dejection."[49] One aspect of the dejection crisis is nostalgia for Sara Hutchinson:

> Indisposed in my Bowels—Observe that this Feeling of ⟨Bowel—⟩ uncomfortableness &c is combined with *Fear*, with *tender* Thoughts, tender & serious recollections—& if I were with one whom my Soul loved, it would rather increase than decrease my Happiness. . . . The rest of the walk I was deeply impressed by the Faith, that my Illness would not materially diminish my Happiness if I were Housemate with Love.[50]

A more direct personal reference to Sara Hutchinson is found in a lengthy description of his mental state in the notebook entry 1577 21.297 written on October 19, 1803, the day before his thirty-first birthday. Coleridge starts with the description of "Slanting Pillars of Light, like Ladders up to Heaven, their base always a field of vivid green Sunshine."[51] Then he moves on to the description of his mental state: "O me! my very heart dies!—This *year* has been one painful Dream / I have done nothing!" He goes on to express his sense of retarded work, mentioning "The Vision of the Maid of Orleans,"

---

[48] See above, p. 218.
[49] Note to the notebook entry 1185 6.160.
[50] *Notebooks*, 1: 1644 21.390 (November 7, 1803).
[51] Ibid., 1577 21.297 (October 19–20, 1803).

"The Dark Ladie," and *Christabel*. The second part of the same entry also begins a description of the gradually changing scenery outside. With the "Rain Storm" pelting against his study window, Coleridge suddenly turns to personal references:

> —[O Σαρα why am I] not happy! why have I not an un-
> encumbered Heart! these beloved Books still before me, this
> noble Room, the very centre to which a whole world of
> beauty converges, the deep reservoir into which all these
> streams & currents of lovely Forms flow—my own mind so
> populous, so active, so full of noble schemes, so capable of
> realizing them / this heart so loving, so filled with noble
> affection—O [Aσρα!] wherefore am I not happy! why for
> years have I not enjoyed one pure & sincere pleasure!—one
> full Joy!—one genuine Delight, that rings sharp to the Beat
> of the Finger!—
> †all cracked & dull with base Alloy!—. . .
>   †But still have said to the poetic Feeling when it has
> awak'd in the Heart—Go!—come tomorrow.

This is followed by a reference to the quarrel between the Fricker sisters, and the entry ends with the description of the weather:

> Storm all night—the wind scourging & lashing the rain, with
> the pauses of self-wearying Violence that returns to its wild
> work as if maddened by the necessity of the Pause⟩ I, half-
> dozing, list'ning to the same, not without solicitations of the
> poetic Feeling / for from † I have written, Oct. 20. 1803, on
> Thursday Morning, 40 minutes past 2° clock.

The pattern closely resembles that of the *Ode*: starting from a description of nature, moving into a description of a mental state, and ending with the description of nature again.

Another, rather curious instance of Coleridge's complaint of the mental torment of his unfulfilled feelings toward Sara Hutchinson raises a question.

> Why we two made to be a Joy to each other, Should for

many years constitute each other's melancholy—O! but the melancholy is Joy.[52]

Perhaps, as in the *Ode*, melancholy arises from emotional involvement, and the poet is pining and fretting. But this is better than mental inertia, and to this extent the melancholy is joy, productive of poetry. This paradoxical relationship is further generalized in another notebook entry.

> The still rising Desire still baffling the bitter Experience, the bitter Experience still following the gratified Desire.[53]

This passage seems to imply that joy and dejection endlessly alternate with each other.

The Ancient Mariner and *Christabel* also show Coleridge's awareness of man's corruptibility, of the ease with which he falls from joy to dejection. As a fallen creature, man is under the control of mutability, and although joy is a momentary vision of eternity, the vision is extremely transient. As a result Coleridge often seeks in vain to preserve the present moment, indulging himself in nostalgia.

> In extreme low Spirits, indeed it was downright despondency, as I was eating my morsel heartlessly, I thought of my Teeth of Teeth in general—the Tongue—& the manifest *means & ends* in nature / I cannot express what a manly comfort † religious resolves I derived from it—It was in the last Days of August, 1803.—I wish, I had preserved the very Day & hour.[54]

Already in Coleridge's earlier poems hope and memory were recurrent, key terms.[55] Hope seems to be the accumulation of desire. Since man is not free from mutability, and eternity is so far from him, only by hoping can he enjoy the illusion that he is allowed to attain to eternity, that he has overcome bitter experience. This is what Coleridge means in the first half of the sixth stanza of the *Ode*

[52] Ibid., 1394 8.122 (April–June 1803).
[53] Ibid., 1456 7.9 (August 23, 1803).
[54] Ibid., 1512 7.64 (September 1–11, 1803).
[55] See nn. 21 and 36, above.

(76–81). The blissful moment is so soon gone that it is enjoyed only in memory. Again, because man is fallen, he may hope or desire the wrong thing, and so end in bitterness. This is what Coleridge anticipated in such lines as "Ah Flowers! which Joy from Eden stole / While Innocence stood smiling by !"[56] In any event, the loss of hope is fatal to Coleridge.

> Painful Sensation and Loss of Hope=castration of the self-generating Organ of the Soul / —Continuousness a true Foliation.[57]

Dejection: An Ode is in a sense a dirge over the decline of Coleridge's "shaping spirit of Imagination" and his mental despondency. Yet it holds a potential for joy: the poet at least knows what joy is, and he wishes that the "Lady" would possess it. We might here recall such a phrase as "inly agonize mid fruitless joy" and the case of the Ancient Mariner, who experiences both dejection and joy throughout his voyage. This paradox derives from the fallen quality of man: he lives in a flux of time distinguished from eternity. His awareness of this fact is in itself torture; he tries to transcend this limitation, and he can aspire to eternity or a blissful moment. But it is so transient that he is driven back into the flux of time that is within reach of him, as a fallen being. This is the general significance of the pattern of Coleridge's "Joy" and "Dejection." The poet aspires to the transient moment of joy, but he is soon taken back to the state of dejection. In this sense he calls himself "a genuine *Tantalus*":

> I write melancholy, always melancholy: You will suspect that it is the fault of my natural Temper. Alas! no. —This is the great Occasion that my Nature is made for Joy—impelling me to Joyance—& I never, never can yield to it. —I am a genuine *Tantalus*—[58]

We see another Tantalus-like, vicious circle of aspiration turning to grief:

[56] "Absence" (1791), lines 11–12.
[57] *Notebooks*, 1: 1552 21.272 (October 1803).
[58] Ibid., 1609 21.369 (October 23, 1803).

When I am sad & sick, I'd fain persuade my heart, I do not wish to see you; but when my nature feels a vernal breeze, a gleam of sunshine, & begins to open, motions felt by me, & seen by none, for I still look sad; as the opening rose in its first opening seems shut, O then I *long* for you, till Longing turns to Grief—and I close up again, in [*sic*] despondent, sick at heart—[59]

Coleridge becomes more and more aware of what is wrong with his mental state. He regards his case as consisting in "the deepest Feeling of my Heart hid & wrapped up in the depth & darkness— solitary chaos—& solitariness—."[60] The statement casts a sidelight upon the significance of the Mariner's loneliness on the sea, on that of the "caverns measureless to man" through which the sacred river Alph ran "down to a sunless sea," and also on that of "the deep romantic chasm." Another entry written about the same period gives the picture of Coleridge at the nadir of his "Dejection":

With a deep groan from the Innermost of my Heart, in the feeling of self-humiliation, & a lively sense of my own weakness, & the distraction of my mind, which is indeed "always doing something else," I yet write down the names of Works that I have planned, in the order in which I wish to execute them, with a fervent prayer that I may build up in my Being enough of manly Strength & Perseverence to do one thing at a time—[61]

Amid such throes and hopes, Coleridge composed *Dejection: An Ode*. The poem reveals a man whose aspirations and sufferings kindled his imagination to produce a troubled, very human poetic expression of joy created from the experience of its loss, and of dejection created by a vision of joy.

---

[59] Ibid., 1669 21.404 (November 15–21, 1803).
[60] Ibid., 1670 16.72 (November 14–19, 1803).
[61] Ibid., 1646 21.392 (November 7–9, 1803).

The Education of George Gissing

Shigeru Koike

My life is richer a thousand times—aye a million times—
than six months ago. I am no longer ignorant of the best
things the world contains. It only now remains for me to go
to Greece, then I shall have all the groundwork of education.
The education itself must be the work of my life.[1]

George Gissing wrote these hopeful sentences to his sister from
Italy in 1888. How this short passage epitomizes all the aspirations,
and the frustrations, too, of Gissing's life. The education itself must
be the work of his life—and it *was*, in fact. But how much he had to
pay for it!

He seems to have been obsessed from his earliest days with the
notion that his "little life" should be "rounded" with persistent
study. A typical illustration of this can be found in a self-caricature
which, according to his sister Ellen, he drew at the age of fourteen.
He represented himself as "a hideous, round-backed figure sitting on
a high stool, and leaning over a very small table on which a large
volume is open entitled 'Ossian' "; and on the wall nearby hangs a
scroll with the motto "Perseverance." "This inscription 'Perseverance,' placed near these books, is significant as referring to the ex-

[1] *Letters of George Gissing to Members of His Family*, ed. Algernon and Ellen Gissing
(London, 1927), p. 269, December 31, 1888, to Ellen. Hereafter referred to as *Letters to
Family*.

traordinary persistence which, even at that early age, characterized his reading and studies in general."[2]

Here we may note the fact that the last articulate words we know to have been uttered by Gissing were "Patience, patience," murmured with a French accent on the day before his death at the age of forty-six, in a small village in southern France.[3] Indeed, his whole life proved to be nothing but a continuation of patience and perseverance: nothing but a hard struggle to educate himself, and other people, too. Can these desperate, and so often futile, exertions of Gissing really be explained only by his psychological idiosyncrasies or by the *Zeitgeist* of England in the nineteenth century, the age of strenuous life and popular enlightenment? A far better approach would be to follow each successive stage and aspect of his education—from the beginning, when he expressed his outlook on life with the boyish motto "Perseverance," to the end, when he recapitulated his life and work with a murmur of "Patience." So doing one may try to answer the paradoxical question: how did it come to pass that this man of perseverance and assiduity, so devoted to serious study and education, was denied the reward that the heroes of all popular success-in-life stories are sure to enjoy and found himself, after all, an obvious failure, alien to his own country, all *because of* his zeal for education?

In his diary entry for September 15, 1870, when he was still twelve years old, he gave the following extract from the book called *That's it, or Plain Teaching*, a present from his father, because he thought it "a fact worthy of attention":

> The number of eggs deposited by certain of the oviparous species of fish is enormous. The sole lays 100,000. The carp 200,000. The tench 400,000. The mackerel 500,000. The flounder 1,300,000. The cod 8,500,000. The salmon 20,000,000.[4]

[2] Ellen Gissing, "Some Personal Recollections of George Gissing," *Blackwood's Magazine*, 225 (May 1929): 658.
[3] *Letters to Family*, p. 398, Appendix A.
[4] Ibid., p. 6.

Of course it is a common thing for a studious boy to cram himself with a heap of dry information about some subject or other so that he may boast to his fellows of his own superiority. And little Gissing had, in fact, a strong inclination toward natural history, imbued and encouraged by his father, a dispensing druggist. Now, the mental state of young Godwin Peak may be identified, more or less, with that of the author as a little boy (we have every reason to believe this highly probable; for Gissing wrote, "Peak is myself—one phase of myself"[5]). And it seems as if the great zeal with which this precocious boy tried to collect information not necessarily useful for any practical purpose and to learn more from books than from life anticipated the tragic end his later intellectual development was bound for.

> Godwin devoured books, and had a remarkable faculty for gaining solid information on any subject that took his fancy. What might be the special bent of his mind one could not yet discover. . . . It might be feared that tastes so discursive would be disadvantageous to a lad who must needs pursue some definite bread-study, and the strain of self-consciousness which grew strong in him was again a matter for concern.[6]

From the first he loved study, not from any ulterior motives, but for its own sake. A liberal education, which might barely enable him to get his bread in the immediate future or to promote his social status— this, truly, was to be hoped for. The aspiration was rather snobbish, however, for a liberal education was too great a luxury for a youth of his class to be indulged with, and he could never afford to educate

---

[5] *The Letters of George Gissing to Eduard Bertz*, ed. Arthur C. Young (London, 1961), p. 153, May 20, 1892. Hereafter referred to as *Letters to Bertz*.

[6] George Gissing, *Born in Exile*, 3 vols. (London, 1892), 1: 51. Another character in whom "one phase" of the author manifests itself as strongly is Emily Hood; she also devours any book out of love of reading: "She had a passionate love of learning; all books were food for her. . . . The strange things she read, books which came down for her from the shelves [of the library] with a thickness of dust upon them; histories of Greece and Rome ('Not much asked for, these,' said the librarian), translations of old classics, the Koran, Mosheim's *Ecclesiastical History*, works of Swedenborg, all the poetry she could lay hands on, novels not a few. One day she asked for a book on *Gymnoblastic Hydroids*; the amazing title in the catalogue had filled her with curiosity; she must know the meaning of everything. She was not idle, Emily" (George Gissing, *A Life's Morning* [London, 1947], p. 78).

himself for education's sake. He knew as much from the painful case of his father, the very man under whose influence he entertained the pure love of study. A self-educated man, his father was fairly liberal-minded for a poor dispensing druggist in a country town; well read in literature, he was very fond of Tennyson and Dürer and possessed sufficient knowledge of botany to publish a little study on ferns. It is no doubt that George loved, respected, and took pride in him, and yet the son later recollected that he could not but be struck by some palpable evidence of his father's ignorance, especially about classical languages (he did not know that Greek and Latin poetry lacked rhyme).[7] Although understandable, these defects in the most important item of a liberal education must have appeared fatal to the son, because they clearly and ruthlessly showed the nature and the limit of his father's education, and most likely *his own*, so long as he should remain contented where he was.

So, he must get out of the environment he was born in, climb up the social ladder somehow or other, and get for himself a ticket of admission into the higher world where, he believed, the fullest scope could be allowed to his capacities. But how? The only way open for this intellectual snob would be to win some sort of scholastic distinction: "It was a great thing to learn what the past could teach, to set himself on the common level of intellectual men."[8] Here is the beginning of his illusion that intellectual power and books would surely help him with the promotion of his social status, or, in any event, with the conquest of the handicap he suffered from, carrying him over into a "room at the top," the world of an aristocracy, not of feudal, but of intellectual power, or "an aristocracy of *brains*,"[9] as he very often put it. Note how glad Godwin Peak felt to hear his brother call him an aristocrat:

By dubbing him aristocrat, Oliver had flattered him in the

[7] Jacob Korg, *George Gissing: A Critical Biography* (Seattle, 1963), p. 7. This account is based on the unpublished MS "Reminscence [*sic*] of My Father" in the Yale University Library.

[8] Gissing, *Born in Exile*, 1: 79.

[9] *Letters to Family*, p. 327, March 14, 1892, to Ellen. Note such similar expressions as "an Aristocracy of mind" (*Letters to Bertz*, p. 151, May 1, 1892), or "*intellectual aristocracy*" (*Letters to Bertz*, p. 172, June 2, 1893).

subtlest way. If indeed the title were justly his, as he instantly felt it was, the inference was plain that he must be an aristocrat of nature's own making—one of the few highly favoured beings who, in despite of circumstance, are pinnacled above mankind. In his ignorance of life, the boy visioned a triumphant career; an aristocrat *de jure* might possibly become one even in the common sense did he but pursue that end with sufficient zeal. And in his power of persistent endeavour he had no lack of faith.[10]

The inscription on the scroll, "Perseverance," assumed a grave significance; it was the first commandment for an intellectual aspirant eagerly awaiting deliverance from the nether world of the scullery to the glorious castle—the castle for Gissing being not in Spain but in ancient Italy and Greece. Thus began his education, or more accurately, what he convinced himself was his education, namely, the pursuit of intellectual prestige (the title of "an aristocrat *de facto* of brains"), which was carried on persistently, desperately. The young "pot-hunter," as he was called, made innumerable conquests at the boarding school and at Owens College, Manchester, until the fatal and inevitable disaster completely destroyed his future.

By the term "disaster," however, I am referring, not necessarily to his liaison with a young prostitute and his consequent thefts, but rather to the disillusionment and loss of self-confidence that stole over him amidst his apparently glorious academic career. At first, he had no doubt that he was steadily making his way to a definite goal, but soon enough his overly self-conscious mind could not help noticing his false position; he studied so hard—but from some ulterior motives, namely, to get over the class barrier and grasp the chance of study for its own sake. In short, his education must be a very *practical* one so that he might enjoy a *liberal* education on some far-off day. He could no longer be sure that the end justified the means. Worse still, neither the professors nor their lectures could satisfy his spiritual hunger. According to Morley Roberts, his college mate and lifelong friend, Morhampton College in those days was not a uni-

[10] *Born in Exile*, 1: 64.

versity in the strict sense of the word, but "could only be regarded, for a boy of his [Maitland's, that is, Gissing's] culture, as a stepping-stone to one of the older universities, probably Cambridge."[11]

> [Godwin Peak] understood that college learning could not be an end in itself, that the Professors to whom he listened either did not speak out all that was in their minds, or, if they did, were far from representing the advanced guard of modern thought. With eagerness he at length betook himself to the teachers of philosophy and of geology. Having paid for these lectures out of his own pocket, he felt as if he had won a privilege beyond the conventional course of study, an initiation to a higher sphere of intellect. The result was disillusion.[12]

On the other hand, there were many students around him who, scornful of the teachers and quite indifferent to the college instruction, had about them an air of culture and refinement which they had acquired without effort as a natural and genuine fruit of the liberal education they had enjoyed. It was true that they were of much lower rank in the academic competition, but he felt himself inferior to them:

> . . . he often regarded with bitter envy those of his fellow-students who had the social air, who conversed freely among their equals, and showed that the pursuits of the College were only a part of their existence. . . . Some of them Godwin could not but admire, so healthful were they, so bright of intellect, and courteous in manner,—a type distinct from any he had formerly observed.[13]

However hard he might try, he could scarcely expect to be on the same level with them, to win the title of "an intellectual aristocrat *de facto*"; the most he could wish for was to become "an intellectual

---

[11] Morley Roberts, *The Private Life of Henry Maitland* (London, 1958), p. 28. This book is a biography of Gissing in the guise of fiction, every person and place given a fictitious, but easily identifiable, name: e.g., George Gissing as Henry Maitland, Owens College as Morhampton.

[12] Gissing, *Born in Exile*, 1: 80–81.

[13] Ibid.

aristocrat *parvenu.*" His incessant study with "perseverance" had, instead of helping him to overcome the handicap, served only to make it greater and to make him aware that education meant more than mere persistent study of books.

This revelation must have been most crushing. The many prizes and scholarships he had won must have seemed to be but vain trophies, and perhaps he even lost his confidence in education itself, his last resort. But then, what else could he have to believe in and live for? Hitherto he had been so arrogant and sure of himself, so far above the other students, and his professors for that matter, that he studied for himself and by himself nothing but "what the past could teach him," never doubting the moral support that books would give him. He had no chance, or rather could not afford, to have his mind cultivated through personal contact with friends and teachers who might have subdued his arrogance and undeceived him of the illusion. These circumstances well explain the fact that, always lonely and avoiding his fellow students, he sought human companionship in a poor girl in the street and, short of the money to save her from the slough, committed many thefts in the common room and the locker room. Such desperate conduct could be ascribed to his sexual and psychological idiosyncrasies, his inferiority complex, his shyness with or rather abhorrence of women of ordinary middle-class families, his idealism and lack of practical sense, and so on. That is no doubt true, to some extent. But he was *not* of abnormal mind. If he had not been aware of the futility of his education, he might have known better; he might have pursued his studies for some practical purpose, or even from some worldly motives. As it was, he could entertain no hope for "room at the top" and, what was worse still, he had grown too proud to be content with the original circumstances he was born in, having already eaten some fruit of temptation. Thus he found himself belonging nowhere, an exile in both the social and the spiritual senses of the word—one of "the unclassed," as he later put it.[14]

---

[14] By this term Gissing meant "not the *déclassés* but rather those persons who live in a limbo external to society, and refuse the statistic badge" (George Gissing, *The Unclassed*, new rev. ed. [London, 1895], author's preface).

In this sense he may be said to anticipate the tragedy of Leonard Bast, the humble clerk, mere scum in the flux of modern London, whom E. M. Forster introduced in *Howards End*.

> He felt that . . . if he kept on with Ruskin, and the Queen's Hall Concerts, and some pictures by Watts, he would one day push his head out of the grey waters and see the universe. He believed in sudden conversion, a belief which may be right, but which is peculiarly attractive to a half-baked mind. . . . But of a heritage that may expand gradually, he had no conception: he hoped to come to Culture suddenly, much as the Revivalist hopes to come to Jesus.[15]

So it was inevitable that Gissing was soon struck by the barrier between himself and the refined world which he could never rise to, "not if he read for ten hours a day."[16]

> Oh, it was no good, this continual aspiration. Some are born cultured; the rest had better go in for whatever comes easy. To see life steadily and to see it whole was not for the likes of him.[17]

What he could do was to find compensation in taking a condescending attitude toward Jacky, his wife, who came of an even lower and further morally degraded class and whom he promised never to forsake.

I do not know whether E. M. Forster had Gissing in mind in portraying Leonard Bast, nor do I think that Leonard is among the most important characters in *Howards End*. But the comparison of Gissing with Forster, which I will return to later, would be well worth further study.[18] What Gissing reveals to us is the real destination of the spiritual self-education of an aspiring youth: his only reward is futility and alienation, quite contrary to the gospel of

---

[15] *Howards End* (New York, 1944), p. 57.
[16] Ibid., p. 64.
[17] Ibid.
[18] But I have seen only a few casual allusions to the resemblance, the earliest of which was made by William Plomer in his introduction to Gissing's *A Life's Morning* (London, 1947): "*The Whirlpool*, which a little foreshadows *Howards End*" (p. 16).

many success-in-life novels or of Samuel Smiles's *Self-Help*, the educational Bible of an age of strenuous life. And such alienation following upon disillusionment with education is a problem that we university people in the twentieth century are now compelled to recognize with graver significance. Besides, he reveals it to us, in terms not of social issues but of those human relationships Forster regards as the essential theme of his novels.

One instance of such human relationships, or rather of failure in, or the absence of them, is shown in that very interesting short story "A Lodger in Maze Pond," which deals with a man foolish enough to be married twice to a poor, uneducated girl of the lower class, just like the author himself. His remark sounds as if it were made by Leonard Bast: "Unfortunately I am not a rascal: I can't think of girls as play-things; a fatal conscientiousness in an unmarried man of no means."[19] This "fatal conscientiousness" can be replaced by some other phrase, namely, his wish, or rather obsession, to *educate* a poor girl—to develop her natural and dormant disposition. He thought "he would educate" his first wife because "she had excellent dispositions";[20] and—though he had to pay so dearly for his foolish attempt —after the death of his first wife, he could not help proposing marriage to another girl of much the same position as the first, "making plans for the future—for her education, and so on."[21]

In fact, driven by the emotional desolation described previously, Gissing tried to reclaim a young prostitute, Marianne Helen (Nelly) Harrison, and gave her the money with which she might buy a sewing machine and get an honest living; finally he *promised to marry her,* as if that were one item in his system of education! Did he, having failed in educating himself, wish to find compensation in the successful results of the education he gave her? A victim of a "Cophetua complex,"[22] he was now as eager and patient as ever to carry out his

[19] George Gissing, *The House of Cobwebs* (New York, 1906), p. 259.
[20] Ibid., p. 248.
[21] Ibid., p. 262.
[22] Of course there is no such term in textbooks of psychoanalysis, and I have only once come across it, in Graham Greene's *The End of the Affair*: "I don't know whether

mission of enlightenment in somebody inferior to him both socially and intellectually, somebody whom he could educate as he would like to, so that he might enjoy vicarious satisfaction, and from whom he might expect the gratitude due to a savior. But here again, he was mistaken. Only disappointment awaited him.

And that was not surprising; for his was the most foolish way to reclaim such a woman, since it served only to make her more conscious of her own inferiority and to create a serious gap between them, as he later realized and showed in the scenes between Arthur Golding and Carrie Mitchell in his first novel, *Workers in the Dawn*. Yet, he seems no more cured of his obsessive sentimentalism about education than the hero of "A Lodger in Maze Pond," and after deliverance from his first wife, for whom he suffered so much and so long, he found another uneducated girl of the working class, Edith Underwood, who, he hoped, would satisfy his passions, sexual and educational, at once. See how he described her: "The girl is peculiarly gentle and pliable, with a certain natural refinement which seems to promise that *she might be trained to my kind of life.*"[23] Of course he was too optimistic in his hope of a new education, and there is no need to give a full account of their tragic married life. But, to do her justice, she was no hypocrite; she did not pretend to be gentle and pliable enough to be trained successfully in his system. It was Gissing who failed in realistic insight, who was the more to blame. I venture a conjecture (a very tenuous one, I admit) that if he had not tried to educate his two wives at all, or if he had known a suitable way to educate them, one, at least, might have become a gentle wife, or a less abominable shrew. Nelly might have had re-

---

psychologists have yet named the Cophetua complex, but I have always found it hard to feel sexual desire without some sense of superiority, mental or physical" (New York, 1957, p. 27). George Meredith wrote fine comedies introducing a number of such male characters, for example, Sir Willoughby.

    [23] *Letters to Bertz*, pp. 115–16, January 23, 1891; italics added. We can see how he found her, in his own words, as later addressed to Gabrielle Fleury, his third wife: "In recklessness (of course *criminal* recklessness) I offered marriage to the first girl I happened to meet—and the result was what might have been expected." (*The Letters of George Gissing to Gabrielle Fleury*, ed. Pierre Coustillas [New York, 1964], p. 29, August 1898. Hereafter referred to as *Letters to Fleury*.)

course to drink less often, and Edith might have had fewer fits of madness. As it was, his attempts were misguided.

Emily Hood, the somewhat idealized heroine of *A Life's Morning* and governess of ten-year-old twin sisters did know how to make a successful impression on her pupils.

> The twins were not remarkably fond of their lessons, but in Emily's hands they became docile and anxious to please. She had the art of winning their affection without losing control over them. . . . The twins were in truth submitting to the force of character. They felt it without understanding what it meant.[24]

This would be the best way to educate innocent children, and for that matter ignorant wives, if their education were necessary. But this seems to be what Gissing was quite incapable of. We know of several instances of his behavior in private tuition, two of which bear mention here: one is a little scene between him and Frederic Harrison's two sons, whom he once tutored, and the other is an extract from his letters to his brothers and sisters.

As one of these two sons, Austin Harrison, bore witness, Gissing was a very gentle, patient, and impressive teacher like Emily Hood, loved and respected by his pupils, who were "lazy and impish enough."[25]

> At first we behaved abominably and once started singing, but he stopped that summarily by suddenly rising and quitting the house—without a word but with a look that appalled us. We rushed out into the street and implored him to return, yet he was adamant. After that we were much better behaved. I can distinctly recall *how pathetic* he seemed to me.[26]

He succeeded, however, in making his naughty pupils repentant

[24] Gissing, *A Life's Morning*, p. 52.
[25] Austin Harrison, "George Gissing," *Nineteenth Century and After*, 69 (September 1906): 460.
[26] Austin Harrison, *Frederic Harrison: Thoughts and Memories* (London, 1927), p. 82; italics added.

244 The Education of George Gissing

not by "the force of character," but by his "pathetic" look, which would move only those who happened to have intelligence and delicate feelings. Under less fortunate and more common circumstances, if the teacher had revealed his weakness and gone out with a pathetic look, it would probably have made pupils (who can be very callous) still more triumphant. To be convinced of that, we have only to read the seventh chapter of *David Copperfield*, where we find the gentle nature and pathetic weakness of Mr. Mell, the teacher, taken advantage of and made a laughing matter by a bullying boy, Steerforth.

Gissing seems to have been well aware that such a demonstration of weakness would not do for women; for he described the awful scene between Edwin Reardon, another alter ego, and his wife Amy, who refuses to live with him, in response to his humiliating suggestion that he earn a livelihood as a petty clerk because he cannot go on writing the novel.

> He lost control of himself; Amy's last reply went through him like an electric shock, and for the moment he was a mere husband defied by his wife, the male stung to exertion of his brute force against the physically weaker sex. . . .
>
> He had but to do one thing: to seize her by the arm, drag her up from the chair, dash her back again with all his force— there, the transformation would be complete, they would stand towards each other on the natural footing. With an added curse perhaps—
>
> Instead of that, he choked, struggled for breath, and shed tears.
>
> Amy turned scornfully away from him. Blows and a curse would have overawed her, at all events for the moment; she would have felt: "Yes, he is a man, and I have put my destiny into his hands." His tears moved her to a feeling cruelly exultant; they were the sign of her superiority. It was she who should have wept, and never in her life had she been further from such display of weakness.[27]

[27] George Gissing, *New Grub Street* (London, 1927), p. 206.

Though he was fair enough to describe Amy, not as a vulgar and ignorant shrew, but as a well-educated and affectionate woman of intellect and refinement who loved her husband, Gissing knew very well that in his century the most effective way "to train a wife to his kind of life," as he put it, was to impress her with "the force of character," or, if necessary, to treat her as Mr. Murdstone, stepfather of David Copperfield and man of "firmness," did his wife;[28] and yet he knew as well that he was too weak and delicate-minded to hold absolute control over her.[29] So, little as we know about the particulars of his married life with Nelly and Edith, we are hardly confident that he was a very competent teacher for those women a great deal coarser and less educated and educable than Amy Reardon.

Compared with these obvious failures, he was more successful with his brothers and sisters. He felt himself responsible for their mental cultivation after his father's death, when he was still thirteen years old. He sent them many letters giving them encouragement and admonitions as to their study. In some of them, especially in those to his sisters, we can very often hear the somewhat priggish and patronizing tone of a preparatory school teacher. Here is one example among many.

> There is nothing worse than desultory reading, without any definite object. Always say to yourself, now I will confine my reading to certain subjects—pretty nearly—till I have a good idea of it. Then, in reading English Poetry—of which

---

[28] "David," he said, making his lips thin, by pressing them together, "if I have an obstinate horse or dog to deal with, what do you think I do?"

"I don't know."

"I beat him . . . I make him wince, and smart. I say to myself, 'I'll conquer that fellow'; and if it were to cost him all the blood he had, I should do it." (*The Oxford Illustrated Dickens* [Oxford, 1947], p. 46.)

[29] Cf. "Could he [Bernard Kingcote] from the first have borne himself like a man . . . then he might have held her [Isabel Clarendon] his own. But that was requiring of him to be another than he was. . . . His passion was that of a woman" (George Gissing, *Isabel Clarendon*, 2 vols. [London, 1886], 2: 229). As for Gissing's attitudes to women, see John Middleton Murry's excellent essay "George Gissing" (in *Katherine Mansfield and Other Literary Studies* [London, 1959]), where Murry compares Gissing's with D. H. Lawrence's. The comparison is altogether convincing. See also Pierre Coustillas, "Gissing's Feminine Portraiture," *English Literature in Transition*, 6 (October 1963): 130–41.

I devoutly hope and trust you read a good deal—don't skip from Chaucer to Tennyson, and from Shakespeare to Crabbe; but read all the principal authors of one period taking for your guide a book like the little Stopford Brooke primer.[30]

In the following, however, we can hear the voice of his truer feelings.

If a girl is to be made a teacher it is certainly right that she should pass examinations; but, as a mere feature in education, I see little good to be effected by these tests. A girl's education should be of a very general and liberal character, adapted rather to expand the intelligence as a whole than to impart very thorough knowledge on any subject.[31]

Anyway, both of his sisters did become teachers and afterward began their school at Wakefield, thus fulfilling their brother's expectation that they should rise above other "quarter-educated" women of their own class. But were they really "emancipated" in the spiritual and intellectual senses of the word, as he would have liked some heroines of his novels to be? Did they enjoy the fruit of a liberal education and turn out to be women in whom he could take vicarious pleasure as the successful achievement of his educational system? Ironically enough, only its negative and less constructive side seems to have taken effect; for, having taken from their mother a provincially rigid moral sense, the Gissing sisters were hardly initiated into their brother's intellectual sphere—especially Margaret, the more obstinately pious, who never could or would understand the free-thinking, provocative thoughts expressed in her brother's novels.[32]

---

[30] *Letters to Family*, p. 54, January 13, 1880, to Margaret. Compare also: "I hope she [Margaret] will choose one or two good books (such as Macaulay) and read them slowly and carefully. I should also advise her to do a little *every* day at French; that is very important" (*Letters to Family*, pp. 75–76, June 20, 1880, to sisters), and "Don't read *too* many novels, but try to know all the best; you should get hold of Jane Austen's novels, they are very healthy" (*Letters to Family*, p. 76, June 25, 1880, to Margaret).

[31] *Letters to Family*, pp. 72–73, May 30, 1880, to Algernon.

[32] "Apropos of 'Born in Exile,' Madge writes to me: 'It is a pity you should write on a subject you so little understand as Christianity.—It would be as reasonable for me to deny the existence of all the beautiful things you have seen & told me of in foreign countries, simply because *I* have not seen them, as it is for you to deny spiri-

And yet, on the other hand, they underwent his brainwashing thoroughly enough to believe themselves too highly educated to be satisfied with the social class to which they belonged and to be destined for anything but the bleak and solitary life of single-blessedness. It may be said, however, that his educational zeal had its reward; for they remained always loyal to him during and after his lifetime, and particularly Ellen, the more "gentle and pliable," felt very grateful for his guidance. Resenting the title of "a mere prig" wrongly given to him, she wrote in 1927:

> His knowledge was no mere affectation, and his desire to instruct others was free from all thought of self: let it but be necessary to help some fumbler in learning, though it were but one step on the way, and all else was forgotten in the wish to be of use. No pains were spared, no patience was too great, so long as the glance of intelligence in the eye of the listener showed that his words had been understood.[33]

She seems quite sure that she at least could understand his words; but was it really so? The implications of her misunderstanding of his idea of education and of his novel *The Emancipated* are our next concern.

The surest way to enjoy the satisfactory results of one's guidance, or to see that "glance of intelligence in the eye of the listener," lies in the creation of imaginary people, and therefore it is quite natural that this recurrent and obsessive theme of education can be detected

---

tual things you have never seen or felt, when there are thousands of people who have seen them, & are therefore as certain of them as of their own existence. How anyone can disbelieve the Bible merely because it is not written in the latest scientific language seems remarkable.' How impossible to reply to such stuff as this!" (*George Gissing's Commonplace Book*, ed. Jacob Korg [New York, 1962], p. 48). It seems that she read "some dirty little pietistic work" during her holidays with George in the Channel Islands (*Diary*, August 25, 1889, quoted in *Letters to Bertz*, p. 71, footnote). See also the very interesting passages where Gissing describes his mother and sisters (*Letters to Fleury*, p. 54, August 30, 1898).

[33] Ellen Gissing, "George Gissing: A Character Sketch," *Nineteenth Century and After*, 102 (September 1927): 418–19.

throughout Gissing's novels. *Workers in the Dawn*, his first novel, already anticipated the *Leitmotif* of some of his later, more important works, in the sense that the process of mental formation and development of its hero and heroine takes a very prominent part in the novel, so that it may be called a novel of adolescence, or a *Bildungsroman*, rather than a novel of social comment. Though so many elements coexist in this work that it gave Mrs. Frederic Harrison the impression that there was "enough stuff in the book to make six novels,"[34] it may safely be said that its main theme is not so much any social problem, general or particular, as the record of its leading characters' "Mind-growth" (which is the title of one of the most important chapters, vol. 1, ch. 14, where Helen Norman, the heroine, gives us through her diary an account of her mental development during her philosophical studies at the University of Tübingen). There is, for example, the hero's dilemma in choosing between two causes, namely, allegiance to social reformation or to the pursuit of artistic beauty (vol. 1, ch. 11, "A Double Life");[35] or the revelation made to Helen by Strauss's *Leben Jesu*, and her doubt of, and "Emancipation" (the title of vol. 1, ch. 13) from, the conventional Christian dogmas with which she had been brought up. Reflecting the author's idea of education, here it means, not instruction of the ignorant mass in the practical information useful for its present work or for promotion to a higher social class,[36] but the spiritual education of the chosen few, "an aristocracy of *brains*." It is also characteristic of his mind that the educations of the hero and the heroine both result in tragic frustration: in the case of the former because of his circumstances and what they lead him to, namely, his moral breakdown—the doom that kept its strong hold upon the author himself and a number of the male characters he created; and in the case of the latter because she could not go through the purgatory of love by which, the author be-

---

[34] *Letters to Family*, p. 79, July 23, 1880, to Algernon. The letter contains a copy of Frederic Harrison's letter.

[35] About this dilemma, see Jacob Korg's "Division of Purpose in George Gissing," *Publications of the Modern Language Association*, 70 (June 1955): 323–36.

[36] Such attempts, if ever made, always end in failure; the evening class organized by Egremont in *Thyrza* is one of the most typical illustrations.

lieved, the true spiritual emancipation of woman could be accomplished, though this consummation of female education was rarely attained even in his imaginary realm.

One of the rare cases where it was attained is that of Miriam Baske, the heroine of *The Emancipated*. The young widow of an industrial potentate, a woman reared under the strictest of puritanical codes, after her husband's death Miriam leaves her sordid Midland industrial town for a vacation in Italy, where, though feeling at first as if in exile,[37] she experiences a most remarkable revelation, just as the people from Sawston do there in some of E. M. Forster's novels. But, while in Forster's work the agent of such revelations is contemporary Italy, the Italians, their real life, or even some mystic power, a *genius loci*, as he prefers to call it, Gissing prefers that a spiritual education be given to the uninitiated woman by an intelligent Englishman like the author himself. In the ninth chapter of Forster's *Where Angels Fear to Tread*, where Philip and Miss Abott (who have come from the civilized community of England) are involved in the shocking scene with Gino, an Italian very crude but full of vitality, the English undergo a wonderful metamorphosis of mind through personal contact with the Italian. And when Lucy, the heroine of *A Room with a View*, sees an unknown Italian stabbed to death in a scuffle on the street in Florence and faints, "something" does happen to her. A quite new phase of life opens, in which she can understand a world and people different from those she has been accustomed to: "It was not exactly that a man had died; something had happened to the living: they [Lucy and George, who held her in his arms] had come to a situation where character tells, and where Childhood enters upon the branching paths of Youth."[38] But in *The Emancipated* Ross Mallard, a middle-aged painter, teaches Miriam in "exile" to love and appreciate Italy and her people, not as it really is or as they really are, but for its classical associations and its cultural heritage.

[37] After calling her past life in the Midland community a "real life," Miriam says in her letter, "I feel it [her stay in Naples] as exile" (George Gissing, *The Emancipated* [London, 1895], p. 5).

[38] E.M. Forster, *A Room with a View* (Harmondsworth, Mddx., 1947), p. 59.

"Don't you like to watch those animals?" [said Mallard, looking at a yoke of oxen drawing a cart along the street in Rome.] "I can never be near them without stopping. Look at their grand heads, their horns, their majestic movement! They always remind me of the antique—of splendid power fixed in marble. These are the kind of oxen that Homer saw, and Virgil."

Miriam gazed, but said nothing.

"Does your silence mean that you can't sympathize with me?"

"No. It means that you have given me a new way of looking at a thing; and I have to think."[39]

Thus, the revelation comes to the uninitiated woman, not through intuition or through some mysterious medium (the brightness of the Italian sky "mesmerized" Lucy),[40] but through an argument that made her feel she had "to think," in other words, in the course of "Learning and Teaching" (the title of vol. 2, ch. 7) about the topics of classical literature and art. The novel closes when Miriam symbolically gives up her original plan to hallow the name and memory of her late husband by building a chapel and offering it to her community and when, fully emancipated, she marries her teacher, Mallard, thus realizing Gissing's idea of the Bildungsroman, that a woman's maturity should be attained by "an education into love, conceived and experienced as an identity or interfusion of the spiritual and the physical."[41]

Gissing's sister Ellen seems to have disapproved of this book, suspecting that her brother had made use of her as the model for Miriam,[42] but since she could not (nor could Margaret, for that matter) experience the purgatory of love and enjoy that crowning moment of education as Miriam could, it is a tragic irony that she, quite ignorant of this crucial difference, and failing to understand the the true meaning of *the* education as her brother used that term, com-

[39] Gissing, *The Emancipated*, p. 322.
[40] Forster, *A Room with a View*, p. 54.
[41] Murry, "George Gissing," p. 68.
[42] Korg, *Gissing: A Critical Biography*, p. 149.

mitted the stupid error of identifying herself with the heroine. It appears that "his words" could *not* be understood even by one most intimate with him. It would be very interesting to know how she reacted to the fortune of two other female characters—one, Maud Enderby in *The Unclassed*, whose love is frustrated because of her religious fanaticism, or rather fatalism; the other, Jessica Morgan, a poor victim of the sham intellectual emancipation of women, whom Gissing describes so ruthlessly:

> She talked only of the "exam," of her chances in this or that "paper," of the likelihood that this or the other question would be "set." Her brain was becoming a mere receptacle for dates and definitions, vocabularies and rules syntactic, for thrice-boiled essence of history, ragged scraps of science, quotations at fifth hand, and all the heterogeneous rubbish of a "crammer's" shop. When away from her books, she carried scraps of paper, with jottings to be committed to memory. Beside her plate at meals lay formulae and tabulations. She went to bed with a manual and got up with a compendium.[43]

Emily Hood's case is a very ambiguous one; she is saved from barren intellectual asceticism by the love of Wilfred Athel, an intelligent young man brought up in a sphere of liberal culture, and by such means her spiritual education is brought to consummation. But, as we know, the present version is the result of reluctant revision forced on the author by James Payne, reader for Smith & Elder (one is reminded of the end of *Great Expectations*, changed by Dickens at Edward Bulwer Lytton's suggestion), and Gissing's original intention was, perhaps, to make the story a chronicle of the "mind-growth" and frustration of an intellectual young woman, who, like Godwin Peak and the author himself, must eventually find herself alien both to her lover's world and to her own original environment —in a spiritual exile to which she has been driven by the education she got "by hook or by crook."[44] As such, *A Life's Morning*, together

---

[43] George Gissing, *In the Year of Jubilee* (New York, 1895), p. 15.
[44] Gissing, *A Life's Morning*, p. 77. But her asceticism has none of Maud Enderby's religious aspect. "The vulgarities of hysterical pietism Emily had never known; she

with *Born in Exile*, may be one of Gissing's finest Bildungsromane. The Bildungsroman, when introduced from eighteenth-century Germany, had a very peculiar reception in England.[45] Some novelists (for example, Bulwer Lytton) made such a superficial use of this design of fiction that the original theme of the hero's spiritual education was confused with, and finally replaced by, the more practical idea of training for success in life. This process was, perhaps, intentional on the part of the author, who wished to make the philosophical design borrowed from the Continent more congenial to his own taste and to that of the contemporary reading public of England as well. Gissing was, then, one of the few novelists with the insight to purge the practical English version of the Bildungsroman of its shallow utilitarian moral and to reestablish its original and genuine function, namely, the pursuit of the "mind-growth" and spiritual education of its principal character. But the rather optimistic conception of the original Bildungsroman developed by the German men of letters in the Enlightenment had to disappear, and the artist was now confronted with the fact that the cultivation of mind leads an intellectual and conscientious man in modern society to the awareness of being lost in the abyss of doubt, tormented with everlasting dilemmas and frustrations, and finally condemned to an exile at once spiritual and physical. As William York Tindall begins his survey of modern British literature with the chapter titled "Exile," referring to *New Grub Street* to illustrate the general literary situation discussed there,[46] such crucial issues as the modern novelists (e.g., Henry James, James Joyce, and Thomas Mann) were later to deal with were already recognized and made by Gissing the most important theme of the Bildungsroman. His *Born in Exile* should be referred

---

did not fear the invasion of such blight as that" (p. 80). She also experiences much the same dilemma as Arthur Golding between the aspiration toward the Palace of Art and the renunciation of it.

[45] But in my opinion what may be called the germ of the Bildungsroman was already detected in the picaresque novels that flourished in eighteenth-century England and France (such as the works by Lesage and Smollett). This point is discussed in my book *Shiawasena Tabibitotachi* [The Fortunate Travelers] (Tokyo, 1962).

[46] *Forces in Modern British Literature: 1885–1956* (New York, 1947), p. 4.

to again, therefore, as the zenith in a series of Bildungsromane begun with *Workers in the Dawn*.

Born in Exile is the record of a youth who was ambitious for a "room at the top," like many of his brothers from Julien Sorel to Joe Lampton, and whose aspiration to educate himself was identified with the wish to get a woman of a class higher than his own.

> "I have no other ambition in life—no other! Think the confession as ridiculous as you like; my supreme desire is to marry a perfect refined woman. Put it in the correct terms: I am a plebeian, and I aim at marrying a lady."[47]

But it is the record not of the practical stratagems and conquests he made but of the mental agonies he suffered; there are as little action and as much argument here as in *Crime and Punishment*, a psychological detective novel, as it is often called, and one that Gissing liked.[48] And, needless to say, all Godwin Peak's ambitions came to nothing; he could find no community for him to belong to in his own country, and, when he left "a social sphere where he must ever be an alien,"[49] he could not find any spiritual shelter abroad. While Miriam Baske's education could bear fruit in Italy, where, though feeling at first as if in "exile," she was awakened to classical beauty by her spiritual teacher and emancipator, *his* could not, even in exile. Expatriation meant to him nothing positive or regenerative but a mere continuation of and, perhaps, the last straw in, his endless frustration. "Dead, too, in exile! . . . Poor old fellow!"[50]—these last words of the novel were, of course, addressed to the hero, Godwin Peak, but do they not seem to allude to the fate of many other heroes and heroines of the modern Bildungsromane written by Gissing and later by twentieth-century writers? And do they not also apply to

[47] Gissing, *Born in Exile*, 1: 223.
[48] As for the influence of *Crime and Punishment* and other novels by the writers of the Continent on Gissing, see Jacob Korg's "The Spiritual Theme of George Gissing's *Born in Exile*," in *From Jane Austen to Joseph Conrad*, ed. Robert Rathburn and Martin Steinman, Jr. (Minneapolis, 1958), and Korg's *Gissing: A Critical Biography*, pp. 171–72.
[49] Gissing, *Born in Exile*, 1: 84.
[50] Ibid., 3: 270.

the fate of the author himself, whose obsessive intellectual zeal was to end blighted, without any fruit, or root?

For Gissing's real life very often imitated fictitious art, and some events and situations in his novels were followed by those in his later life as the last stage of his education. The most striking instance was that Godwin Peak's dream to marry a woman of refinement came true, and Gissing did in fact experience the "frantic exultation" of Edwin Reardon, who "had always regarded the winning of a beautiful and intellectual wife as the crown of a successful literary career."[51] He at long last found the ideal woman, one intellectually equal to him, and won her love. His letters to Gabrielle Fleury are marked by a passionate tone that we had been led to expect from the mouths or pens of people in his novels, but hardly from himself. At all events, such a strong outburst of personal emotion and sanguine hope shows itself nowhere in his letters to his family or to his German friend Bertz. Gissing finally seemed almost sure that the crowning moment of his lifelong education was coming to him.

> I believe that you will make of me a far better man, intellectually and morally, than I could ever otherwise be; and I believe that you, my sweet, will find a freer development of all your beautiful and noble qualities than would be possible if you did not marry me.[52]

But what most surprises us is that he was so modest here that he dared neither try to train her to his kind of life, as he had done with his former wives, nor offer her that intellectual guidance in which he had so often indulged himself with his sisters.

> Darling, I should think it impertinent to say that you must not read this or that. . . . You are my intellectual equal, Gabrielle, and I shall *never* presume to dictate to you in such matters.[53]

[51] Gissing, *New Grub Street*, p. 56.
[52] *Letters to Fleury*, p. 69, October 1, 1898.
[53] Ibid., p. 91, December 24, 1898.

He refrained even from encouraging her to master the classical languages, an indispensable part, in his mind, of a liberal education, for want of which he had been almost ashamed of his own father.

> Don't grieve, dear, that the old languages are unknown to you. As I said, life is so short, and the knowledge you already possess is far more than enough for our intellectual communion. It delights me that you know many things of which I am ignorant. You will often be my teacher. In one thing—all that concerns the higher life of the soul—I shall always be your pupil.[54]

In Gissing's words, the comparison of teacher and pupil is more than mere lover's nonsense; but here we see that the table was turned and the "learning and teaching" relationship between Mallard and Miriam was just reversed—it was *he* who was to learn and *she* to teach in the actual realization of his ideal scheme of an education into love. That, however, does not necessarily mean that he was ever after to be subjected to Gabrielle; she was not so stupid as to gloat over his humiliation. She seems to have been very eager to learn what she didn't know, and she later asked him to teach her Italian and Greek.[55] Nevertheless, as Pierre Coustillas points out in his introduction to these letters, Gissing must have felt just as Edwin did when he took Amy as his wife—that it was amost too great a reward for his long suffering and "Perseverance."[56] And perhaps it was due in part to this sense of indebtedness on his part, and also to his homage to her culture and, through that, to French literature in general, that he represented himself as a pupil rather than a teacher.

Thus he bade farewell to his own country and began the last period of his education as an exile in the physical as well as the spiritual sense of the word. But was he able to reach the crowning stage of his life and art after achieving "intellectual communion" with one he loved? Alas, here again the answer is no. He seems to have grown spiritually very little under the new *ménage*, and physically much

[54] Ibid., p. 53, August 30, 1898.
[55] Ibid., p. 104, February 4, 1899; and p. 106, February 12, 1899.
[56] Ibid., p. 13.

weaker under the new system of diet. There was also little growth in his art—unlike Joseph Conrad and Henry James, two novelists he admired, who achieved their artistic maturity through expatriation, who learned so much from life in exile. Perhaps Gissing had experienced spiritual exile too early and too thoroughly in his own country. Although in earlier years he had always been learning more from books than from life and had been more interested in "the minuter difference between Dochmiacs and Antispasts" than in actual events in real life,[57] yet he could create out of this intellectual passion fine works of fiction. Some of his Bildungsromane, which will have their place in the history of the English novel, were at once an autobiographical and impersonal representation in art of his obsessive idea of spiritual education, whether its outcome be success or failure. There *Wahrheit* and *Dichtung* were indivisibly combined.

But in his later and apparently calm days his passion could assume only the very personal form of a delightful account of travel or quasi-autobiographical wish-fulfillment. It could not elevate itself into the impersonal world where a group of imaginary people can live freely.

> Foolishly arrogant as I was, I used to judge the worth of a person by his intellectual power and attainment. I could see no good where there was no logic, no charm where there was no learning. Now I think that one has to distinguish between two forms of intelligence, that of the brain, and that of the heart, and I have come to regard the second as by far the more important.[58]

To learn to recognize these two kinds of intelligence, and to subdue his own intellectual arrogance, was, to be sure, an advance in his education to a philosophic wisdom, to maturity. But why should he express it in such a personal form—why not in the impersonal form of fiction? It seems as if he had learned to distinguish between two forms of his art, the impersonal and the personal, and to produce better personal writings than novels. Was this complete discord

[57] Roberts, *Henry Maitland*, p. 68.
[58] George Gissing, *The Private Papers of Henry Ryecroft* (London, 1903), p. 43.

between *Wahrheit* and *Dichtung* one step nearer to artistic maturity?

His exodus—the last stage of his education—did not turn out to be the beginning of a great epoch in his life, a time when something new and positive would be born; rather, it was a mere continuation of the same endless education to which he had been, and would be, submitted all his life, and which was again to end in frustration. His personal study, of course, was still carried on patiently. He wrote in his commonplace book that his "modest" intellectual ambitions were "a thorough knowledge of Greek & Roman Literature, of the period covered by Gibbon, of English history, of the history of Christian church, of the topographical history of London, of French fiction & memoirs, of Goethe, Heine & a few of the Germans, of all English literature, of the English flora, of the Bible, of classical Geography, of the history of Magna Graecia & Sicily, of the Renaissance, of Dante, [and] of the history of Painting & Sculpture."[59] And he was very pleased to have learned enough Spanish to read *Don Quixote* in the original—the achievement he had looked forward to for so long. But what did these vast intellectual exertions of his come to?

Nothing. After toilsome documentation prolonged over many years, he at last set to work on *Veranilda*, his first attempt at a historical romance—a work which he had dearly wished to write for more than twenty years, one that was dearer to him than, and so different from, any of those he had written for money during that period, and one that was based on the materials on which he had worked so long and diligently. It was doomed to be left unfinished. But the most painful thing about it is not that it was left unfinished but that nobody, however sympathetic, dares to assert that with *Veranilda* Gissing's art would have attained its consummation, if he had lived to finish it. This is only to repeat the familiar truism that the hardest work will not necessarily produce a good piece of art. To the very last, his study with "Perseverance" was for its own sake indeed and availed him nothing—not even for artistic creation. The only consolation is that he seemed quite unaware that this effort

[59] *Gissing's Commonplace Book,* p. 26. The date of entry is unknown but is assumed to be toward the end of his life.

would prove to be his last and that it would also prove to be futile. For he murmured "Patience, patience," now with a French accent, his language in exile, still convinced, perhaps, that his education, "the work of his life," was continuing, continuing forever.

The Dissociation of Ideas in Whitman's *Democratic Vistas*

Masayuki Sakamoto

Thomas Carlyle published an essay entitled "Shooting Niagara: And After?" in the August 1867 edition of *Macmillan's Magazine*, charging democracy with bringing the death of culture. This essay, reprinted in the New York *Tribune* for August 16 by Horace Greeley, understandably started a series of heated discussions in the United States. Walt Whitman, too, in compliance with the request of the editors of *The Galaxy*, contributed an essay entitled "Democracy" to the magazine. Needless to say, as an ardent defender of American democracy, Whitman intended it to be a refutation of Carlyle's charge. Nevertheless, the current inclination of American society did not allow him to settle himself entirely as Carlyle's critic: he could not help discovering some propriety in Carlyle's charge. He even felt somewhat justified in criticizing America himself. The dilemma, in which Whitman had to act simultaneously as a defender and a critic of America, is confessed in one of his own notes to *Democratic Vistas*.

> I was at first roused to much anger and abuse by this essay from Mr. Carlyle, so insulting to the theory of America—but happening to think afterwards how I had more than once been in the like mood, during which his essay was evidently cast, and seen persons and things in the same light . . . I have since read it again, not only as a study . . . but have read it with respect as coming from an earnest soul, and as contribut-

ing certain sharp-cutting metallic grains, which, if not gold or silver, may be good hard, honest iron.[1]

The fact that Carlyle's "feudal" criticism of America seemed to this wholehearted lover of democracy to be, "if not gold or silver," at least "good hard, honest iron," suggests that some change was secretly taking place in his mind. The complete account includes the sequel to "Democracy," "Personalism," published in *The Galaxy* for May 1868, and a final part which was to have been entitled "Literature" but which was rejected; these three pieces were fused into *Democratic Vistas* in 1871.

Post-bellum America, in which *Democratic Vistas* was written, had set up industrial capitalism as her definite goal, and with all the difficulties incidental to any postwar period was nonetheless making steady strides toward achieving it. It was, according to Arthur M. Schlesinger, "an Economic Revolution which brought changes so sudden and far-reaching that ever since the country has been trying to adjust itself to them."[2] Those domestic industries that had already been given impetus, even during wartime, from war supplies, inflation, and protective tariffs now began to take big strides in earnest, until in the eighties industrial output had exceeded agricultural. In short, the rapid development of post-bellum industry brought fantastic prosperity and radical changes to American society.

It was this very prosperity, however, that turned Whitman from a defender to a critic of America. The thriving materialism of his contemporary America was the blow that broke to fragments his integral (or, in Whitman's own terms, "kosmic") image of the world. "With such advantages at present fully, or almost fully, possess'd . . . and with unprecedented materialistic advancement—society, in these States, is canker'd, crude, superstitious, and rotten" (*Democratic Vistas*, p. 369). Society, then, can be "rotten" in spite of

[1] "Democratic Vistas," in Floyd Stovall, ed., *Prose Works 1892*, 2 vols., Collected Writings of Walt Whitman (New York, 1964), 2: 375–76.
[2] Arthur Meier Schlesinger, *The Rise of Modern America, 1865–1951* (New York, 1951), p. 27.

its "unprecedented materialistic advancement." The maturity of human society cannot be reaped as the *natural* harvest of its "materialistic advancement." However "unprecedented" the advancement may be, it does not necessarily follow that it can be expected to turn itself sometime into some superior sphere. "In vain do we march with unprecedented strides to empire so colossal, outvying the antique, beyond Alexander's, beyond the proudest sway of Rome. In vain have we annex'd Texas, California, Alaska, and reach north for Canada and south for Cuba" (*Democratic Vistas*, p. 370).

Here we must recall, however, that Whitman in the 1850s, (or "myself" in *Song of Myself*) had found no difficulty in transcending "things." The suspicion probably never occurred to him then that things might be "canker'd, crude, superstitious, and rotten." He could enjoy them and easily liberate himself from them. "I mind them or the show or resonance of them—I come and I depart." "I but use you a minute, then I resign you, stallion" (*Song of Myself*, 32.24).[3] "Your facts are useful, and yet they are not my dwelling, / I but enter by them to an area of my dwelling" (*Song of Myself*, 23.15–16).

Even if he did "resign" or "depart from" things and then "enter by them to an area of [his] dwelling," this does not mean that he despises the materiality of those things. He does not "abate . . . the angular distinctness of objects," as Emerson does.[4] For Emerson nature is "an appendix to the soul" (*Nature*, p. 31), and "every natural fact is a symbol of some spiritual fact" (*Nature*, p. 15); while for Whitman the universe is first of all composed of innumerable individual objects, and he admires each of them without reserve.

To admire objects as such and to praise them in ecstatic songs constituted Whitman's "first step" ("Beginning My Studies," 1) as a poet. He, as it were, made love indifferently to each of his objects, including even the bride with whom he would stay, turning "the

[3] *Song of Myself*, 8. 19. All quotations from Whitman's poetry are from Harold W. Blodgett and Sculley Bradley, eds., *Leaves of Grass: Comprehensive Reader's Edition*, Collected Writings of Walt Whitman (New York, 1964); references are to section and line, or, in the case of unsectioned poems, to line number only.
[4] "Nature," in Brooks Atkinson, ed., *The Complete Essays and Other Writings of Ralph Waldo Emerson* (New York, 1950), p. 27.

262 The Dissociation of Ideas in Whitman

bridegroom out of bed" (*Song of Myself*, 33.109–10), and sought to merge with the particular lover. The instances of his merging with objects, or his metamorphosis, abound in *Song of Myself*: for example, "My voice is the wife's voice, the screech by the rail of the stairs, . . . / I am the hounded slave, I wince at the bite of the dogs, . . . / I am the mash'd fireman with breast-bone broken, . . . / I am an old artillerist, . . ." (33.111–49).

Against this impulse to merge is the other impulse working in "myself." If to merge means to die as "myself" and to metamorphose into some non-ego, then, in order to be restored to life, "myself" must necessarily "depart from" its particular love. Whitman describes this mode in which "myself" moves as "living always, always dying" ("O Living Always, Always Dying," 1) or treats himself as "one of that centripetal and centrifugal gang" (*Song of Myself*, 43.16).[5] Thus in the fifties things had enough power neither to retain nor to reject him. They were, so to speak, "garments" (*Song of Myself*, 33.135) which he could change one after another at his pleasure.

Why, then, did it come to pass in the sixties that Whitman could no longer believe in things? Why did he complain that "with unprecedented materialistic advancement—society . . . is canker'd . . . and rotten"? It is at least certain that the relationship between human consciousness and external things, with the radical change of the society, had undergone a considerable change itself: "Unwieldy and immense, who shall hold in behemoth? who bridle leviathan?" (*Democratic Vistas*, p. 422). The external world has grown too huge and "unwieldy" for human consciousness to "bridle." Things, which once yielded themselves willingly to the touch of "the caresser of life" (*Song of Myself*, 13.8), now commenced to assert themselves: "But wo to the age or land in which these things . . . stopping *at themselves*, do not tend *to ideas*" (*Democratic Vistas*, p. 419; italics added). Whitman's vehement condemnation of the materialistic inclination of the external world ironically testifies in effect to the

[5] Cf. "And as to you Life I reckon you are the leavings of many deaths, / (No doubt I have died myself ten thousand times before)" (*Song of Myself*, 49.9–10).

fact that he has fallen into a gap too wide for him to bridge and has no other choice than to complain about his own predicament.

Hitherto his human consciousness had been capable, as a "loafer," of embodying itself freely in various individuals. But now, divested of those carnal "garments," it has no other choice than to weave *out of itself*. Whitman compares this destiny of human consciousness to that of "a noiseless patient spider."

> A noiseless patient spider,
> I mark'd where on a little promontory it stood isolated,
> Mark'd how to explore the *vacant* vast surrounding,
> It launch'd forth filament, filament, filament, *out of itself*,
> Ever unreeling them, ever tirelessly speeding them.
>
> And you O my soul where you stand,
> Surrounded, detached, in measureless oceans of space, . . .
> Till the bridge you will need be form'd, till the ductile
>   anchor hold,
> Till the gossamer thread you fling catch somewhere, O
>   my soul.
> ["A Noiseless Patient Spider"; italics added]

This metamorphosis of Walt Whitman from a caresser of life to a patient spider may be illustrated in various ways. For instance, in *Democratic Vistas*, he directs his bitter complaint against "the people's crudeness, vice, caprices," and asks, "Are there, indeed, *men* here worthy the name? Are there athletes? Are there perfect women, to match the generous material luxuriance? . . . Is there a great moral and religious civilization—the only justification of a great material one?" (p. 371). He asks if there are men worthy of the name because there are no men worthy of the name in the "surrounding space"; he asks if there is a great moral and religious civilization because there is no such civilization anywhere: in short, he asks these questions precisely because he cannot find any answers.

The "vacant vast surrounding" space compels the poet to cease to be a poet. His ideas can be expressed no longer in sensuous forms but only by themselves. Where there was once an actual living people, he now substitutes the naked idea of the people.

This process of Whitman's transformation from a poet to a prophet (or a "national bard"), or of his ideas dissociating themselves from their embodiments, can be traced in the movement of "Scented Herbage of My Breast." In this poem, while admiring the "slender leaves" and "blossoms of my blood" growing from his breast, the poet yet finds himself unable to grasp their meaning. Then helplessly he "permits" them "to tell in *your own* way of the heart that is under you" (italics added). This seems to suggest that the identity of himself and his soul, formerly so closely tied together and never known to part, is now lost. Once he could "stand with [his] robust soul" (*Song of Myself*, 44.36); once he could conceive of his soul as his "mistress" ("Starting from Paumanok," 5.15). And the soul, too, could rejoice in "receiving identity *through materials* and loving them, observing characters and absorbing them" ("A Song of Joys," 98; italics added). In short, he could easily understand the meaning of his soul "through materials" and to understand his soul he had only to see individual things.

> Was somebody asking to see the soul?
> See, your own shape and countenance, persons, substances,
>   beasts, the trees, the running rivers, the rocks and
>   sands.
>   ["Starting from Paumanok," 13.1–2]

But now he fails to understand what his own soul means, which is undebatably because he can no longer see the reflex of his soul in "materials." Things now will not serve as the soul's incarnations but, as we have seen, have already grown into a "leviathan" too huge for him to "bridle."

It is quite natural, therefore, that, however coaxingly he may request the herbage of his own breast to tell its meaning, it should not comply at all.

> Grow up taller than sweet leaves *that I may see!* grow up
>   out of my breast!

Spring away from the conceal'd heart there!
Do not fold yourself so in your pink-tinged roots, timid
    leaves!
Do not remain down there so ashamed, herbage of my
    breast!
    ["Scented Herbage of My Breast," 17–20; italics added]

They feel ashamed to grow up, probably because they know that the
external world will no longer "celebrate" them, that in fact it has
already gone back on them. In other words, they are another
"noiseless patient spider," isolated and detached in the midst of "the
vacant vast surrounding."

    Thus it is that the herbage makes him "think of death."

    O I think it is not for life I am chanting here my
        chant of lovers, I think it must be for death.
        ["Scented Herbage of My Breast," 12]

The death the herbage here seems to be growing "to ascend to" is
altogether different from the death "the caresser of life" ardently
desired as being the fulfillment of his love. The latter was really a
premise of life and so was always followed by rebirth, or the regaining of identity. But the death celebrated in "Scented Herbage of My
Breast" is simply a negation of life: "Nor will I allow you to balk
me any more with what I was calling life" (30). Here life is one
thing, and death another. Between them gapes an unbridgeable
"hiatus" (*Democratic Vistas*, p. 365). Life and death can no longer
hope to be tied closely together in one dynamic dialectic of "living
always, always dying."

    Now that his soul has decided once and for all to turn its back on
the external world, he is made to confront the necessity of choosing
antinomically either to follow his soul and isolate himself, or else to
maintain the old tie with the external world and to try to save it
from damnation. The poet seems to have chosen the latter and to
have decided to transform himself into a prophet, or a national bard,
for in this poem he gives up the herbage of his own breast after repeated efforts to understand its meaning.

Emblematic and capricious blades *I leave you*, now you
  serve me not,
I will say what I have to say *by itself*.

[22–23; italics added]

Henceforth ideas are to be put in words by themselves (that is, not in
"indirections") and to be given as directions from outside to the depraved external world.

  If we compare Whitman's poems of the 1850s with *Democratic
Vistas*, we can clearly see how definitely ideas had dissociated themselves from their creative source, the poet's private soul, and changed
into mere ideas. To take one example, Whitman could once sing:

Logic and sermons never convince,
The damp of the night drives deeper into my soul.

[*Song of Myself*, 30.6–7]

(I and mine do not convince by arguments, similes,
  rhymes,
We convince by our presence.)

["Song of the Open Road," 10.15–16]

A healthy presence, a friendly or commanding gesture,
  are words, sayings, meanings.

["A Song of the Rolling Earth," 13]

  But turning to *Democratic Vistas*, we find that ideas there are set
forth as nothing but ideas. For example,

> We shall, it is true, quickly and continually find the origin-
> idea of the singleness of man, individualism, asserting itself,
> and cropping forth, even from the opposite ideas. But the
> mass, or lump character, for imperative reasons, is to be ever
> carefully weigh'd, borne in mind, and provided for. . . . The
> two are contradictory, but our task is to reconcile them.
> [*Democratic Vistas*, p. 373]

It is simply because his "materials" are now nothing but ideas that he
can expect "the singleness of man" to assert itself and crop forth,
even from its "opposite" pole, or that he can assign to himself the

task to "reconcile" the "contradictory" two. They can be easily and endlessly spun out, "filament, filament," because the spinning is done all along *within* the spinner's mind. His consciousness never goes out and troubles itself to see whether its ideas are pertinent to the living world.

And against this autonomous spinning of ideas, or weaving of the prophet's "vista," is his interminable complaint over the external world, which is, as it were, mechanically opposed.

> We live in an atmosphere of hypocrisy throughout. The men believe not in the women, nor the women in the men. A scornful superciliousness rules in literature. . . . Conversation is a mass of badinage. From deceit in the spirit, the mother of all false deeds, the offspring is already incalculable. . . . The depravity of the business classes of our country is not less than has been supposed, but infinitely greater. The official services of America . . . are saturated in corruption. [*Democratic Vistas*, p. 370]

Thus his complaint and his vista are never to be interwoven. It seems as if they were made at different levels of his mind. When he finishes with his complaint, he shifts to another sphere of his mind and commences to spin out his ideal vista. For him the external world is there only to be complained of and will never yield any vista out of itself.

Such ideas as "personalism" or "Comradeship," which Whitman spun out in *Democratic Vistas*, are, then, nothing but ideas substituted for what the living world lacks. In *Democratic Vistas*, Whitman generally tries to transcend the evils of the external world by substituting some autonomously created ideas. Besides, Whitman goes on to presume that democracy itself is the "law" of substitution.

> Democracy too is *law*. . . . Many suppose . . . that it means a throwing aside of law, and running riot. But, briefly, it is the superior law, not alone that of physical force, the body, which, adding to, it *supercedes* with that of the spirit. Law is

the unshakable order of the universe forever; and the law over all, and law of laws, is the law of *successions*; that of the superior law, in time, gradually *supplanting and overwhelming* the inferior one. [*Democratic Vistas*, p. 381; italics added]

Whitman had to enact a law named "Democracy," just because there was "a throwing aside of law" in the world. This anarchic "running riot" made it urgent for him to establish a law. Things in the actual world are going steadily and obstinately their own way and, "stopping at themselves, do not tend to ideas." And Whitman as a national bard assumes the task of making them "tend to ideas," furnishing those depraved things with "a lofty and hitherto unoccupied framework or platform, broad enough for all" (*Democratic Vistas*, p. 403). The framework must be "broad enough for all" to be reoriented in it. It compels all the anarchic atoms of the actual world to obey its totalitarian will and to come into unity again. All of them, without a single exception, are told to concentrate upon "faithfully partaking of their source, and indeed only arising either to betoken it, or to furnish parts of that varied-flowing display, whose centre was one and absolute" (*Democratic Vistas*, p. 390). Briefly, all things are directed to subordinate themselves to the "one and absolute" center and become its mere "parts." And this center is, in Whitman's own terms, "the *idea* of All" (*Democratic Vistas*, p. 420; italics added).[6]

Whitman's pertinacious devotion to the "idea of All" throughout *Democratic Vistas* distinctly shows how far he has departed from that former "myself," who could boast of his very contradictions.

> Do I contradict myself?
> Very well then I contradict myself,
> (I am large, I contain multitudes.)
> [*Song of Myself*, 51.6–8]

---

[6] Cf. "From Paumanok starting I fly like a bird, / Around and around to soar to sing the *idea of all*, . . . / To sing first, . . . / The *idea of all*, of the Western world *one and inseparable*, / And then the song of each member of these States" ("From Paumanok Starting I Fly Like a Bird," lines 1–11; italics added).

Even the fact that he contradicted himself could, in the *Song of Myself*
period, be something to be proud of. The anarchical state of things
did not yet inspire any fear in him but was rather the source of his
rejoicing, thanks to its infinite diversity. In *Democratic Vistas*, however, contradicting oneself is an undesirable situation which one has
fallen into in spite of oneself and which one must get away from at
any cost:

> ... how can we remain, divided, contradicting ourselves, this
> way? I say we can only attain harmony and stability by con-
> sulting ensemble and the ethic purports, and faithfully build-
> ing upon them. [*Democratic Vistas*, p. 409]

Whitman can no longer remain "imperturbe" ("Me Imperturbe,"
1) among contradictions. The contradictoriness of the world now
is simply a menacing "leviathan" to him, or, to be more exact, *he*
has been reduced to a mere outsider to the world. Certainly, Walt
Whitman, "of Manhattan the son" (*Song of Myself*, 24.1) is no more
the center of the "kosmos."

Thus the contrast of *Democratic Vistas* with Whitman's earlier
poems shows clearly the process of transformation through which
his mind had passed from the eve of the war of secession to the post-
bellum period. In the period preceding the war, when America was
separated into the North, the South, and the West, and each of those
districts was comparatively independent of the others, it was almost
impossible to discern where America was heading. It was possible,
therefore, to have various prospects of what the future America
should be like. Each of a number of young men of genius, with his
self-consciousness enhanced and infinitely magnified by the flow of
the upsurging energy of the rapidly changing society, had created
his own vision of America, with his own apotheosized self at its
center. The world had afforded ample room for Whitman to create
his vision. But once America emerged from the Civil War, her
destination came into plain view. The external world turned out to
be not "a metaphor of the human mind" (*Nature*, p. 18) but its own

master. Thus the romantic haze named Transcendentalism at last lifted, leaving human consciousness exposed to the cold dry air of post-bellum industrial America. The romantic ego had been dethroned and made to confront its own nakedness as an outsider.

In this sense, Whitman's *Democratic Vistas* seems to me to be not only one of his own more memorable works but also one of the monuments that tell the story of the fall of the American ego from an apotheosized being to an isolated outsider.

Isabel's Freedom: On Henry James's *Portrait of a Lady*

Tsugio Aoki

H enry James's novel *The Portrait of a Lady* is a complex and highly finished work of art, which can be appreciated in a variety of ways. If, however, we seek to understand the American character of James's fiction, we must examine the question of freedom in Isabel's attempt and failure to explore life. She was freed, of course, from economic restrictions by wealth inherited from her uncle. Freedom meant for her, however, not only a deliverance from restrictions but also a positive responsibility toward herself and toward the world. And at the core of her sense of duty there was an idealistic conviction that she could develop and that the world could be changed for the better. The title of the novel itself suggests not only James's technique of presenting the heroine in a succession of pictorial scenes, but also the heroine's desire to create her ideal self in a visual form, and to perpetuate it. The promise and danger inherent in such a view of the self form the basic tension in this novel. James presents a portrait of a charming but presumptuous heroine who attempts a self-portrait not in pigments but in actual life. This double vision—James's portrait of Isabel's attempt at self-portraiture—shows his realistic grasp of the heroine's romantic temperament. Our understanding of James's ironic distance from the heroine, however, must not obscure his sympathy. James's irony in this novel is never without sympathy for the heroine.

The differences between the two distinguished James brothers warn us not to take any simple view of their resemblance in character. According to William H. Gass, both of them were "consumed by a form of the Moral Passion. Both struggled to find in the plural

world of practice a vantage for spirit. But William was fatally en-
meshed in the commercial."[1] They shared, however, an interest in
the flow of psychological processes, and both found in the discovery
of this inner fluidity the condition of human freedom, the possibility
of an Emersonian self-culture. William regarded "the self as known"
as the sum total of all that a man can call his, including his psychic
powers, his body, his clothes, his house, his bank account, and so
forth. In his discussion of "the material me," "the social me," and
"the spiritual me," as also in his analysis of "the hierarchy [of the
me's]," the basic moral concern underlying his apparently scientific
approach to psychology becomes clear. His analysis of the con-
stituents of the self is a preparation for affirming the necessity and
efficacy of conscious efforts toward achieving the ideal self.[2] I am not
prepared to discuss the brothers' mutual influences, but William's
view of the plastic fluid character of personality seems very like
Mme Merle's philosophy: "What shall we call our 'self'? Where
does it begin? where does it end? It over-flows into everything that
belongs to us—and then it flows back again. I know a large part of
myself is in the clothes I choose to wear. I've a great respect for
things!" (1. 287).[3] As Isabel's story reveals, such a philosophy of the
self as a fluctuating entity can lead to either a parasitic attitude to life
or a creative one. If life is regarded, as by Mme Merle, primarily as
an established order of things from which one is excluded by the
accident of birth or any other mishap, then the best that one can do
is to exploit it. But life can also be viewed as one's creative relation
to oneself and to the preexisting order of things, as in Isabel's case.

In James's view, America was a young nation freed from old
fetters but lacking a culture capable of expressing the spirit of its
people and conducive to bringing out their potential capacities. So
that, for an American of Isabel's aspirations, the freedom for self-

---

[1] William H. Gass, "The High Brutality of Good Intentions," in William T.
Stafford, ed., *Perspectives on James's "The Portrait of a Lady"* (New York, 1967), p. 207.

[2] William James, *Psychology: The Briefer Course*, ed. Gordon Allport (New York,
1961), ch. 12.

[3] All quotations from the novel are from *The Novels and Tales of Henry James*, 26
vols. (New York, 1907–17), in which *The Portrait of a Lady* comprises vols. 3 and 4.
References to the novel are by volume *of the novel* and page.

improvement, to choose her ideal mode of existence, became a destiny, rather than a choice. Given Isabel's temperament, the wish to make her life an art form was not merely an innocent and presumptuous delusion, nor was choosing Osmond as her husband simply a result of machinations. In the background of her efforts was a felt necessity to embody her spirit in a visible or artistic form like those of the supreme examples of the European tradition. At the same time, James was fully aware of the dangers inherent in the concept of the self as a plastic entity susceptible to conscious improvement; his awareness led him to show Isabel falling a willing, inevitable victim to a sterile dilettante and Mme Merle. Moreover, in his sympathy with the heroine he never ignored the fact that, if the will was not nourished by a living cultural tradition, it could operate, even in so admirable a character, as a force destructive of that inner harmony which is its source of energy. The darkly ambiguous ending of the novel was inevitable.

When, early in the novel, Isabel disagreed with Mme Merle's philosophy of the self as "made up of some cluster of appurtenances" and declared that nothing that belonged to her was any measure of herself (1. 287–88), she was not merely giving vent to her characteristic impulse to be contrary. It was clear, without Mme Merle's telling her, that she should not go without clothes even if they were, as she asserted, imposed upon her by society. She was asserting a crucial point about the kind of relationship she wanted to establish between herself and the world of things. She was a product of a rapidly developing, unstable society; she was aware of the cultural poverty of her background but full of hope, and anxiety, for the possibilities of her unknown future. Inevitably she found her freedom both exhilarating and fearful. "Do you know where you're drifting, Isabel Archer?" Henrietta asked after she had turned down two marriage offers. "No," Isabel answered, "I haven't the least idea, and I find it very pleasant not to know. A swift carriage, of a dark night, rattling with four horses over roads that one can't see—that's my idea of happiness" (1. 235). In spite of the consciously frivolous tone, there is serious ambivalence in these words. The dilemma she has to face in her pursuit of freedom is shown first in the fact that, in spite of her attraction to Lord Warburton, she could not accept his hand. When he proposed, she was still in the stage of seeing the world, of not yet having decided what to do, and of fearing that her freedom would be circumscribed. In spite of his progressive character, Lord Warburton was a refined product of a very well-established society, and all the security society could offer was his. When this man "of a happy temperament fertilized by a high civilisation" (1. 5) explained, in his marriage proposal, that he had "filled all the other relations of life very creditably," and insisted, "I don't see why I shouldn't fill this one—in which I offer myself to you" (1. 148), it was clear that he belonged to a stable old world where human relations were determined by a preestablished order and in which the individual could achieve a sense of fulfillment by accepting and conforming to a prescribed social role. Isabel belonged to a radically different world, in which one had constantly to face the necessity of choosing and even creating the role one played. The difference between her world and that to which Lord Warburton wanted, Isabel thought, to confine her will be clearer when we compare her with Lord Warburton's sisters. We may recall Henrietta's ironic comment to them: "I suppose in your position it's sufficient for you to exist" (1. 189).

In spite of the rich variety of personal characteristics depicted in the novel, the American characters share one important characteristic. We recall that, in Mrs. Touchett's "thoroughly arranged and servanted life," for example, her sick son Ralph's "turn always came after the other nearest subjects of solicitude, the various punctualities of performance of the workers of her will" (1. 48). Caspar Goodwood was "a mover of men" whose jaw was "too square and set and his figure too straight and stiff," suggesting "a want for easy consonance with the deeper rhythms of life" (1. 164–65). And Osmond made his life an art form and lived "in a sorted, sifted, arranged world." These are all typical products of the American condition in that they all shared, in varying degrees and qualities, the necessity of imposing their wills upon life to give it form. In marked contrast with the typical passivity of Lord Warburton and his sisters, their attitude toward life may be characterized as more or less aggressive.

What brought Isabel and Osmond together was, in the last analysis, this peculiarly American fate of freedom. There was a complicated interplay of motives among Isabel, Osmond, and Mme Merle, which found its inevitable but tragic solution in Isabel's unhappy marriage to Osmond. Mme Merle's machinations only helped Isabel to decide on the course of an action ideal, she thought, for the right disposal of that money which was after all a burden on her conscience. The story of eager innocence betrayed by worldly cunning becomes only a minor aspect of *The Portrait of a Lady* when we understand that Isabel's choice of Osmond as her husband was an inescapable conclusion of her search for an ideal life at that particular moment. What she found on Osmond's hilltop overlooking a large expanse of Florentine landscape lying in perfect harmony and classic grace was the kind of intentionally ordered life that seemed to be the perfect realization of her own vague yearnings. Her meeting with Osmond occurred at the right structural moment in the novel, when her rather roving disposition was beginning to feel the desirability, even the responsibility, of settling down. She was sincere when she told him that she was ashamed of her constantly changing plans. When she told Osmond that "one ought to choose something very deliberately, and be faithful to that," and when he described his "studied, willful renunciation" (1. 381), she was ready to accept his esthetic world at its face value and to find in it an ideal opportunity to serve a higher cause.

The Portrait of a Lady has often been discussed as a novel about "seeing," and Isabel's freedom has sometimes been defined as the free cultivation of the life of consciousness. Another aspect of the novel that must be emphasized, however, is its "doing" and "becoming." Isabel comes to think that "to be rich was a virtue because it was to be able to do" (1. 301) and she imagined herself doing great deeds after inheriting the fortune from her uncle. "Her life should always be in harmony with the most pleasing impression she should produce; she would be what she appeared, and she would appear what she was" (1. 69). This was her ideal, as explained by the narrator. And this was the ideal that became possible for her to achieve, she innocently dreamed, with Osmond as the high priest of the altar of beauty. The emphasis of the story returns to her "seeing" only

when she realizes that her attempt has been frustrated. Isabel's romance is sharply defined against the background of dark reality. She
may regard her mind as a garden, where even the introspection into
the recesses of the spirit is a harmless excursion for a lapful of roses;
but this view is offset by the presentiment of "dusky pestiferous
tracts, planted thick with ugliness and misery" (1. 72). In James, the
realistic form of the novel is a perfect medium for containing the
romantic, "the things that can reach us only through the beautiful
circuit and subterfuge of our thought and desire," as James put it in
his preface to *The American*.[4]

It should not be thought, however, that James shared Isabel's idea
that her fate was a total denial of freedom. She was a person with a
sense of high mission; and although this is no doubt presented in an
ironic light, it survives and retains its relevance, because the structure
of the novel itself gives validity to it. In the admirably composed
opening scene set in the garden of Gardencourt, her role in the novel
is explained with highly finished but unobtrusive artistry. The pleasant, joking conversation of the three male characters conceals, under
the surface of their bantering mood, the author's clear-cut intention
to prepare for the first entrance of the heroine. The words of Old
Touchett, "I'm convinced there will be great changes; and not all
for the better" (1. 10), reflect the historic sense of the author, who
was to write, four years after *The Portrait of a Lady*, a novel about the
underground political movement in England. In the most enjoyable
atmosphere, "the increasing seriousness of things" only provided a
"great opportunity of jokes" (1. 10). And the idea of Old Touchett
that in the coming social changes "you ought to take hold of a pretty
woman" was treated as an amusing subject for continuing the light
bantering. But a momentary silence fell when the old man insisted
that "the ladies will save us ... that is the best of them will.... Make
up to a good one and marry her, and your life will become much
more interesting" (1. 11). The silence did not refer directly to the
seriousness of the historical situation but referred, rather, to the
magnanimity of the old man whose own "experiment in matri-

---

[4] Henry James, *The Art of the Novel: Critical Prefaces*, introd. R. P. Blackmur (New
York, 1934), p. 32.

mony" had not been a felicitous one. James never does anything so awkward as to mar the perfect atmosphere of a scene by inserting obtrusive comments or by pointing out the moral. Yet the underlying seriousness and relevance should not be missed. The conversation also defines, in exchanges of witty remarks, Isabel's mission in the novel. When Ralph said, "I should like to see your idea of an interesting woman," Lord Warburton answered, "My dear fellow, you can't see ideas—especially such highly etherial ones as mine. If I could only see it myself—that would be a great step in advance" (1. 12). And as Isabel finally appeared in person, as if introduced by the comments of the three men about the independent girl of whom Mrs. Touchett telegraphed from America, Lord Warburton decided she was exactly his idea of the interesting woman. Isabel's sense of her mission and freedom is central to the whole structure of the novel.

If we accept such a concept of the self and of its freedom in Isabel, then her tendency to watch herself imaginatively as if she were a figure in a picture cannot be dismissed as a form of narcissism. When Lord Warburton is about to propose to her, she has in her mind the picture of "the park of an old English country-house, with the foreground embellished by a 'great' (she supposed) nobleman in the act of making love to a young lady who, on careful inspection, should be found to present remarkable analogies with herself" (1. 146). This may read more like a narcissistic daydream with a dash of sexual fantasy, as "making love" suggests, but this tendency of hers begins to have a more serious meaning as the story develops. When she inherited her uncle's fortune, she lost herself in a maze of visions of wonderful things she would do as a rich, free, and generous person: "her fortune . . . became to her mind a part of her better self: it gave her importance, gave her even, to her own imagination, a certain ideal beauty" (1. 321–22). As might be expected, her self-image completed itself when Osmond proposed to her. Told by Osmond that for him she would "always be the most important woman in the world," she "looked at herself in this character—looked intently, thinking she filled it with a certain grace" (2. 19). Just before she chose her fate in Rome, she told Ralph that "a large fortune means freedom. . . . It's such a fine thing, and one should make such a good use of it" (1. 320). Since her freedom was the freedom of the beautiful spirit to become and exist as a beautiful form, it is significant that her choice was made in Rome. To James, Rome was specially attractive for the moral and esthetic significance it had to the rest of the world. "We go to Italy," James wrote in a review of Howell's *Italian Journeys* in 1868, "to gaze upon certain of the highest achievements of human power—achievements, moreover, which, from their visible and tangible nature, are particularly well adapted to represent to the imagination the *maximum* of man's creative force."[5] Adeline Tintner says, "James's *œuvre* is the record of an attempt to balance the material aspect of civilization, art—with its spiritual aspect, life."[6] It was exactly this balancing of the material and the spiritual that Isabel hoped to achieve in Rome with Osmond and Pansy.

There are also religious overtones. Isabel's efforts to become an ideal lady have slight but unequivocal associations with the Virgin Mary. There was of course irony in Mrs. Touchett's comment that Isabel "looked as solemn . . . as a Cimabue Madonna" (1. 300) when she was deciding that to be rich was a virtue because it was to be able to do. There may seem but slight relation between her and the Madonna by Collegio that James chose for the background of the scene when Henrietta met Caspar in Florence, asking him to go to see Isabel as a friend. But it was another matter when Pansy imploringly told Isabel how much she wished to marry Mr. Rosier— "as if she were praying to the Madonna" (2. 256). As "the Madonna" responded to Pansy "with unusual frigidity," the reader has no doubt of the author's view of the cleavage between Isabel's ideal and her reality. But this association surely proves his intention of giving the reader the impression that indeed "from the Roman past to Isabel Archer's future was a long stride, but her imagination had taken it in a single flight" (1. 415) at its most hopeful moment.

No scene in *The Portrait of a Lady* presents James's sympathetic but

---

[5] Albert Mordell, ed., *Literary Reviews and Essays by Henry James* (New York, 1957), pp. 199–200.

[6] Adeline Tintner, "The Museum World," in *Henry James: A Collection of Critical Essays*, ed. Leon Edel (Englewood Cliffs, N.J., 1963), p. 140.

realistic understanding of Isabel's difficulties so clearly as that in the Capitol in Rome. When Isabel parts from the dejected Lord Warburton, there follow unusual passages in which the author talks in the first person and in the present tense:

> It is impossible, in Rome at least, to look long at a great company of Greek sculptures without feeling the effect of their noble quietude; which, as with a high door closed for the ceremony, slowly drops on the spirit the large white mantle of peace. I say in Rome especially, because the Roman air is an exquisite medium for such impressions. [2.8]

Immediately after the description of Isabel's religious rapture, however, James reintroduces Osmond into the scene, and the chapter comes to an end as he finds "a new attraction in the idea of taking to himself a young lady who had qualified herself to figure in his collection of choice objects by declining so noble a hand" (2. 9). An immense difference may seem to lie between Isabel's creative concept of the self and Osmond's satisfaction in Isabel as an object of art. Once she loses, however, her youthful illusion about the future and wakes up to the fact that her world of beauty is the product of the past, there is but a single step from her life to Oswald's sterile dilettantism. "The portrait of Isabel is the portrait of a mind rather than that of a person with physical form and body," said Cornelia Kelley.[7] I might add that *The Portrait of a Lady* successfully reveals the frustration of trying to create a living portrait with the self itself as material. In spite of interpretations that try to make Isabel's future in Rome seem hopeful, her story may be regarded as a continuation or an expansion of the feeling of the hero in "The Madonna of the Future." In both, the great creative period of European civilization is over, and the light that has inspired older masters is now gone. This may sound too simple, in view of the complex meanings and feelings structured into the novel. But if this novel is a mirror, it is certainly the mirror of which James talked in his essay "The Future

---

[7] Cornelia Pulsifer Kelley, *The Early Development of Henry James* (Urbana, 1965), p. 299.

of the Novel," the mirror in which will be reflected varied images of the collapse, even when the world is an unpeopled void.[8]

Three years after her marriage we see Isabel again with Rosier, first as the "picture of a gracious lady," "framed in the gilded doorway," high, splendid, and radiantly gentle. "The years had touched her only to enrich her; the flower of her youth had not faded, it only hung more quietly on its stem" (2. 105). But after this dramatic presentation of Isabel as the perfection of a veritable portrait of a lady, James masterfully reveals her inner truth. Certain that something had gone wrong with her, her friends kept concerned watch over her apparently happy life. Never cheated by appearances, and blessed with the lover's instinct, Ralph penetrated into the reality behind her mask. To his eye it was clear that the once keen, free girl had now become a lady who represented Gilbert Osmond. Gradually the point of view shifts into the inner world of Isabel's consciousness, revealing how she herself perceived her self-imposed situation. She knew that she had been cheated, that her freedom was denied, and that the very fact that she had a mind of her own had aroused her husband's hatred. Hers was "the house of darkness, the house of dumbness, the house of suffocation" (2. 196). To make her situation worse, she could not reproach Osmond alone; she had to admit that he had his own reasons for disappointment. When she met him on the Florentine hilltop, did she not try to give a better impression of herself than the facts warranted? She, too, had failed to make her appearance one with her ideal. Because she could not confess the mistake she had made in spite of the advice of her friends, her life became of necessity a mask, a vain theatricality in which she increasingly resembled Mme Merle. "There was a corner of the curtain that never was lifted; it was as if she had remained after all something of a public performer, condemned to emerge only in character and in costume" (2. 39). Once this was what she thought of Mme Merle. Now it was Isabel herself who exercised her will in insisting on wearing the mask.

In James's novels, the world of fine appearances, however bril-

---

[8] Henry James, *The Future of the Novel, Essays on the Art of Fiction*, ed. Leon Edel (New York, 1956), p. 41.

liantly presented, never has the solid permanence of the artistic beauty it strives to attain, and the tension between appearance and reality often finds expression in sophisticated and tense theatricality. "Women find their religion sometimes in strange exercises," the narrator explains,

> . . . and Isabel at present, in playing a part before her cousin, had an idea that she was doing him a kindness. It would have been a kindness perhaps if he had been for a single instant a dupe. As it was, the kindness consisted mainly in trying to make him believe that he had once wounded her greatly and that the event had put him to shame, but that, as she was very generous and he was so ill, she bore him no grudge and even considerately forbore to flaunt her happiness in his face. Ralph smiled to himself . . . at this extraordinary form of consideration; but he forgave her for having forgiven him. [2. 204]

The novel might have resembled a melodrama about the machinations of evil characters for the fortune of an innocent girl, if Isabel's complex psychology had not been presented convincingly. To quote an ironical comment of the narrator: "The depths of this young lady's nature were a very out-of-the-way place, between which and the surface communication was interrupted by a dozen capricious forces" (1. 45). This rather amusing figure of speech, however, points to a serious feature of her psychological make-up. This emerges from her excitement with power and fear of herself when she succeeded in sending Caspar back to England. Another example was her refusal of Lord Warburton's marriage offer, which was motivated not only by fear lest her freedom should be restricted but also by fear of his masculinity. There seems to be something forced in her conscious relation with her deeper self. Her fear of sexuality was something more than the natural fear of a young and inexperienced girl for the violence involved in sexual passion. As a consequence, her efforts to create an ideal and tangible self functioned as a restrictive force on her potentialities, instead of liberating and realizing them. Read from this point of view, a major irony in the novel is found in the fact that, with her consciously moral and esthetic intention to be a lady, she failed to arrive at any satisfactory concept of womanhood, which obviously must be the basis of any sound definition of the lady.

The same theme is sounded at other places in the novel. Isabel could not offer wholehearted congratulations to Henrietta when she became engaged to Mr. Bantling. It made her feel disappointed and melancholy to find that "Henrietta, after all, had confessed herself human and feminine" (2.400). Of course, Henrietta's engagement was a rather banal conclusion to her own version of the free exploration of life. But we must compare Isabel's attitude, in the next to last chapter, with the magnanimity of the Old Touchett in the opening scene (see above) in order for her peculiar narrowness of outlook, and even of humanity, to become clear. Henrietta's remark that "we're too infatuated with mere brain-power . . . a woman has to change a good deal to marry" (2. 400) must be meant by the author as a penetrating criticism of one aspect of Isabel's personality. It is relevant here to recall that she never thought, as far as one learns, of the six-month-old baby she had lost. There is undeniable frigidity in her answer, "Oh my brother," to Ralph's passionate deathbed confession: "And remember this . . . that if you've been hated you've also been loved. Ah, but, Isabel—adored!" (2. 417). When she was to visit Italy for the first time, Ralph advised her:

> Take things more easily. Don't ask yourself so much whether this or that is good for you. Don't question your conscience so much—it will get out of tune like a strummed piano. Keep it for great occasions. Don't try so much to form your character—it's like trying to pull open a tight, tender younger rose. Live as you like best, and your character will take care of itself. Most things are good for you. [1. 319]

With its excessive self-consciousness and its belief in the power of the will over the self, Isabel's kind of freedom could work as a restrictive force on Ralph's kind of freedom, which meant the self's inherent and essentially good power for harmonious development.

This is, again, not to suggest that Ralph represents James and his total rejection of Isabel's concept of freedom. The dichotomy between freedom as the will's control over the self and the self's natural capacity for growth reflects an unresolved problem in James himself. In order to be a great poet, James wrote in his review of Whitman's *Drumtaps* (1865), "you must be *possessed*, and you must strive to possess your possession."[9] Not only to be a great poet but also to live life fully, he might have added. But obviously no amount of conscious striving alone can unite the active striving to possess with the passive state of being possessed by a superhuman force. The concept of the plasticity of the self and the esthetic attitude toward life in this novel are based, in the last analysis, on a ritualistic view of life. Isabel's life took the form of an unanswered prayer that she might be possessed by the great spirit of Europe. She strove, but only to discover that answering prayers was not the function of human will. From this discovery she derived her feeling, at the end of the novel, that the world had become a very small place.

James's fictional world may seem, at first glance, to be remote from the actualities of his time. That world is securely founded, however, on his understanding of the changes the age was undergoing. W. B. Stein's view is relevant here. Doubt still remains whether or not James was influenced by Henry Adams in his revision of *The Portrait* for the New York edition, but certainly, as Stein asserts, "manners and customs in this period, according to *The Education* and *The Portrait*, were tending to redefine the role of woman in determining the life-goals of civilization. Artificial values, like money and social station, usurped her biological autonomy, falsifying her responsibilities to herself and to mankind." Isabel's own values, if they could be defined as artificial, could never be exemplified by money and status. Stein is indeed at once extreme and bold in saying that "in Isabel . . . the *vis inertiae* of female sexuality succumbs to the irresponsible force of a male who has lost his sense of function in a culture which has destroyed the natural basis of relation between the opposite sexes."[10] There is, however, much

[9] Henry James, *Selected Literary Criticism*, ed. Morris Shapiro (New York, 1965), p. 5.

[10] W. S. Stein, "The Portrait of a Lady: *Vis Inertiae*," in Stafford, *Perspectives*, pp. 170, 182.

to this view. James saw a cleavage between life as the formless primordial force seeking realization in formal expression, and life as a visible, tangible order and process. The European world of beauty presented in *The Portrait of a Lady* is a museum world, as Adeline Tintner has aptly called it, a world from which the energy that created it had already receded. Isabel's was essentially the wish to have the world in the process of becoming, of being made, so that the order she might achieve moment by moment would constantly be one with her creative energy. And her tragic realization was that she had to accept what Caspar called "that ghastly form" (2. 433), the vain ritual of lifeless convention in which she had no hope of ever being possessed.

"The world, in truth, had never seemed so large; it seemed to open out, all round her, to take the form of a mighty sea, where she floated in fathomless waters. She had wanted help, and here was help; it had come in a rushing torrent" (2. 435)—in Caspar's last passionate embrace. But no, she could not let herself be carried away by the saving rush of waters. Even apart from the question of her fear of sexuality, to do so would have been to let herself be possessed from below, whereas her hope had been to be possessed from above, to borrow Paul Tillich's terms. And this was exactly the conclusion impossible for James to envision. His knowledge of Europe and its traditions was so vast, and his love of it so deep, that it would have been impossible for him to imagine a revitalizing energy welling up after Isabel's self-image as a lady had crumbled away.

In the strict sense, James seems not to have been a religious person. But *The Portrait of a Lady* may rightly be thought to present Isabel in a state of sin as defined by Tillich—"sin as separation, estrangement from one's essential self."[11] Obviously Isabel was not an evil character. She was more sinned against than sinning. It is also true, however, that Mme Merle and Osmond were, not the primary cause, but rather the occasion of clarifying her tragic human predicament. In this, her fate finally represents more than those particularly American difficulties faced by men for whom the great tradition belonged to an alien culture and to whom the shape of the future was

[11] Paul Tillich, *Theology of Culture* (New York, 1964), p. 132.

not yet in view. It may be more appropriate to say that her fate is the fate of any person in any age and place where history is in constant and rapid flux. Torn between the receding past and the uncertain future, such a character resembles Isabel in failing to discover any sense of the solidity of a reliable present.

T. S. Eliot on Hamlet and His Problems

Shoichi Yamada

In 1919 T. S. Eliot wrote a critical essay on Hamlet and his problems well known today for his judgment of "artistic failure" passed upon Shakespeare's play and also for the phrase "objective correlative," which he employed in an argument well seasoned with the words "feeling" and "emotion."

My purpose is not to investigate this essay from the standpoint of a Shakespearean scholar, since I am not one. But I do not think a thorough knowledge of Shakespearean criticism is indispensable to understanding Eliot's work as poet or critic. My concern is rather with trifles, or seeming trifles, that is, with the words "feeling" and "emotion." These words are similar in meaning and difficult to define in their relation to each other. But can we not say that they are used consciously or half-consciously by Eliot the critic, based on his understanding of their meanings? And can we not say that they are key words for us as we try to understand the fundamental attitude of Eliot the poet? My essay seeks to answer these questions.

In the second part of Eliot's "Tradition and the Individual Talent," which was written in the same year as "Hamlet and His Problems," the two words appear frequently enough to be noticeable. They are employed to explain the relation of the poem to its author. Eliot suggests, to begin with, through the analogy of a catalyst, that

> the mind of the mature poet differs from that of the immature one not precisely in any valuation of "personality," not being necessarily more interesting, or having "more to say," but rather by being a more finely perfected medium in which

special, or very varied, feelings are at liberty to enter into new combinations.[1]

Setting aside Eliot's view of "personality," which would require a whole thesis, perhaps, to examine closely, I would like to observe here as far as possible how the two different words are used by the author. Eliot goes on to say:

> When the two gases previously mentioned are mixed in the presence of a filament of platinum, they form sulphurous acid. This combination takes place only if the platinum is present; nevertheless the newly formed acid contains no trace of platinum, and the platinum itself is apparently unaffected; has remained inert, neutral, and unchanged. The mind of the poet is the shred of platinum. . . . The experience, you will notice, the elements which enter the presence of the transforming catalyst, are of two kinds: emotions and feelings. The effect of a work of art upon the person who enjoys it is an experience different in kind from any experience not of art. It may be formed out of one emotion, or may be a combination of several; and various feelings, inhering for the writer in particular words or phrases or images, may be added to compose the final result. Or great poetry may be made without the direct use of any emotion whatever: composed out of feelings solely.[2]

Eliot's explanation thus far, as is shown in these passages, would not be sufficient in itself for us to discern the respective meanings of the two words. Nor is it likely that further explanation by Eliot would enable one to understand the two different and yet related words precisely. But our understanding can be informed by examining the works or parts of works discussed by Eliot. Take the following, for example:

> Canto XV of the *Inferno* (Brunetto Latini) is a working up of the emotion evident in the situation; but the effect, though

[1] T. S. Eliot, *The Sacred Wood*, 7th ed. (London, 1950), pp. 53–54.
[2] Ibid., p. 54.

single as that of any work of art, is obtained by considerable complexity of detail. The last quatrain gives an image, which "came," which did not develop simply out of what precedes, but which was probably in suspension in the poet's mind until the proper combination arrived for it to add itself to. The poet's mind is in fact a receptacle for seizing and storing up numberless feelings, phrases, images, which remain there until all the particles which can unite to form a new compound are present together.[3]

Consider also such a brief and terse remark as "the episode of Paolo and Francesca employs a definite emotion";[4] or, "Canto XXVI, the voyage of Ulysses, which has not the direct dependence upon an emotion."[5] Eliot does not quote from Dante, so one must refer to Dante oneself. Is it not "a definite emotion" that is evoked in the lines where Dante, seeing the souls of Paolo and Francesca, says to Virgil:

> "Poet," said I, "fain would I speak those two
> That seem to ride as light as any foam,
> And hand in hand on the dark wind drifting go."[6]

Or in the lines where Francesca speaks:

> "One day we read for pastime how in thrall
> Lord Lancelot lay to love, who loved the Queen;
> We were alone—we thought no harm at all.
>
> As we read on, our eyes met now and then,
> And to our cheeks the changing colour started,
> But just one moment overcame us—when
>
> We read of the smile, desired of lips long-thwarted,
> Such smile, by such a lover kissed away,
> He that may never more from me be parted

---

[3] Ibid., pp. 54–55.
[4] Ibid., p. 55.
[5] Ibid., p. 55.
[6] *The Comedy of Dante Alighieri the Florentine, I: Hell*, trans. Dorothy L. Sayers, Penguin Classics (Harmondsworth, Mddx., 1951), p. 99.

Trembling all over, kissed my mouth."[7]

Is not the episode of Paolo and Francesca "a working up of the emotion evident in the situation," in their love affair? This conclusion
surely must be reached, if one places the above-cited lines side by
side with those describing the voyage of Ulysses. Ulysses narrates his
adventures as follows:

"I and my fellows . . .
    . . . made the straits where Hercules
        Set up his marks, that none should prove so hardy

To venture the uncharted distances. . . .

'Brothers,' said I, 'that have come valiantly
    Through hundred thousand jeopardies undergone
    To reach the West, you will not now deny

To this last little vigil left to run
    Of feeling life, the new experience
    Of the uninhabited world behind the sun.

Think of your breed; for brutish ignorance
    Your mettle was not made; you were made men,
    To follow after knowledge and excellence.'

My little speech made everyone so keen
    To forge ahead, that even if I'd tried
    I hardly think I could have held them in.

. . . at long last hove up a mountain, grey
    With distance, and so lofty and so steep,
    I never had seen the like on any day.

Then we rejoiced; but soon we had to weep,
    For out of the unknown land there blew foul weather,
    And a whirlwind struck the forepart of the ship;

And three times round she went in a roaring smother
    With all the waters; at the fourth, the poop

[7] Ibid., pp. 100–01.

Rose, and the prow went down, as pleased Another,

And over our heads the hollow seas closed up."[8]

If these lines can be said to be "composed out of feelings solely," or out of a feeling, at least one feeling can be identified that commands a man like Dr. Faustus who cannot help striving after infinite knowledge and excellence. It persists throughout the narration but has nothing particular to do with any event or thing. It comes from no particular place. It is not "evident in the situation," and therefore is not to be confused with "emotion." It is to be presumed that the word "feeling" means something that has nothing particular to do with any one event or object, while the word "emotion" means something that is "evident in the situation."

In "Hamlet and His Problems," Eliot says:

> The intense feeling, ecstatic or terrible, without an object or exceeding its object, is something which every person of sensibility has known; it is doubtless a study to pathologists. It often occurs in adolescence: the ordinary person puts these feelings to sleep, or trims down his feeling to fit the business world; the artist keeps it alive by his ability to intensify the world to his emotions.[9]

It may safely be said that, for Eliot, "feeling" is "without an object or exceeding its object." My previous assumption and this inference find support in another remark of the poet:

> The ode of Keats contains a number of feelings which have nothing particular to do with the nightingale, but which the nightingale, partly, perhaps, because of its attractive name, and partly because of its reputation, served to bring together.[10]

Although there are cases like that of Dante, who made great poetry "without the direct use of any emotion whatever . . . out of feelings solely," "the business of the poet is," generally speaking, "not

---

[8] Ibid., pp. 236–37.
[9] Eliot, *Sacred Wood*, p. 102.
[10] Ibid., p. 56.

to find new emotions, but to use the ordinary ones and, in working them up into poetry, to express feelings which are not in actual emotions at all. And emotions which he has never experienced will serve his turn as well as those familiar to him."[11] But "it is not the 'greatness,' the intensity, of the emotions, the components, but the intensity of the artistic process, the pressure, so to speak, under which the fusion takes place, that counts."[12] Eliot quotes a passage from Tourneur and explains the "whole effect" of that passage as follows:

> The whole effect, the dominant tone, is due to the fact that a number of floating feelings, having an affinity to this emotion (i.e., the structural emotion) by no means superficially evident, have combined with it to give us a new art emotion.[13]

It should be pointed out that the remarks by Eliot that have been quoted thus far concern almost always emotions and feelings as the material of poetry. Problems of communication do not intrude, or at least they are not brought out into the open. Dubious cases may be found in which the question might intrude whether Eliot is speaking from the viewpoint of a writer or a reader of poetry. But close examination will reveal that he always speaks of poetry as a writer rather than as a reader. The subtle difference in meaning he sees between the two words "emotion" and "feeling," which appear to differ little theoretically, serves to confirm the hypothesis that he writes primarily as a poet in the throes of artistic creation.

According to his use of these two words, the total effect of a work of art is to be called not "feeling" but "emotion." That is because it is evoked by the external facts or events arranged in a particular way in that work of art; because, in short, it has its object. But this is a special kind of emotion, which Eliot, at times, calls "a new art emotion" or "an artistic emotion" or, simply, "the emotion in his poetry" (meaning the poet in general by "his") as in the following sentence: "The emotion in his poetry will be a very complex thing, but not with the complexity of the emotions of people who have

[11] Ibid., p. 58.
[12] Ibid., p. 55.
[13] Ibid., p. 57.

very complex or unusual emotions in life."[14] Careful reading is necessary to decide whether Eliot means the material of poetry or the effect of a work of art by the word "emotion."

After making these observations, the theory of the "objective correlative" can be better understood, because the two words "emotion" and "feeling" are used in "Hamlet and His Problems" in the same way as in "Tradition and the Individual Talent." The famous argument runs as follows:

> The only way of expressing emotion in the form of art is by finding an "objective correlative"; in other words, a set of objects, a situation, a chain of events which shall be the formula of that *particular* emotion; such that when the external facts, which must terminate in sensory experience, are given, the emotion is immediately evoked. If you examine any of Shakespeare's more successful tragedies, you will find this exact equivalence; you will find that the state of mind of Lady Macbeth walking in her sleep has been communicated to you by a skillful accumulation of imagined sensory impressions; the words of Macbeth on hearing of his wife's death strike us as if, given the sequence of events, these words were automatically released by the last event in the series. The artistic "inevitability" lies in this complete adequacy of the external to the emotion; and this is precisely what is deficient in *Hamlet*.[15]

Here Eliot speaks of emotion as the artistic equivalent of a set of objects, a situation, a chain of events. This is the artistic emotion immediately evoked by the external facts, which are different from those in actual life. A work of art is not a mere reproduction of the relations between external facts and emotions in practical life. The poet adopts or rejects external facts, considering the results of his choice. His external facts must evoke an artistic emotion that is satisfactory to himself. To express emotion in the form of art means, to him, to evoke an artistic emotion by the choice of external facts;

[14] Ibid., p. 57.
[15] Ibid., pp. 100–01.

the artistic emotion commands their choice. Therefore, emotion comes first, and thereafter its "objective correlative." Consciously or half-consciously, Eliot is, I think, placing emphasis upon this phase of thinking in his famous passage.

There is another passage that also needs to be read attentively:

> Hamlet (the man) is dominated by an emotion which is inexpressible, because it is in *excess* of the facts as they appear. And the supposed identity of Hamlet with his author is genuine to this point: that Hamlet's bafflement at the absence of objective equivalent to his feelings is a prolongation of the bafflement of his creator in the face of his artistic problem. Hamlet is up against the difficulty that his disgust is occasioned by his mother, but that his mother is not an adequate equivalent for it; his disgust envelops and exceeds her. It is thus a feeling which he cannot understand; he cannot objectify it, and it therefore remains to poison life and obstruct action. None of the possible actions can satisfy it; and nothing that Shakespeare can do with the plot can express Hamlet for him. And it must be noticed that the very nature of the *données* of the problem precludes objective equivalence. To have heightened the criminality of Gertrude would have been to provide the formula for a totally different emotion in Hamlet; it is just *because* her character is so negative and insignificant that she arouses in Hamlet the feeling which she is incapable of representing.[16]

Here is a problem of Hamlet the man, and the use of the word "emotion" in the first sentence seems to contradict our earlier observations. But we should read this psychologically. Hamlet the man is dominated by something which might be called "feeling," in view of the suggestion that it "is inexpressible, because it is in excess of the facts as they appear." But he is struggling desperately to make out what it is, where it comes from, by any means. He wants to find its "objective correlative" in actual life; for him there must be a reality that can account for everything; in him there should be an emotion in

[16] Ibid., p. 101.

place of a feeling. I suspect that Eliot was here looking at the situation from the muddled inside of the man Hamlet, and thus he employed the word "emotion" instead of "feeling." Hamlet was baffled "at the absence of objective equivalent to his feeling," and no wonder.

And finally, in this essay, comes the remark quoted above to the effect that intense feeling without an object, or exceeding its object, often occurs in adolescence; Eliot concludes as follows:

> The Hamlet of Laforgue is an adolescent; the Hamlet of Shakespeare is not, he has not that explanation and excuse. We must simply admit that here Shakespeare tackled a problem which proved too much for him. Why he attempted it at all is an insoluble puzzle; under compulsion of what experience he attempted to express the inexpressibly horrible, we cannot ever know.[17]

Under compulsion of what experience, we might ask, did Eliot write a critical essay like this? The fact that the author had been making strenuous efforts as a poet ought not go unheeded. Without these efforts, he could not have made the daring statement, in terms of "emotion" and "feeling," that the *Hamlet* of Shakespeare is an artistic failure, praising the minute studies by J. M. Robertson and others. He was at that time, and had been for years before, working very hard on the problem of expressing precisely subtle and complex artistic emotions. His approach to artistic emotions, one is led to think, made him write this essay, which presents a precise emotion first, treating its form of art subsequently. In order to satisfy an artistic emotion, one might say, he had been seeking its form. Of the two kinds of elements, or material, to be transmuted into an artistic emotion, he was concerned more with feelings than with emotion; what to do with feelings was the graver issue at stake. We should recall that his essay on Hamlet was written only three years after the publication of *Prufrock and Other Observations*. The dangerous venture undertaken by Shakespeare was, I think, one against which Eliot himself felt he should be ever on guard. Reading *Prufrock*, one can scarcely deny that the author is keeping alive feelings

[17] Ibid., p. 102.

that are intense almost to the point of breakdown. It was, I suppose, his particular interests, apparently narrow but actually concentrated upon the writer's problem, that made him criticize the process of composing a work of art in terms almost exclusively of such words as "thoughts" and "thinking."

Anyone who reads Eliot, whether his poetry or prose, will be compelled to recognize, among other things, that he is very sensitive to ethical matters. He was so from the first, at least from the time of his first appearance in the literary world. This does not mean that the poet from the beginning was provided with a definite system of ideas, moral or philosophic, congenial to him; rather, it means that he was apt to be bothered or obsessed in his thinking by the complex emotions and intense feelings that hung about him. It is a well-known fact that he read widely in philosophy, especially when he was a young student at Harvard and at Oxford. It was his desire, perhaps, to get a perspective on human activities. But he could not settle down with a philosophy or philosophies; he could not see things from a purely philosophical point of view. It is easy to imagine that a little observation and a little thinking brought out in him too much emotion to be discarded and too many feelings to be trimmed down even by means of philosophy; that the more observation and the more thinking he undertook, the more emotion and feelings he discovered; and that, finding that the best way to relieve these was to write poetry, he was delighted to fabricate a wide range of them into artistic patterns and to concentrate his critical attention upon subtleties of a technical sort. "Poetry is not a turning loose of emotion, but an escape from emotion,"[18] he wrote, and yet the function of poetry "is not intellectual but emotional."[19] As far as thinking is concerned, he was interested not in thought itself but in "the emotional equivalent of thought."[20] The poet must have been developing an aversion to the transformation of reality subsequent to an excessive idealization.

Mario Praz says that

[18] Ibid., p. 58.
[19] T. S. Eliot, *Selected Essays*, 3d enlarged ed. (London, 1951), p. 138.
[20] Eliot, *Selected Essays*, p. 135.

> Pound's idea of poetry . . . as of "a sort of inspired mathema-
> tics, which gives us equations, not for abstract figures, tri-
> angles, spheres, and the like, but equations for the human
> emotions," may be said to be the starting point of Eliot's
> theory of the "objective correlative."[21]

There is much to be pondered in that; but it is not my purpose to
consider either the influence of Pound upon Eliot or a common
literary situation of the time that might lead them to make similar
statements. It will be enough to concentrate on Eliot's usage of the
two crucial words.

Eliot's theory of the "objective correlative" becomes even clearer
if one reads with some attention another essay of his, "Lancelot
Andrewes" (1926).

> Andrewes's emotion is purely contemplative; it is not per-
> sonal, it is wholly evoked by the object of contemplation, to
> which it is adequate; his emotion is wholly contained in and
> explained by its object. But with Donne there is always the
> something else, the "baffling" of which Mr. Pearsall Smith
> speaks in his introduction. Donne is a "personality" in a sense
> in which Andrewes is not: his sermons, one feels, are a
> "means of self-expression." He is constantly finding an object
> which shall be adequate to his feelings; Andrewes is wholly
> absorbed in the object and therefore responds with the
> adequate emotion. Andrewes has the *goût pour la vie spiri-
> tuelle*, which is not native to Donne.[22]

Here Eliot introduces "feeling" and "emotion" again, and their relations to their objects. The two words may be said to be used in the
same manner as before. Their senses are not altered, but a firm attitude toward "object" is recognizable. Here "object" is put before
"emotion" or "feeling."

As we have seen, in his early days Eliot was occupied above all
with the task of capturing the artistic emotion. His observations and

[21] Mario Praz, *The Flaming Heart* (New York, 1958), p. 351.
[22] Eliot, *Selected Essays*, p. 351.

his thoughts were haunted by the complex emotions and intense feelings he had been struggling to mold into a new artistic emotion. And that yet to be created artistic emotion commanded the choice of external facts that provided the objective correlative. To find an object or objects adequate to that emotion, to find its objective correlative, was the most urgent task confronting him, and I strongly suspect that, despite his efforts, some actual emotions or feelings in his life were apt to enter in place of that artistic emotion.

For the poet Eliot, his own private feelings must have been especially important. His insight into Hamlet as a man suffering from vain efforts to find an objective correlative for an intense feeling incomprehensible to himself, and the hesitant, vacillating states of mind that are found in "Prufrock" and "Portrait of a Lady"—these lead one to surmise that Eliot the man was suffering through the same or similar efforts or states. One cannot help thinking that he himself was haunted in his own life by an intense feeling which was persistent but lacked a definite object. I suspect that he often sought vainly to discover the objective correlative of intense feeling through the selection of external facts, and that he often wondered whence his feeling arose. But he must have been somewhat if not fully conscious already of the danger of seeking "constantly" to find "an object which shall be adequate to his feelings." Eliot the man was working hard to see things as they were.[23] Not, perhaps, that he was unable to find such an object, but that actually he was prone to. He was conscious of the danger, so he made strenuous efforts, wrestling with his emotions and feelings. Because of the presence of feelings strong enough sometimes to make him forget the danger, I think that he was led to seek consolation in a work of art which succeeded, to his satisfaction, in expressing similar feelings. It may be that such feelings motivated him to write poetry.

Such feelings contribute to the writing of poetry through a process so complicated that it would be impossible for him or anyone else to analyze it ultimately. But the poet as poet, who must secure an objective correlative, was to be warned against the man in him who was apt to find "an object which shall be adequate to his feel-

---

[23] Cf. "The Perfect Critic" in Eliot, *The Sacred Wood*, pp. 1–16.

ings." It can be imagined that Eliot, after being attracted by the rare delights produced by poetry after the demanding process of creation, wanted to avoid the awkward state of mind in which the creative power would be baffled unduly by the suffering of actual life. The following passage indicates not so much the actual as the ideal state of mind cherished by the poet.

> The more perfect the artist, the more completely separate in him will be the man who suffers and the mind which creates; the more perfectly will the mind digest and transmute the passions which are its material.[24]

The perfect artist conceived here should not be confused with the actual poet Eliot, who seems in these words to be giving stringent orders to himself. The famous analogy of the catalyst should be viewed as the words of a poet who consciously took great pains in writing his poems, line by line, even though the analogy seems to claim that poetry is created automatically in the mind of the poet. For that matter, one might be reminded of another of Eliot's remarks:

> His [i.e., Blake's] method of composition, in his mature work, is exactly like that of other poets. He has an idea (a feeling, an image), he develops it by accretion or expansion, alters his verse often, and hesitates often over the final choice. The idea, of course, simply comes, but upon arrival it is subjected to prolonged manipulation. In the first phase Blake is concerned with verbal beauty; in the second he becomes the apparent naïf, really the mature intelligence. It is only when the ideas become more automatic, come more freely and are less manipulated, that we begin to suspect their origin, to suspect that they spring from a shallower source.[25]

That was the attitude of the earlier Eliot, manifested in his first book of collected essays, The Sacred Wood (1920), and in several essays written a little later. For that Eliot, Donne as a poet was a great master, while Donne as a man was simply a kind of precarious

[24] Eliot, The Sacred Wood, p. 54.
[25] Ibid., pp. 153–54.

being like Eliot himself, and no more. But in "Lancelot Andrewes," which opens his third book of collected essays, *For Lancelot Andrewes* (1928), he goes so far as to declare that Donne "lacked spiritual discipline"[26] and was therefore "constantly finding an object which shall be adequate to his feelings." There is now no question of his poetry, of his poetic composition. Eliot is now surprisingly concerned with the attitude of Donne the man. The earlier Eliot would have pointed out the necessity of "the free intelligence . . . which is wholly devoted to inquiry"[27] and have gone no further; while the later Eliot gives Andrewes a place "in the spiritual hierarchy . . . higher than that of Donne,"[28] by reason that "Andrewes is wholly absorbed in the object and therefore responds with the adequate emotion," which "is not personal" and "is wholly evoked by the object of contemplation." Here is a manifestation of an attitude more positive than that in *The Sacred Wood*.

I cannot put from my mind the thought that the essay on Andrewes concerns mainly the style of his sermons, and that the examples of "objects" in the passages quoted from his sermons are largely of a religious order. The problem of depersonalization might be relevant here, a problem already made much of in "Tradition and the Individual Talent," if as a purely literary problem, in 1919.[29] But, for the present, I cannot enter on an inquiry into Eliot's idea of tradition or personality. *For Lancelot Andrewes* contains the preface in which Eliot confesses that he is "classicist in literature, royalist in politics, anglo-catholic in religion." How and why it came about, how and why he came to be interested in religion to so remarkable a degree and to reveal this in his critical and other writings, is a question not to be answered here. I will leave this matter for another occasion, reflecting only that the attitude previously mentioned— which the earlier Eliot, trying to see things as they are, seems to be on guard against—is declared by the later Eliot to belong to a man who

---

[26] Eliot, *Selected Essays*, p. 345.
[27] Eliot, *The Sacred Wood*, p. 12.
[28] Eliot, *Selected Essays*, p. 352.
[29] Cf. T. S. Eliot, *After Strange Gods* (London, 1934), p. 15.

had no taste for the spiritual life. It may be said, moreover, that it is viewed by the later Eliot as decidedly undesirable.

About 1926, Eliot was wrestling with religion, adopting a new, positive attitude. One can see the man in him suffering very much from private feelings which persisted in spite of his will to respond to the (religious) object with the adequate emotion. But the mind in him which creates ought to have been, or would have been, receiving the motive, as before, from his actual feelings, rather than from the religious object he was tackling resolutely. He says in *After Strange Gods* (1934):

> Why, I would ask, is most religious verse so bad; and why does so little religious verse reach the highest levels of poetry? Largely, I think, because of a pious insincerity. The capacity for writing poetry is rare; the capacity for religious emotion of the first intensity is rare; and it is to be expected that the existence of both capacities in the same individual should be rarer still. People who write devotional verse are usually writing as they want to feel, rather than as they do feel.[30]

Ash-Wednesday (1930) and other ensuing poems are composed of material including, no doubt, religious emotion of an intensity yet to be assessed. That emotion must have been obtained in consequence of Eliot's efforts to entertain an emotion which is "not personal" and "wholly evoked by the object of contemplation, to which it is adequate." But the feeling which "has an affinity to this emotion by no means superficially evident" I believe to have been as important as before, for both "the mind which creates" and "the man who suffers."

[30] Ibid., pp. 30–31.

Index

Except for anonymous writings, works are entered under their authors' names. Since the notes are at the foot of the pages, no distinction is made in this index between appearance in the text and in the notes.

Foquières, L. Becq de, 19
Ford, Boris, 128
Ford, John, 101–114; *The Broken Heart*, 101–02, 104, 107, 109, 112; *The Lady's Trial*, 108; *The Lover's Melancholy*, 105, 107; *Love's Sacrifice*, 104, 110, 111–12; *Perkin Warbeck*, 113; *'Tis Pity She's a Whore*, 102, 105, 107, 109, 111
Forster, E. M., 240–41, 249; *Howards End*, 240; *A Room with a View*, 249–50; *Where Angels Fear to Tread*, 249
Fraser, Russell A., 53–54
Freud, Sigmund, 188, 190
Frost, William, 49, 50
Frye, Northrop, 74, 115
Furness, H. H., 53, 85, 87, 88–89

Galle, Theodore, 65
Gardner, Dame Helen, 29, 82
Gass, William H., 271–72
Geoffroi de Vinsauf, 4, 7, 10–11, 13; *Poetria Nova*, 10
Gilio, Giovanni Andreo, 71
Gillman, James, 202
Gissing, Algernon, 233
Gissing, Ellen, 233–58 *passim*
Gissing, George, 233–58; *Born in Exile*, 235, 236, 237, 238, 252–54; *The Emancipated*, 247–50; *The House of Cobwebs*, 241; *In the Year of Jubilee*, 251; *Isabel Clarendon*, 245; *A Life's Morning*, 235, 243, 251; "A Lodger in Maze Pond," 241–42; *New Grub Street*, 244, 252; *Thyrza*, 248; *The Unclassed*, 239, 251; *Veranilda*, 257; *Workers in the Dawn*, 242, 248, 253
Gissing, Margaret, 246
Godwin, William, 224
Godyere, Henry, 77
Goethe, Johann Wolfgang von, 185, 189
Golding, Arthur, 252
Gordon, Donald, 57
Gower, John: *Confessio Amantis*, 4
Green, Henry, 77
Greene, Graham: *The End of the Affair*, 241–42
Grierson, Sir Herbert, 132, 140–41, 148, 149
Griggs, Earl Leslie, 206
Guillaume de Lorris, 5, 7; *Le Roman de*

la Rose, 6, 7, 17. *See also* Chaucer, Geoffrey
Guillaume de Machaut, 7, 10–11; *Jugement dou Roy de Behaingne*, 5

Hadrianus, 56, 57, 78
Hall, Edward, 34
Harrison, Austin, 243
Harrison, B. S., 10
Harrison, Mrs. Frederic, 248
Hartley, David, 193, 196, 215
Hazlitt, William, 101
Heninger, S. K., Jr., 19
Henley, W. E., 42
Henry V, 34
Henry VII, 44
Herford, C. N., 25, 39
Hoccleve, Thomas, 12
Holinshed, Raphael, 85, 89
Holland, Norman N., 167
Holmes, P., 133
Hone, William, 65
Hooker, Richard, 135
Horace, 19
House, Humphry, 195, 207
Huizinga, Johan, 36, 39
Hutchinson, Mary, 213, 220
Hutchinson, Sara, 173, 176, 205, 206–32 *passim*

Iwasaki, Takeo, 127

James I, 35
James, D. G., 49, 56, 77, 81, 94
James, Henry, 252, 256, 271–85; *The American*, 276; *The Art of the Novel*, 276; *The Future of the Novel*, 279, 280; *The Portrait of a Lady*, 271–85
James, William, 272
Jones, A. R., 182
Jones, John, 174, 178
Jordan, Thomas: *London in Luster*, 35; *The Triumphs of London*, 40
Jorgensen, Paul A., 80, 81
Joyce, James, 252; *The Portrait of the Artist as a Young Man*, 182
Jung, Carl Gustav, 188
Jünger, Ernst, 155

Kant, Immanuel, 145